MEXICO

MICHAEL D. COE
& REX KOONTZ

MEXICO

FROM THE OLMECS TO THE AZTECS

Fifth edition, revised and expanded

With 174 illustrations, 19 in color

Thames & Hudson

Ancient Peoples and Places
FOUNDING EDITOR: GLYN DANIEL

On the cover: Stone *hacha* of a ballplayer wearing a dolphin headdress, Veracruz, Late Classic. Ht 27 cm. The Art Archive/National Anthropological Museum, Mexico/Dagli Orti.

Frontispiece: Monument 1 from San Lorenzo, Veracruz, a Colossal Head in basalt. Olmec culture, Early Preclassic Period. Ht 2.84 m.

Published in the United States of America in 1984 by
Thames & Hudson Inc., 500 Fifth Avenue, New York, New York 10110

thamesandhudsonusa.com

Fifth edition 2002

Library of Congress Catalog Card Number 2001094767
ISBN 0-500-28346-X

Printed and bound in Singapore by CS Graphics

Contents

Cerro de las Mesas 121   The Classic Veracruz civilization 122
Classic Monte Albán 124   The Classic downfall 130

Preface

The subject matter of this book is the story of the pre-Spanish peoples of Mexico, who with their neighbors the Maya were the most advanced of the American Indians north of the Andes. The term "Mexico" will here refer to all the land in that Republic which lies between the western border of the Maya civilization and the northern frontier where Mexican farmers once met the nomadic tribesmen of the desert. This is roughly the area covered by the old Viceroyalty of New Spain in early Colonial times.

We have found it both feasible and justifiable to exclude the ancient Maya from this survey, although part of their territory was, in fact, within the boundaries of the present-day *Estados Unidos de México*. The Maya civilization of the Yucatan Peninsula and Central America was so extraordinarily complex that to do it justice would be impossible within the confines of the present volume. With a few notable exceptions, those remarkable people would appear to have remained within their own borders throughout the centuries; accordingly, other native cultures of the Republic can be considered quite independently without the problem of Maya influences seriously conflicting with the development of our theme. The latest revised edition of *The Maya*, the companion volume in the series, should be read with it; we have made every effort to give each volume the same format and general approach.

We have incorporated in this present edition of *Mexico* many of the most recent findings, from a number of disciplines. The reader will here be brought up to date on the thorny problem of maize origins; on the shaft-tomb cultures of western Mexico, with their remarkable circular, temple-oriented settlements; and on the nature of the Olmec civilization in the light of newer excavations at San Lorenzo, La Venta, and elsewhere on Mexico's Gulf Coast. Spectacular discoveries have been made in Teotihuacan's Temple of Quetzalcoatl and Pyramid of the Moon. We have begun to appreciate the key role that northern and northwestern Mexico played during the Epiclassic and Early Post-Classic periods, when local mining of precious stones and contacts with the turquoise-producing Pueblo cultures of the American Southwest resulted in the florescence of sites such as Alta Vista, La Quemada, and Casas Grandes. And we have tried to present a balanced discussion of the continuing controversy over the relation between Tula of the Toltecs and the great city of Chich'en Itza in distant Yucatan.

Some may be disappointed to find the Aztec empire confined to a chapter and a half. "Aztec" and "Mexico" seem almost synonymous, but we now know that in the total span of human occupation of that country, the Aztecs were late arrivals, their empire but a final and brilliant flicker before the light of native civilization was put out once and for all. Nevertheless, thanks to the accounts of Spanish friars and conquistadores, and to native and creole (Mexican-born) historians, we have more information on this civilization than on any other native culture of the New World. Each generation of scholars brings new insights and understandings to the study of the Aztecs, and we have tried to incorporate some of the latest into this volume.

It is all too easy to treat the pre-Spanish cultures of Mexico and Central America as "dead," yet in spite of the cataclysm of the Conquest and the ensuing epidemics which decimated the native peoples, the indigenous populations have survived through the Colonial period and into the present; in fact, much of the flavor of modern Mexico derives, both consciously and unconsciously, from its ancient heritage. Accordingly, we have included an Epilogue which takes these peoples through the Conquest up to our own day, and have done likewise with *The Maya*.

A matter which must be touched upon is the pronunciation of the very formidable-looking words and names of ancient Mexico. Most of these are in Nahuatl, the national tongue of the Aztec state, and were transcribed in Roman letters by the early Spanish friars in terms of the language spoken in central Spain in the sixteenth century. Thus, vowels and most consonants are generally pronounced as they would be in modern Spanish, with these exceptions:

x has the sound of the English *sh*, as it once had in Spanish (witness the derivation of "sherry" from the Spanish *Xerez*).

tl - this cluster is a voiceless surd consonant, much like the Welsh *ll*.

hu followed by a vowel is pronounced like English *w*.

In Nahuatl, word stress always fall on the penultimate (next-to-last) syllable. We have therefore omitted all accents in such words and names. However, various corruptions have crept into Nahuatl from Spanish, including occasional stress placed on the final syllable (e.g. in many books, *Teotihuacán* is found in place of the more correct *Teotihuácan*).

We have used the correct Nahuatl form *Motecuhzoma* ("Angry Like a Lord") for the third and seventh Aztec kings, although *Moteuhczoma* is also permissible. The familiar "Montezuma" of numberless boyhood romances and the Marine Corps Hymn is hopelessly wrong and merely reflects the inability of most Spaniards to pronounce native names.

In recent years, there have been important advances in the accurate correlation of dates derived from radiocarbon determinations with those of the Christian calendar (or "sidereal years"). Dendrochronological studies of the bristlecone pine now affirm that prior to the Christian era, radiocarbon dates are significantly younger than "true" years. For example, according to radiocarbon determinations, the Olmec civilization at San Lorenzo begins around 1200 BC, but the new calibration curve would more accurately place this some 300 years earlier. In this edition, all ages based upon the radiocarbon method have been so calibrated, as they have in *The Maya*.

Many scholars have aided us in the preparation of this and earlier editions, if only through their published work, but we would like to acknowledge here

DATES (calibrated)	PERIODS	CENTRAL HIGHLANDS	NORTH AND CENTRAL GULF	SOUTHERN GULF COAST	OAXACA	SIGNIFICANT DEVELOPMENTS
1521						*Spanish Conquest, fall of Tenochtitlan*
	Late Post-Classic	Aztec Empire	Isla de Sacrificios	Independent states	Monte Albán V (Mitla, Mixtec states)	*Aztec Triple Alliance formed*
1200		"Feudal" states				*Aztecs reach Valley of Mexico*
	Early Post-Classic	Tollan / Mazapan				*Toltec state*
900				Villa Alta	Monte Albán IV	
	Epiclassic		El Tajín		Monte Albán III-B	*Competing regional capitals*
650		Coyotlatelco				*Destruction of Teotihuacan*
	Classic	Metepec / Xolalpan-Tlamimilolpa (Teotihuacan III)	Late Remojadas / Classic Veracruz	Cerro de las Mesas / Late Tres Zapotes	Monte Albán III-A	*Height of Teotihuacan influence*
		Miccaotli (Teotihuacan II)				
150 AD BC		Tzacualli (Teotihuacan I)	Early Remojadas	La Mojarra		*Isthmian script* / *Building of Pyramid of the Sun, city planning at Teotihuacan* / *Invention of Long Count calendar*
	Late Preclassic	Chupícuaro / Cuicuilco		Early Tres Zapotes	Monte Albán II	
		Ticomán				
400					Monte Albán I	*Construction of Monte Albán* / *First writing at San José Mogote*
		Zacatenco				
	Middle Preclassic			La Venta	Rosario	*Spread of La Venta Olmec influence*
		Chalcatzingo				
		El Arbolillo		Nacaste	Guadalupe	
1200				San Lorenzo B		
	Early Preclassic	Tlatilco { Manantial / Ayotla	El Trapiche	San Lorenzo A	San José	*Spread of San Lorenzo Olmec influence* / *Early Olmec civilization at San Lorenzo*
				Chicharras / Bajío / Ojochi	Tierras Largas	
1800		Nevada-Tlalpan				*Origins of village life, pottery, figurines*
		Purrón?			Gheo-Shih, Oaxaca Archaic	
	Archaic	Abejas				*Early agriculture; hunting, fishing, gathering*

9

the constant support and sound advice we have continued to receive from an old friend and colleague, Richard A. Diehl. George Cowgill, whose knowledge of the Classic civilizations of central Mexico is unparalleled, has also given us many suggestions for revision. We are grateful also for the continued inspiration of that great Mexican expert on all things Aztec, the *nahuatlato* and scholar Dr Miguel León-Portilla. And lastly, we thank the staff of Thames & Hudson for their help in enabling us to present often complex archaeological research to the general reader.

1 · Introduction

The ancient cultures of Mexico along with the Maya civilization comprise the larger entity known to archaeologists as "Mesoamerica," a name first 1 proposed by the anthropologist Paul Kirchhoff and including much of the great constriction that separates the masses of North and South America. Above all, the peoples of Mesoamerica were farmers, and had been somewhat isolated for thousands of years from the simpler cultivating societies of the American Southwest and Southeast by the desert wastes of northern Mexico, through which only semi-nomadic, hunting aborigines ranged in pre-Spanish times. Beyond the southeastern borders of Mesoamerica lay the petty chiefdoms of lower Central America, distinguished by a high production of fine ceramics and quantities of jade or gold ornaments, lavishly heaped in the tombs of their great.

Further south yet, in Ecuador, Peru, and Bolivia, was the Andean area, most noted for its final glory, the immense Inca empire, but having native civilizations as far back in time as the tenth century before Christ, and large temple constructions even earlier than that. The Andean area and Mesoamerica were the twin peaks of American Indian cultural development, from which much else in the Western Hemisphere seems both peripheral and sometimes derived; yet this picture may be oversimplified, because recent research in the Pacific lowlands of Ecuador, the Caribbean coast of Colombia, and the upper reaches of the Amazon has shown that the important criteria of settled life – agriculture, pottery, and villages – may have had a precocious start in those areas.

Setting them off from the rest of the New World, the diverse cultures of Mesoamerica shared in a number of features most of which were pretty much confined to their area. The most distinctive of these is a complicated calendar based upon the permutation of a 260-day sacred cycle with the solar year of 365 days. Others are hieroglyphic writing (the Andean area never developed a script); bark-paper or deer-skin books which fold like screens; maps; an extensive knowledge and use of astronomy; a team game resembling basketball played in a special court with a solid rubber ball; large, well-organized markets and favored "ports of trade"; chocolate beans as money; wars for the purpose of securing sacrificial victims; private confession, and penance by drawing blood from the ears, tongue, or penis; and a pantheon of extraordinary complexity.

Naturally, the peoples of Mesoamerica followed a number of other customs which are widespread among New World Indians, such as ceremonial tobacco smoking, but their typical method of food preparation as a unified

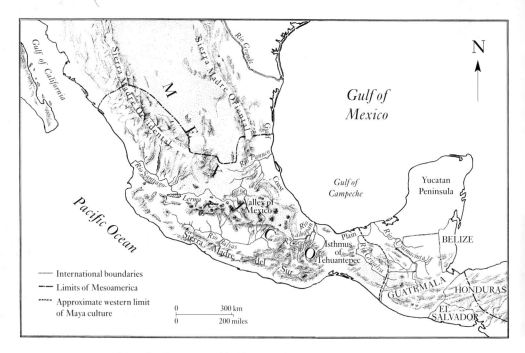

1 Map of major topographical features of Mexico.

complex appears to be unique. The basis of the diet was the foursome of maize, beans, squash, and chile peppers. Maize was, and still is, prepared by boiling it with lime, then grinding the swollen kernels with a hand stone (Spanish *mano*) on a trough- or saddle-shaped quern (*metate*, from the Nahuatl *metlatl*). The resulting dough is either toasted as flat cakes known in Spanish as *tortillas*, or else steamed or boiled as *tamales*. Always and everywhere in Mesoamerica, the hearth comprises three stones, and being the conceptual center of the world, is semi-sacred.

The geographic setting

On the map, Mexico resembles a great funnel, or rather, a cornucopia, with its widest part toward the north and its smallest end twisting to the south and east, meeting there the sudden expansion of the Maya area. There are few regions in the world with such a diverse geography as we find within this area – Mexico is not one, but many countries. All the climatic extremes of our globe are found, from arctic cold near the summits of the highest volcanoes to the Turkish-bath atmosphere of the coastal jungles. Merely to pass from one valley to another is to enter a markedly different ecological zone.

This variation would be of interest only to the tourist agencies if one neglected to consider the effect of these contrasts upon the human occupation of Mexico. A topsy-turvy landscape of this sort means a similar diversity of natural and cultivated products from region to region – above all, different

2 Central highlands of Mexico, near Puebla, with Popocatepetl volcano in the distance.

crops with different harvest times. It means that no one region is now, or was in the past, truly self-sufficient. From the most remote antiquity, there has been an organic interdependence of one zone with the others, of one people or nation with all the rest. Thus, no matter how heterogeneous their languages or civilizations, the people of Mexico through exchange of products were bound up with each other symbiotically into a single line of development; for this reason, great new advances were registered throughout the land within quite brief intervals of time.

Most of this funnel-shaped country lies above 3,000 ft (900 m), with really very little flat land. The Mexican highlands, our major concern in this book, are shaped by the mountain chains that swing down from the north, by the uplands between them, and by numerous volcanoes which have raised their peaks in fairly recent geological times. The western chain, the Sierra Madre Occidental, is the loftiest and broadest of these, being an extension of the Rocky Mountains; it and the Sierra Madre Oriental to the east enclose between their pine-clad ranges an immense inland plateau which is covered by mesquite-studded grasslands and occasionally even approaches true desert. Effectively outside the limits of Mesoamerican farming, the Mexican plateau was the homeland of partially or wholly nomadic hunters and collectors. As we move south, the two Sierras gradually approach each other until the interior wastelands terminate some 300 miles (480 km) north of the Valley of Mexico.

The Valley of Mexico, the center of the Aztec empire, is one of a number of natural basins in the midst of the Volcanic Cordillera, an extensive region of intense volcanism and frequent earthquakes. A mile and a half high with an area of 3,000 sq. miles (7,800 sq. km), much of the Valley was once covered by a shallow lake of roughly figure-eight shape, now largely disappeared through ill-advised drainage and general desiccation of central Mexico in post-Conquest times. Since the Valley of Mexico has no natural outlet, changing rainfall patterns have produced severe fluctuations in the extent of the lake. As will be seen in Chapter 10, the Aztec table was amply supplied by foods raised on its swampy margins in the misnamed "floating gardens," or 3   *chinampas*. Surrounded by hills on all sides, the Valley is dominated on the southeast by the snowy summits of the volcanoes Popocatepetl ("Smoking Mountain") and Iztaccihuatl ("The White Lady").

Other important sections of the highlands are the Sierra Madre del Sur, its steep escarpment fronting the Pacific shoreline in southern Mexico, and the mountainous uplands of Oaxaca; both of these fuse to form a highland mass heavily dissected into countless valleys and ranges. Separated from this difficult country by the Isthmus of Tehuantepec, the southeastern highlands form a continuous series of ranges from Chiapas down through Maya territory into lower Central America.

Although snow falls in some places at infrequent intervals, the Mexican highlands are temperate; before denudation by man, they were clothed in pines and oaks, with true boreal forests in the higher ranges. As elsewhere in Mexico, there are two strongly marked seasons – a winter dry period when rain seldom if ever falls, and a summer wet spell. The total rainfall is less than half that of the lowlands, so that occasionally conditions are arid and somewhat precarious for the farmer, in spite of the general richness of the soil. This is especially true of the boundary zone between the agricultural lands and the northern deserts.

The lowlands are confined to relatively narrow strips along the coasts, of which the most important is the plain fronting the Gulf of Mexico. Of alluvial origin, this band of flat land extends unbroken from Louisiana and Texas down through the Mexican states of Tamaulipas, Veracruz, and Tabasco to the Yucatan Peninsula, and played a critical role in the origins of settled life and the growth of civilization in Mexico.

A bridge between the Gulf Coast plain and the narrower and less humid Pacific Coast plain is provided by the Isthmus of Tehuantepec, a constriction in the waist of Mesoamerica, with a gentle topography of low hills and sluggish rivers.

Lowland temperatures are generally torrid throughout the year, except when winter northers come down the Gulf Coast, bringing with them cold rains and drizzle. So heavy is the summer precipitation that in many places the soils are red in color and poor in mineral content as a result of drastic leaching. However, when these rains cause flooding of rivers, the soils can be highly productive since they are annually replenished with silt along the natural river levees. The winter dry season is generally well marked, so that many of the tropical trees lose their leaves in that season. But where there is an unusually great amount of rain (along with winter northers), one encounters the evergreen canopies and lush growth of the fully developed rain

3 *Chinampas* or "floating gardens" in the vicinity of Xochimilco, Valley of Mexico.

forest. Dotting the lowlands are patches of savannah grassland, sometimes quite extensive, and of little use to the once plowless Mexican farmer.

In response to the opportunities presented by these surroundings, contrasting modes of land cultivation have been developed over the millennia. Highland farmers are quite efficient about their land, since only a moderate period of fallowing is necessary for the fields. On the other hand, many lowland cultivators, faced with immense forests, the low potential of the soil, weed competition, and winter desiccation, have evolved a shifting form of horticulture which they share with other peoples of the world. This system entails the cutting and burning of the forest from the plot to be sown; a very extensive territory is required for the support of each family since exhausted and weed-infested fields have to be left fallow for as much as ten years. Such a mode of food-getting could never have supported a large population, and we have every evidence to suggest a light occupation of much of the lowland zone throughout its history.

Nonetheless, it is easy to exaggerate the limitations of the lowlands; there are not one but many lowland environments, and a diversity of human responses to them. For instance, one could point to the use of fertile river levees by ancient and modern farmers of the southern Gulf Coast plain, which could have led and *did* lead to increased population density.

Tragically reduced in today's Mexico, game abounded in ancient times. The most important food animals are the white-tailed deer and the collared peccary, found everywhere. Confined to the lowlands are the tapir, the howler monkey, and the spider monkey, all of which are still eaten with relish by the native inhabitants. The lowlands also harbor the now-rare jaguar, the largest of the spotted cats and the source of much-desired skins for the nobles of civilized Mexico; it must have been an object of primitive terror to the early dwellers of the coastal plains. Waterfowl, especially ducks, teem on the lakes and marshes of the uplands, and wild turkeys in the more isolated reaches of the country. Feathers from tropical birds such as the cotinga, the roseate spoonbill, the hummingbird, and above all, the quetzal, with iridescent blue-green plumage, provided rainbow-like splendor for headdresses and other details of costume.

The larger highland lakes, such as Lake Pátzcuaro in Michoacan and the great lake of the Valley of Mexico, teemed with small fish, while the lowland rivers and the coasts provided such an abundance of fish (such as snook and snappers) and turtles that these food resources were more important to ancient peoples than game mammals.

There were no wild species in the New World suitable for domestication as draught animals. The native American horse was exterminated at the end of the Ice Age, probably by human hunters; the South American llama is amenable only as a pack animal; and modern efforts to tame the North American bison have shown that beast to be completely intractable. As a consequence, none of the American Indians prior to the European arrival had wheeled vehicles. Ancient Mexico did without any form of overland transportation other than the backs of men, although the principle of the wheel was known and applied to toys and idols of clay. The only warm-blooded animals kept in domestication were the dog and the turkey, the former as well as the latter valuable for its meat. Hives of tiny, stingless bees were exploited for honey by tropical lowlanders.

Languages and peoples

An amazing number of languages were spoken in native Mexico. The situation would be even more confusing if it had not been for the efforts on the part of linguists to group them into families, of which some fourteen have been defined within our area.

4

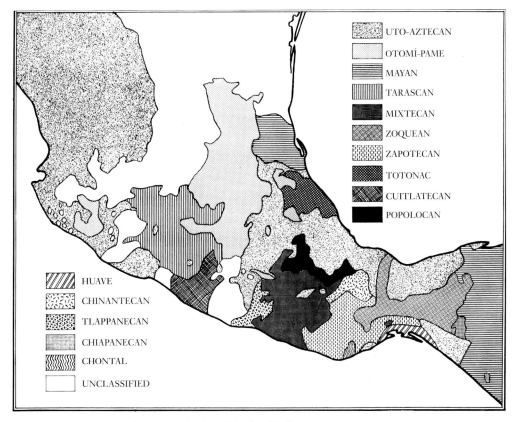

Legend:
- UTO-AZTECAN
- OTOMÍ-PAME
- MAYAN
- TARASCAN
- MIXTECAN
- ZOQUEAN
- ZAPOTECAN
- TOTONAC
- CUITLATECAN
- POPOLOCAN

- HUAVE
- CHINANTECAN
- TLAPPANECAN
- CHIAPANECAN
- CHONTAL
- UNCLASSIFIED

4 Native language groups of Mexico at the time of the Spanish Conquest.

Of these, the largest and most important to the history of Mexico is Uto-Aztecan, comprising dozens of languages distributed from the northwestern United States as far south as Panama. Since the greatest diversity within this family is found in northwestern Mexico, this wild region has been suggested as the probable heartland of the Uto-Aztecan peoples. By all odds the major language group within Uto-Aztecan is Nahua, the most significant member of which is Nahuatl, the language of the Aztecs and the *lingua franca* of their empire, still spoken by hundreds of thousands of farmers in the central Mexican highlands and in the state of Guerrero. Since the Conquest, Nahuatl has greatly enriched Mexican Spanish with loan words, and has contributed such words as ocelot, coyote, tomato, chocolate, tamale, and copal to the English language.

Tarascan or Purépecha, the tongue of a large, independent kingdom at the time of the Aztecs centered on Lake Pátzcuaro in the western part of the Volcanic Cordillera, is totally unrelated to any other language in the world. Otomí-Pame was spoken by peoples who followed a semi-nomadic way of life to the north of the Valley of Mexico, on the fringe of Mesoamerica. Totonac is spoken on the middle Gulf Coast, significantly in the region of the old Tajín civilization. Mixtec and Zapotec are the dominant languages of the state of Oaxaca in southern Mexico, and Zapotec written records go back to at least 500 BC. The Mixe-Zoquean language family is distributed from the Isthmus of Tehuantepec to the Grijalva Depression, and as we shall see in Chapter 5, may have been the language of the ancient Olmecs. Huave was and is spoken by primitive fishermen (now largely turned to cattlemen) on the Pacific Coast of the Isthmus. To the east is the large group of Mayan languages; this family has an enigmatic outlier, Huaxtec, in the area of the Gulf Coast north of the Totonac that is called, naturally enough, the Huaxteca. The location of Huaxtec remains a puzzle for Mesoamericanists. Evidence from the branch of linguistic research known as glottochronology, or lexicostatistics, suggests that it separated from the main group of Mayan languages about 900 BC, but what this means for the development of Mesoamerican cultures has yet to be ascertained.

It would be a fruitless task to try to reconstruct Mexican history merely on the basis of these distributions. Nevertheless, it is evident that the expansion of Uto-Aztecan through much of Mexico must have been drastic; the isolated islands of Nahua speech as far south as lower Central America, Nahua placenames, and the presence of Nahua words in many other languages testify to large-scale movements of peoples. We know in this case of Nahua conquests and migrations having taken place long before the imperialism of the Nahuatl-speaking Aztecs, events recorded in the traditional histories of these peoples. The role that they have played on the stage of New World history has certainly been in the grand style.

Other peoples have probably been more sedentary. But, contradictory as it may seem, while there is fairly good knowledge of the geographic position of most language groups in Mexico at the time of the Conquest, archaeologists are often loath to apply linguistic names to past civilizations unless they are sure beyond any doubt of the identification, as in the case of the Zapotecs and the Maya, whose writings we have, or the Aztecs. Stones and pottery fragments do not tell us who made them, so that we must be content with the noncommittal names which archaeologists have given us for past peoples.

Periods

The Aztecs encountered by the Spanish conquistadores and missionaries knew that they had not been the first occupants of the land of Mexico. Time and time again they told their interlocutors that they had been preceded by a marvelous people called the Toltecs, the "People from Tollan." And beyond that epoch lay a mystical, never-never land known as Tamoanchan, a paradise inhabited by the gods and ancestors of humans. Further, the Aztec thinkers said that the world had been created and destroyed four times, and that we were now living in the fifth age or "Sun," doomed – like the rest – to annihilation. The Aztecs knew of the great, ruined city of Teotihuacan, to the northeast of their island capital, and said that the gods had met there to create our present era, and the Sun that was to give it life and substance.

It was not until the first decades of the twentieth century that the new science of archaeology began to render the outlines of the real prehistory of Mexico and its peoples. The first stratigraphic excavation carried out in the Valley of Mexico demonstrated not only that Teotihuacan was substantially earlier than Aztec, but that the Teotihuacan culture was underlain by the remains of a far simpler, pottery-using people. How early were these pre-Aztec cultures? There was no real way to know, and most archaeologists were reluctant to think of these ceramic cultures as pre-dating the Christian era. They looked enviously at the American Southwest, where dendrochronology, or tree-ring dating, gave an absolute, year-to-year chronology for the ancient adobe pueblos, and at the Maya area, where a similarly accurate time scale had resulted from the correlation of the Maya and Christian calendars.

All this was changed by the advent of radiocarbon dating in the mid-twentieth century. Some of those early cultures turned out to date to the beginning of the first millennium BC; and Teotihuacan proved to be a contemporary of the earlier part of the Maya Classic (AD 250-900) period, and had nothing to do with the Toltecs, as some had thought. The Toltecs, in fact, appeared on the scene as the Classic came to an end (see below), and as the Aztec ethnohistories had affirmed.

There is general agreement among scholars about the periods or stages of development in pre-Conquest Mexico, even though certain details remain unclear. The first occupation is here called Early Hunters (identical to the Paleo-Indian period of some specialists), and extends from the time of the earliest migrants into the area – a topic still under debate – until about 7000 BC. During this era, people lived in tiny, nomadic bands, following a way of life centered on the hunting of now-extinct large game and on the collection of wild plant foods. During the subsequent Archaic (or "Incipient Agricultural") period, ancestral Mexicans began to domesticate those food plants – above all, maize – upon which all subsequent civilizations in this hemisphere rested. With the introduction of pottery and village life at about 1800 BC, the Preclassic (or Formative) period opens, lasting until c. AD 150. It was once considered that the Preclassic was some sort of New World counterpart to the Old World Neolithic, but radiocarbon dating and field archaeology have shown that Olmec and other ancient civilizations flourished in this epoch. The Classic period which follows on its heels marks the apogee of Mexican civilization, with the rise and decline of mighty states like those of Teotihuacan and Monte Albán. The Epiclassic witnesses the decline of these two giants, while smaller, innovative cities such as El Tajín replaced the Classic powers in the Mesoamerican world. During these latter two periods the lowland Maya civilization to the east experienced its zenith, with cities dotting the jungle, several of which had important ties to Mexican peoples. Many Maya and Mexican cities were extinguished or fast-fading by AD 900, to be replaced by the supposedly more militaristic states of the Post-Classic, beginning with the Toltecs and culminating in the great empire of the Aztecs.

First encountered by the Spaniards in 1519, Aztec civilization was still in full flower until it was finally destroyed by the intruders in 1521, bringing at least 15,000 years of native American prehistory and history to a tragic end.

2 · Early Hunters

High on the flanks of the hills fringing the Valley of Mexico are clearly visible the remains of beaches left by the great lake which once covered much of the Valley – from these alone it would be obvious that rainfall conditions in the distant past were very different from what they are today, or even from what they were in Aztec times. A close study of pollen from weather-sensitive plants recovered from deep cores has revealed that many thousands of years ago the amount of annual precipitation was very much higher, and that it has drastically declined since then.

To understand such changes, we must go back in time more than two million years. Then, for reasons still under debate by geologists, the generally warm and humid climate of the globe suffered a profound alteration, and the Pleistocene, or Ice Age, was initiated. Temperatures dropped and vast quantities of snow were deposited on the ever-rising mountain masses of far northern latitudes, to turn into massive ice sheets that ground their way south over much of northern Eurasia and North America. There were numerous glacial advances in the Pleistocene, separated by long interglacial periods during which more moderate conditions prevailed. In more southerly regions, such as Mexico, which actually lies within the Tropics, such advances of the northern ice are believed to have been reflected by pluvials, that is, by rainy, cool periods interspersed with dry intervals – hence those relict beaches in the Valley of Mexico.

While the broad outline of what happened during the late Pleistocene in the New World is becoming clearer with every new discovery of very early artifacts and sites, it is still not established exactly when humans first entered this hemisphere. Even the how is now controversial. The last major stage of the Pleistocene, the Wisconsin in North America, began around 50,000 years ago and continued, with many fluctuations, until 10,000 years ago. Because their water was taken up into ice, the oceans of the world during the advances of the late Wisconsin were 200 ft (60 m) lower than they stand at present, sufficiently exposing a platform to form a land bridge at least 1,000 miles (600 km) wide between Siberia and the western coast of Alaska. Although an enormous sheet of ice then covered much of North America as far south as the Great Lakes of today, the land bridge was ice-free, as was western Alaska and the Yukon Valley. Many of the earliest migrant hunters into America would then have crossed from Asia through a tundra-covered, treeless, cold region, covered with thin and patchy snows in winter, and inhabited by small herds of woolly mammoth, horse, bison, and other ungulates.

Archaeologists have divided broadly into two camps over the date and

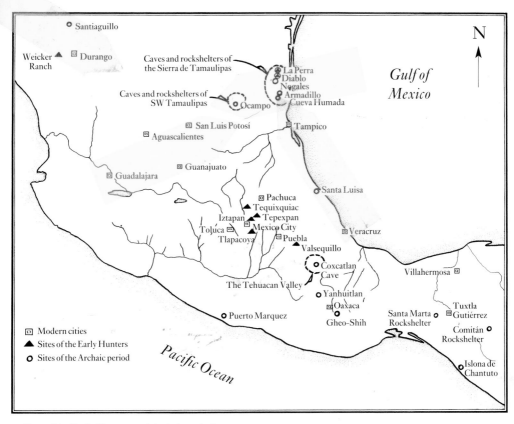

N

Santiaguillo

Weicker ▲   Durango
Ranch

Caves and rockshelters of
the Sierra de Tamaulipas

La Perra
Diablo
Nogales
Armadillo
Cueva Humada

*Gulf of
Mexico*

Caves and rockshelters of
SW Tamaulipas

Ocampo

San Luis Potosí
Aguascalientes

Tampico

Guanajuato

Guadalajara

Santa Luisa

Pachuca
Tequixquiac
Iztapan ▲ Tepexpan
Toluca   Mexico City
Tlapacoya   Puebla
Valsequillo

Veracruz

Coxcatlan
Cave

Villahermosa

The Tehuacan Valley

Yanhuitlan

Puerto Marquez

Oaxaca
Gheo-Shih

Santa Marta
Rockshelter

Tuxtla
Gutiérrez

Comitán
Rockshelter

Modern cities
▲ Sites of the Early Hunters
O Sites of the Archaic period

Pacific Ocean

Islona de
Chantuto

5 Sites of the Early Hunters and Archaic periods.

mode of entry of these earliest Americans. One camp firmly believes in a "short chronology": that the first movements into this hemisphere from Asia could only have taken place when there was a land bridge in place (this would have been drowned by rising sea levels beginning about 10,000 years ago), and that this occurred no earlier than 14,000-16,000 years ago. The other school holds to a "long chronology," pointing to far older – if often disputed – radiocarbon dates than this for early human remains in the hemisphere. The argument regarding the land bridge put forward by the "short chronology" school only holds weight if boat travel was unknown in the world during the late Pleistocene. Yet early humans had reached Australia, which was never connected to the Asiatic mainland by a land bridge, by 50,000 years ago, surely by boat. This raises the possibility of perhaps equally early migrations into North America, although there is yet no evidence for them.

All the early skeletons that we have from the Early Hunters stage indicate that these peoples were ancestral American Indians belonging to the great Mongoloid branch of humanity; no remains of Peking Man (*Homo erectus*), Neanderthal, or any other archaic form of our genus have ever been discovered in this hemisphere. Since no indisputably Last Interglacial artifacts have

5

come to light in North or South America, we may surmise that humans entered Alaska at the earliest during the Wisconsin, both by land and by sea.

Certain finds tend to back up the "long chronology" for human entry into the hemisphere. At Valsequillo, near Puebla in southern Mexico, Cynthia Irwin-Williams found cultural remains associated with an extinct fauna which included mammoth, mastodon, horse, antelope, dire wolf, and smaller mammals; the lack of bifacially worked projectile points suggests an early date, supported by a single radiocarbon determination of about 21,000 years ago. In the Valley of Mexico itself, dates ranging from 21,000 to 24,000 years ago are possible at the island site of Tlapacoya for a crude industry of choppers, scrapers, flakes, and a blade and burin.

The New World must have been an untouched paradise for the first hunting people. Extensive herds of large grazing animals such as mammoths, mastodons, camels, horses, and giant bison roamed through both subcontinents. With ideal conditions such as these, population expansion and spread were probably fairly rapid. Radiocarbon dating has demonstrated that people were hunting sloth, horse, and guanaco at the Straits of Magellan by at least 10,000 BC, and Tom Dillehay's work at Monte Verde, Chile, has produced compelling evidence for a significantly older occupation, at 12,500 BC.

To understand the significance of finds of late Pleistocene date that have been made in Mexico, it is necessary to consider them in the light of the Early Hunters stage as we now know it for North America as a whole, especially for the United States, where research on this problem has been most intensive. The opinion of many New World archaeologists is that the earliest known remains are those of a very simple culture of hunters and gatherers in which the majority of tools were inconceivably crude, percussion-chipped, pebble artifacts. Coarse choppers, chopping tools, scrapers, and knives are found at a number of campsites and open stations in the western United States under conditions of seemingly great antiquity; since this rudimentary inventory is exactly that of the late Pleistocene population of east Asia, it is believed to represent the non-perishable part of the tool-kit of the first immigrants.

By approximately 11,000 BC an immense technological change had taken place, with the introduction or invention of fine percussion- and pressure-flaked stone points of the type known as Clovis. These have, extending up from the base on one or both sides, a broad channel or flute formed by the removal of long, narrow flakes by a technique that is not yet well understood. Clovis points are found over much of North America, from Alaska down to Panama; some magnificent specimens come from mammoth "kill" sites in Arizona near the Mexican border. In the American Midwest and West, at about 10,300 BC, a refinement in fluting produced the well-known Folsom point; specimens of this type supersede Clovis, and are often associated with bison "kills." All these points, because of their size and weight, are considered to be the "business end" of spears which were hurled with the aid of a spearthrower (or *atlatl*, to use the Nahuatl term). Experiments carried out by Dennis Stanford of the Smithsonian Institution have shown the high efficiency of this weaponry over the hand-held spear: the atlatl-hurled spear has 15 times the speed and 200 times the impact. It comes as no surprise that the atlatl stayed in favor until the Spanish Conquest. The bow and arrow was a late arrival in Mexico and was not adopted at all in many areas.

Concurrently with Folsom, in the Great Plains as far south as Texas appeared a number of related industries all characterized by bifacially chipped, lanceolate points (Angostura, Scottsbluff, etc.); in actuality, this lanceolate point "horizon" covers much of Latin America as well. The origin of the techniques and concepts involved in the production of bifacially chipped spear points in this hemisphere is not known, although some have looked to the Old World where very similar industries have existed from a much earlier time level.

Of course, all the above-mentioned tool inventories were the equipment of peoples who were without agriculture and who lived mainly by the chase and the gathering of wild plant foods. From what we know about still extant societies with a similar way of life, such as the Australian Aborigines, concentrations of population larger than the small band were quite impossible. The late Edward Deevey once estimated that on this level of development, corresponding roughly to the Upper Palaeolithic of Europe, 25 sq. miles (65 sq. km) of territory are required for the support of one person. In all the New World prior to 7000 BC there may never have been at any one moment in time more than half a million persons, with about 30,000 of these in Mexico – a crude guess, to be sure, but not unreasonable.

Late Pleistocene Mexico presented a landscape considerably different from that which we see at the present. Rain poured then on places where it hardly touches today, and many semi-deserts must have been in those remote times a sea of grass. The great lake in the Valley of Mexico, where the most significant finds of the Early Hunters stage have been found, was a great deal broader and deeper, as testified by old strand lines on the surrounding hills.

A single spear point of the Clovis type of quartzite, about 2 inches (5 cm) long, was found on the surface of the Weicker Ranch, some 30 miles (48 km) west of the city of Durango in northwestern Mexico. Like all Clovis specimens, this is a fluted point fashioned by a combination of percussion- and pressure-flaking and shows the characteristic dulling of the edges at the sides and base (presumably to prevent abrasion of the lashing by which it was bound to the shaft). By analogy with radiocarbon-dated Clovis sites in the United States, this artifact represents an occupation of Mexico as early as the eleventh millennium BC.

Freshwater sediments over 250 ft (75 m) thick underlie Mexico City and all areas of the now dry beds of the great lake in the Valley of Mexico. Geological work has established a stratigraphy for the upper part of these deposits that corresponds to the later part of the Pleistocene and all the post-Pleistocene climatic sequence. Crucial to the problem of the ancient occupation in the Valley is the Becerra Formation, divided into an Upper and a Lower. The latter probably pertains to the early or middle Wisconsin Stage, while the Upper Becerra Formation can be assigned with some confidence to the Valders Advance of the late Wisconsin (11,000–8000 BC), on the basis

6 (right) Clovis point about 5 cm long from the Weicker Ranch, Durango.

of a single radiocarbon date and the kind of artifacts associated with this stratum.

The Upper Becerra is a fine, green muck, and has lenses of ash deposited by the volcanoes that were then in frequent eruption. Over this is a layer of brown, sandy sediments that were deposited at a time when the great lake was shrinking. Presumably this layer represents the first part of the warmer period known as the Hypsithermal Interval, broken by the sudden readvance of the ice sheet in Canada about 6000 BC. A turn to really dry conditions and desiccation of the lake bed is indicated by a layer of *caliche*, or calcium carbonate, marking the climax of the Hypsithermal. From the *caliche* layer to the surface are several layers which probably date from the late Hypsithermal to modern times and which contain abundant potsherds.

As long ago as 1870 the Mexican naturalist Mariano Bárcena discovered the sacrum of an extinct camelid which had been carved to represent the head of an animal, apparently a large member of the dog family, at the locality of Tequixquiac, 42 miles (67 km) north of Mexico City. This specimen lay at a depth of 40 ft (12 m) below the surface, in deposits of unknown age. One can only indulge in guesswork, but several other lesser finds at Tequixquiac in subsequent years have been ascribed to the base of the Upper Becerra Formation, and the carved sacrum may well have been found in this layer.

Few finds in Mexico have aroused such general interest as the famous "Tepexpan Man" (in fact a woman). In 1949 the geologist Helmut de Terra was engaged in a search for mammoth skeletons in the vicinity of Tepexpan, on the northeastern edge of the old beds of Lake Texcoco, a locality known to be rich in Pleistocene fossils. Almost as an accidental by-product of his survey, a human skeleton was exposed in one trench. "Tepexpan Man" appears to have been deliberately buried by her fellows, face down and with the legs drawn up under the body, unaccompanied by any offerings. According to a study by Santiago Genoves, the dead person was a woman of no more than thirty years of age, about 5 ft 3 in (160 cm) tall, and not particularly different from Mexican Indians in general. The major problem, it should be unequivocally stressed, is the actual stratigraphic position of the skeleton when discovered. According to de Terra, it was found in the Upper Becerra Formation, a stratum known to have fossil elephant remains as well, and underlying the *caliche*. Unfortunately, the inept handling of the excavation makes it unlikely that we shall ever know whether this was so or not. As Marie Wormington has pointed out, the type of burial represented by the Tepexpan Woman suggests the subsequent Archaic period, when flexed, unaccompanied interments are common, at least in the United States. However, fluorine tests have pretty well demonstrated the contemporaneity of the skeleton with mammalian fossils known to be of Upper Becerra age. The Tepexpan Woman may be our First Mexican, after all.

Far more satisfactory and less enigmatic results have been obtained on the old lake flats near Santa Isabel Iztapan, only a few miles south of Tepexpan. In 1952, Mexican prehistorians, following up a chance find by workers opening a drainage ditch, excavated the skeleton of an imperial mammoth

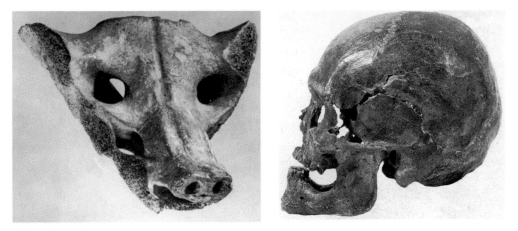

7 Animal head carved from the sacrum of an extinct camelid, from Tequixquiac, state of Hidalgo. Early Hunters period.

8 Fossil human skull from Tepexpan, Valley of Mexico. Early Hunters period.

(*Mammuthus imperator*) which lay entirely within the green muck of the Upper Becerra Formation, and which was therefore Valders in age. The animal had been butchered *in situ*, a fact that could be deduced from the disarticulated position of the bones alone. Most importantly, six human artifacts were indisputably associated with the skeleton. These included a flint projectile point of the type known as Scottsbluff, one of the most widely distributed artifacts of the lanceolate point horizon on the Great Plains of the United States. The other artifacts were utilized in cutting up the mammoth, and comprised a scraper, knife, and fine prismatic blade, all of obsidian, and an endscraper and retouched blade of flint.

In 1954, the construction of another ditch by the Santa Isabel Iztapan villagers resulted in the lucky find of a second mammoth "kill," again with artifacts that had been lost during the butchering process. Here a hind leg of the animal had been caught in the Upper Becerra muck, probably as it was fleeing its human pursuers. During the butchering process, the head and tusks had been dragged back across the body, and some bones showed deep cuts made by stone knives while the meat was being hacked off. Three chipped-stone artifacts found among the bones comprise an Angostura point of a dark igneous material, a Lerma point of flint, and a chert, bifacially worked knife. The first two named are of some interest. Angostura points also can be ascribed to the lanceolate point horizon on the Great Plains, known to be later than the Clovis horizon. Lerma points have an even wider spread in the late Wisconsin Glacial, being found in Texas and northeastern Mexico (where they appear as early as 8000 BC), and are one of the most common types of point ascribed to the Early Hunters stage in South America as far south as Argentina. We have no radiocarbon dates on the Santa Isabel Iztapan finds, but charcoal from a hearth next to a skeleton of still another slaughtered mammoth in the same formation has been dated to 9200 BC by this process.

We can reconstruct something of the life and environment of these lacustrine hunters of the Valley of Mexico some 11,000 years ago, although it must

9 The second fossil mammoth from Santa Isabel Iztapan, Valley of Mexico. The hind leg which had become caught in mud can be seen in the foreground. During butchering, the head and tusks had been dragged back across the body. Early Hunters period.

10 (*opposite*) Chipped stone tools found in association with mammoths at Santa Isabel Iztapan. *a*, flint Scottsbluff point; *b*, flint Lerma point; *c*, Angostura point. Over 1/2.

be remembered that we lack all knowledge of their campsites and have the chance evidence only of their hunting prowess. The climate was more humid and cooler than that of today; in fact, the now barren outskirts of the Valley were covered with pine forests. In the distance, the young cones of the active volcanoes poured out smoke, ash, and lava, perhaps disturbing the tempo of life in the Valley from time to time, but not seriously disrupting it. The imperial mammoth seems to have favored the swampy margins of the wide, shallow lake. These beasts must have been relatively easy game to organized groups of hunters, who, armed with spears hurled from atlatls and equipped with stone knives and other butchering tools, drove the heavy beasts into shallower water where they became hopelessly mired in the treacherous lake bottom. There each mammoth was isolated and dispatched, although probably not without danger since the risk of impalement by the formidable tusks of the surrounded animal must have been considerable – to kill any elephant with spears would require pluck.

On the northeastern frontier of Mexico, in the state of Tamaulipas, Richard S. MacNeish revealed in his excavations a long cultural sequence that begins with our primitive Early Hunters. The earliest of these phases, the Diablo Complex, is of some simplicity, comprising only crude, bifacially flaked and uniface tools made from flints or pebbles; choppers, ovoid blades, pebble endscrapers, and crude flake sidescrapers suggest an unspecialized hunting and gathering way of life on the most rudimentary level. Since these artifacts are found in a high terrace of the Canyon Diablo, formed when the river was running very much higher and the climate was obviously much wetter than today, MacNeish has suggested that the Diablo Complex is contemporaneous with the Mankato Advance of the Wisconsin, 13,500–12,000 BC.

A far better picture of Ice Age life in Mexico comes from the Tehuacan Valley in Puebla, where a large-scale project directed by MacNeish disclosed a late Pleistocene occupation called the Ajuereado phase. Radiocarbon dates suggest that it ended before 8000 BC, but it must have been in part coeval with the Iztapan kills. The evidence shows that the climate was cooler and drier than that now prevailing, with open steppe covering the valley floor. In this setting grazed subsequently extinct horse and pronghorn antelope, which were hunted with spears fitted with Lerma points. The inhabitants also sought smaller game, such as jack rabbits, gophers, and rats. The tool technology was totally based upon chipped stone; in addition to projectile points, there were knives, choppers, sidescrapers (for dressing hides), and crude blades. Ground stone tools, which could have been used to prepare vegetable foods, are absent, although some wild plants such as prickly pear cactus and *Setaria* grass were surely harvested by crude means.

The inhabitants of Tehuacan during Ajuereado times were probably grouped into about three nomadic families or microbands of four to eight people each, and the evidence of cave-floor occupations shows that camps were changed three or four times a season, since there never was enough food in any one ecological niche to support settled life, a state of affairs which also prevailed throughout the succeeding Archaic stage.

It would be a dangerous misconception to consider this period, viewed as a whole, as merely the time when people hunted huge Pleistocene animals such as mammoth, horse, and so forth. As a matter of fact, in actual habitation sites of this date in Texas and elsewhere in the United States, the vast majority of animal bones and remains come from relatively small animals, as humble as rodents, snakes, snails, and mussels. These people gathered and ate everything that was edible, and probably had to survive some very lean seasons. Since most of the sites that we have are large and conspicuous "kills," we have been deluded into thinking that we are dealing with some sort of ancient "big-game hunters" who disdained smaller animals or plant foods. True, large herbivores were slaughtered, but from this we must not assume that the late Pleistocene was a time of plenty. Like the modern Pygmies of the African rain forest, who also hunt elephants, success in the chase probably meant a short feast marked by voracious gluttony, with long intervals of eating whatever they could lay their hands on.

11 Probable community patterns, Ajuereado phase in the Tehuacan Valley. Groups moved from wet-season camps (circles), to fall camps (squares), to dry-season camps (triangles).

3 · The Archaic Period

Six thousand years of almost uninterruptedly high temperatures, as much as 2°C (3.6°F) above present averages in some places, set in on the heels of the final advance of the ice, around 7000 BC. The pleasant term "Climatic Optimum" has been invented for this Hypsithermal period in western Europe, for there the inhabitants of the lands facing on the Atlantic enjoyed significantly wetter as well as warmer weather, perhaps the most balmy ever seen in those regions. Such favorable conditions hardly obtained elsewhere in the world, and in much of North America this long interval was largely one of desiccation. In contrast to the oak forests of humid Europe, vast areas of the New World were transformed into desert wastes.

Odd though it may seem, during the Hypsithermal people continued to live throughout even the most desiccated zones of North America. Species after species of large game perished not long after its onset, or even before it; while climate change has often been advanced as a cause of this ecological disaster, several scholars are convinced that this was a case of Pleistocene overkill by the American Indians themselves. Among the animals that disappeared at this time were the mastodon, mammoth, horse (not to reappear until the coming of the Spaniards), camel, giant bison, ground sloth, and dire wolf. But the native Americans survived. New tools, especially food-grinding implements, new hunting methods, other sources of food, perhaps different forms of shelter, all these enabled people to adapt to radically altered conditions of life.

The new stage of cultural adaptation attained by the inhabitants of the New World is called the Archaic, and it is the full equivalent of the Meso-lithic stage in the western part of the Old World. Denied the rich hunting economy of their late Pleistocene predecessors, small bands of American Indians concentrated on more efficient methods of killing smaller game, on fishing and gathering of molluscs, and to an ever-increasing extent on the collection of specific plant foods.

The Desert Culture in North America

In the dry semi-deserts of the Great Basin and southwestern United States, as well as north to Oregon and south to Texas and Mexico, these Archaic hunters and collectors inhabited caves and open sites near the ever-dwindling lakes or by seepages of water. The region that concerns us here, Mexico, must have been quite hot and dry, as shown by known shrinking of the great lake of the Valley of Mexico and by the overwhelming appearance of dry pollen indicators in the cores at this time. The pattern that enabled humans to eke out a livelihood in this inhospitable environment has been named the Desert Culture, which persisted into the nineteenth century among the nomadic Indians of the Great Basin. Its salient features include a sparse population with no groups larger than the band; caves and rockshelters favored for settlements; a subsistence pattern based on the seasonal exploitation of food resources such as rabbits, wild plant seeds, and even insects; preparation of plant foods by grinding them on a flat milling stone with a cobble mano; abundant basketry, matting, and sandals (known as early as 7000 BC in caves in Oregon); spears tipped with relatively small, percussion-chipped points and hurled by means of the atlatl; a wide variety of scrapers, choppers, scraper planes, and so forth, of quite crude manufacture; and the dog, present for the first time in North America early in this development.

The discovery of an Archaic period of Desert Culture type in Mexico has unexpectedly thrown light on one of the great problems in New World archaeology: where, when, and how were the major food plants domesticated by the American Indian? For it was the cultivation of maize, beans, and squash that made possible all the higher cultures of Mexico, and, to a certain degree, those of Peru as well. In the effort to bridge the gap between the ancient hunting peoples and the first indications of full-blown village life, the researches of Richard S. MacNeish from the 1950s onward have produced particularly important results, and most later researchers build on his work while debating his conclusions. The most important results from Mac-Neish's work and the central remaining questions surrounding the onset of village life are described in this chapter.

The origins of Mexican cultivated plants

There is no simple definition of the term "domestication." Quite obviously, there is a difference between the domestication of an animal like the dog or pig, which can and often do revert to the "wild" state, and a creature, the reproduction of which entirely depends upon the presence of human populations, such as the Egyptian chicken, which has lost the ability to incubate its own eggs. We are clearly dealing here with a broad spectrum, in which the *degree* of domestication may vary widely; one might thus adopt the definition proposed many years ago by the Russian geneticist Nikolai Vavilov, and say that it is evolution directed by the interference of humans. Basically, this implies that human beings have in some systematic way tampered with the reproduction of a certain species, a process that may be totally unwitting.

As in animals, in its most extreme form plant domestication ends up with species which cannot reproduce by themselves and which are therefore without wild populations. In the case of cereals and other plants that reproduce by means of seeds, this implies that artificial selection has resulted in species which lack the ability to disperse their seeds. Not until that state has been reached can botanists be sure of the presence of domestication in ancient plant remains. It is no accident that all the important food plants of the world belong in this category of totally captive populations, since the reduction of the ability to self-reproduce has resulted in greatly increased food values in the plants concerned.

The importance of maize

The Aztecs believed that their hero-god Quetzalcoatl, who created humanity with his own blood, turned himself into an ant so as to be able to steal a single grain of maize that the ants had hidden inside a mountain; this he gave to humans so that they might be nourished. Maize was and is the very basis of settled life in Mexico and, in fact, throughout the regions of the New World civilized in Pre-Columbian times. Speculation as to the origin of this staple has therefore been freely indulged in, with many theories proposed which are no more firmly grounded than the Aztec myth recorded above.

There are in fact two central problems still facing the student attempting to understand the domestication of corn: the identity of its ancestor or ancestors, and the date at which fully domesticated maize (*Zea mays*) first appears. An older generation of archaeologists was raised in the belief that the story of the domestication of maize was completely known. Since maize (*Zea mays*) is a grass with no known wild forms, the search was early started for a closely related species in the wild state. In the highlands of Chiapas and Guatemala, very near the heart of the so-called "Old Empire" of the Maya, a grass called *teosinte* (*Zea mexicana*) grows in and near Indian cornfields as an unwanted weed; this species is the closest relative of maize. It was very early claimed that this was the wild ancestor of maize, and that the process of taming it to meet human needs was the achievement of the notably advanced Maya. From these people maize was supposed to have spread, along with the arts of civilization, far and wide throughout the New World. Although this theory has been subjected to a number of criticisms, there still exist strong arguments for *teosinte* as the ancestor of maize, but there is no evidence that the Maya were the overseers of domestication. In a slightly more complex scenario, the late Paul C. Mangelsdorf and his colleagues finished forty years of research by suggesting that perennial *teosinte* must have crossed with an extinct wild ancestor of maize to produce annual *teosinte* which then led to maize. The eminent geneticist, George Beadle, however, had long ago proclaimed that any theory based on an extinct or unknown ancestor was not satisfactory. Beadle countered Mangelsdorf's scenario with the contention that the simplest explanation was also the best: that maize arose solely from the process of human selection of *teosinte* plants, and thus *teosinte* is the only ancestor of maize.

Recent studies of the molecular biology of maize and its putative ancestors also point to *teosinte* as the sole progenitor of maize. Through the isolation of genes that control the traits separating maize and *teosinte* in a cross-bred population, for example, John Doebley has proposed specific steps in the transformation of ancestor to domesticate. Other similar studies propose to trace the origin of maize to a particular strain of *teosinte* found in the Balsas River Drainage of western Mexico. These studies have been criticized, however, for their tacit acceptance of *teosinte* as the sole progenitor.

Another relative of maize is tripsacum (*Zea tripsacum*), a wild grass distributed throughout North and South America. Although not as closely related as *teosinte*, it has long played a role in certain explanations of maize development, largely because of properties produced when crossed with *teosinte* or maize itself. By crossing tripsacum with *teosinte*, Mary Eubanks has recently been able to produce some plants that resemble the oldest archaeological maize remains, as well as others that resemble reconstructed "wild maize," suggesting to that researcher that perhaps tripsacum did play a role in the earliest domestication of maize.

While the researches above focus mainly on the semi-arid highlands of Mexico as the hearth of domestication, a scenario defined largely by the work of Richard S. MacNeish, several researchers are now investigating the role of the tropical lowlands in these developments. Unlike the dry caves of the highlands, rarely if ever are large plant remains preserved in this hot, humid environment, so other sources of information must be consulted. Phytoliths (fossil evidence of plant cells) related to maize have been found as early as 7000 BC in Panama and Ecuador, far to the south of the generally accepted hearth of maize domestication. Pollen related to maize also appears just after 5000 BC in Panama. It is very difficult, however, to distinguish closely related plants using such molecular methods, so that it may be unclear whether these phytoliths and pollen are maize, *teosinte*, or even tripsacum. This identification problem does not disprove any role for the lowlands, but does make it difficult to argue unequivocally for maize domestication in the area at those early dates. This situation hampers scenarios that depend heavily on molecular data, such as the Balsas River Drainage hypothesis described above. When molecular data is combined with other evidence of human occupation and domestication, however, it makes a much stronger case. Recently archaeologists Mary Pohl and Kevin Pope have found large maize phytoliths (probable domesticates) dated to 4800 BC on the Gulf Coast of Tabasco, very near the later Olmec site of La Venta. There are no known wild species of *Zea* native to coastal Tabasco, so these plants were introduced to the region, almost certainly by humans. At the same level the archaeologists found evidence of large-scale forest clearance of the type associated with maize cultivation in this area. If this Tabasco material is true maize cultivation, then it would be the earliest record of such activity that we have.

In the highlands, the earliest firmly dated maize cob was found in Guilá Naquitz cave in Oaxaca and dated to 4300 BC. Cobs from caves in Tehuacan, Puebla, found by MacNeish and long thought to date to *c*. 5000 BC through radiocarbon dating of associated materials, have recently been subjected to direct dating of the cobs themselves and found to date to 3500 BC and after. This Tehuacan sequence is crucial for the domestication of maize in particular and the Archaic period in general, for it is mainly through the work of MacNeish and his colleagues that we obtained our first systematic picture of this period (see "The Tehuacan Valley" below). Any major revision in the sequence would cause a certain amount of readjustment in our vision of the entire Archaic period. MacNeish was vehement in his defense of the earlier dates for these cobs, citing contamination in the samples as the cause of the

The principal domestic plants of pre-Spanish America

COMMON NAME	LATIN NAME	COMMENTS
* Avocado	*Persea americana*	
Agave (century plant)	*Agave* spp.	Fiber from leaves, pulque from base of flower stalk
Amaranth	*Amaranthus hybridus*	Pot herb, grain
* Annatto	*Bixa orellana*	Flavoring, food coloring
* Arrowroot	*Maranta arundinacea*	Root crop
Black nightshade	*Solanum nigrum*	Pot herb
Black sapote	*Diosbyros ebenaster*	Fruit tree
Bottle gourd	*Lagenaria siceraria*	Container
* Cacao	*Theobroma cacao*	Beans, the source of chocolate, used for money
* Calabash tree	*Crescentia cujete*	Rind of fruit used as container
* Cashew	*Anacardium occidentale*	Fruit tree
Chayote	*Sechium edule*	Squash-like fruit
Chía	*Salvia hispanica*	Seeds used for beverage, oil
Chile pepper	*Capsicum frutescens, C. annuum*	
Common bean	*Phaseolus vulgaris*	
Copal	*Protium copal*	Resin used as incense
Cotton	*Gossypium hirsutum*	
Dahlia	*Dahlia* spp.	Flower
Goosefoot	*Chenopodium* spp.	Pot herb
* Guava	*Psidium guajava*	Fruit tree
* Hog plum	*Spondias mombin*	Fruit tree
Husk tomato or tomatillo	*Physalis ixocarpa*	Vegetable
Indigo	*Indigofera suffruticosa*	Dye
Jack bean	*Canavalia ensiformis*	
Jícama	*Pachyrhizus erosus*	
Maize	*Zea mays*	
* Manioc	*Manihot esculenta*	Root crop
Marigold	*Tagetes erecta*	Flower, medicine
* Papaya	*Carica papaya*	Fruit tree
Peanut	*Arachis hypogaea*	Of Andean origin
* Pitahaya	*Hylocereus undatus*	Fruit of epiphytic cactus
Prickly pear	*Opuntia* spp.	Fruit and cactus pods eaten
Pumpkin	*Cucurbita pepo*	
* Rubber	*Castilla elastica*	Trunk tapped for latex
* Sapota	*Pouteria mammosa*	Fruit tree
Scarlet runner-bean	*Phaseolus coccineus*	
* Soursop	*Annona muricata*	Fruit tree
* Star- apple	*Chrysophyllum cainito*	Fruit tree
Sweet potato	*Ipomoea batatas*	
Tepary bean	*Phaseolus acutifolius*	
Tobacco	*Nicotiana tabacum*	
Tomato	*Lysopersicon esculentum*	
* Vanilla	*Vanilla planifolia*	An epiphytic orchid
Walnut squash	*Cucurbita mixta*	
Warty (crookneck) squash	*Cucurbita moschata*	
White sapota	*Casimiroa edulis*	Fruit tree
* Yam bean	*Pachyrhizus erosus*	Has edible tuber
Yucca	*Yucca elephantipes*	Hedges; flowers edible

* grown mainly in the lowlands

discrepancy. Whatever the final outcome of the Tehuacan date debate, it is clear from the cob shape of both the Tehuacan and Oaxaca examples that considerable evolution of maize had already occurred, throwing open the question once again of when and where domestication first happened. We have some way to go before we answer these questions, but the most important general fact remains: many thousands of years before Christ, the Indians of Mesoamerica had brought a very primitive, wild form of maize under their control. This was indeed the most crucial step along the road leading to the great Pre-Columbian civilizations.

Other cultigens

Although maize was certainly the most important plant for ancient Mexicans, it was not the first to be domesticated. Recently Bruce D. Smith has found evidence of domesticated squash (*Cucurbita pepo*) as early as 8000 BC, which would make it easily the earliest reliably dated Mesoamerican domesticate. The seeds and other plant remains used to date the domestication were found in Guilá Naquitz cave in Oaxaca, and it has been suggested that the type of squash found there is a distant relative of today's pumpkin. Around this same time Archaic foragers were probably domesticating the bottle gourd (*Lagenaria siceraria*), which is a relative of the early squash. While the squash seeds provided a source of protein that was easy to store and transport, the bottle gourd provided a portable container for drinking water, so important to these early nomadic peoples.

While maize is at the center of the Mesoamerican food complex, other vegetable foods, especially chile peppers, always accompany it. The pre-Spanish Mexicans consumed an extraordinary array of plant foods, from various kinds of beans to squashes to chile peppers to fruits. In fact, it is difficult to imagine what the world's cuisines were like before the discovery of Mexico and Peru. The list in the accompanying table is incomplete, and does not, of course, give all the varieties or races of each plant.

The common bean, known in many varieties today, is the most popular in Mexican diets and presumably has been so since very early periods. Its nutritional importance stems from the fact that its proteins complement those of maize. On the basis of a distribution of wild forms, Nikolai Vavilov suggested a primary domestication in Mexico or Guatemala.

Of the squashes, there are three major species in Mexico: pumpkin, warty or crookneck squash, and walnut squash, the forms of all of which are virtually legion, as any visitor to a Mexican food market can readily testify. The origins of all of these from wild ancestors or through hybridization are very little understood, although a very early domesticate has been identified, and the sequence of their appearance in Mexico is now established. The same might be said of chile peppers, today the major ingredient in "hot" foods the world over, but of Mexican and Peruvian origin; the major problem with this particular seasoning (also an important source of vitamins to Indian populations) is the difficulty of distinguishing between wild and domesticated seeds.

Archaeological evidence for the origins of many other cultigens is rare to non-existent, in part due to the perishable nature of root crops. Thus, the antiquity and role of manioc in the tropical lowlands of Mesoamerica are not known, in spite of the fact that this is an important food plant there today. Also important are the decorative plants of Mexico, such as the dahlia, marigold, and zinnia; the marigold, for instance, has a significant part to play in the long roster of Mexican medicinal plants. Omitted from the table are economically important trees which are protected rather than actually domesticated, such as the breadnut tree, the sacred ceiba (symbolic of the Tree of Life), mahogany, and the sapodilla tree, which produced valuable fruit, wood, and chicle latex for chewing gum.

Caves and rockshelters of northeastern Mexico

Richard S. MacNeish's search for the origins of agriculture and settled life in Mexico first led him to the almost rainless, semi-desert environment of Tamaulipas, the northeasternmost Mexican state. It is actually beyond the frontier of Mesoamerica: the tribes encountered by the Spaniards in this backward region were, with few exceptions, hunters and collectors without knowledge of cultivation. MacNeish was drawn to this region because the aridity of Tamaulipas has meant ideal conditions of preservation in cave and rockshelter sites, of which a good many were discovered. In the course of his excavations, he uncovered the first evidence for an entirely new stage in the prehistory of Mexico: the Archaic or "Incipient Agricultural" period, lasting from about 7000 BC to after 2000 BC.

The Archaic Tamaulipas tool inventory is fairly typical of the Desert Culture throughout western and southern North America. In chipped stone, there were scrapers, choppers, pebble hammerstones, and disk scrapers, most of which were probably used in the preparation of vegetable foods; projectile points, used in the hunting of deer, were fixed with resin to shafts of darts (short spears hurled with the atlatl). Plant products were also processed
12 with ground stone tools, such as mortars, pestles, manos, and crude milling stones. MacNeish concludes that the economy largely rested upon hunting, collecting, and the grinding of wild seeds. As part of this complex, there were simple nets and turned and coiled baskets, while cordage was made from the
13 fiber of wild plants like yucca and agave. People slept on twilled mats; these, known as *petates*, are still standard sleeping gear for millions of Indians in back-country Mexico.

12 Characteristic stone tools of the Archaic in Tamaulipas. *a*, mortar; *b*, hand stone or mano; *c*, milling stone. 1/4.

13 Ovoid biface of obsidian and matting fragment, Archaic period of Tamaulipas. Over 1/2.

Plant materials and dried feces, or coprolites, were remarkably well preserved and abundant, for the ancient inhabitants of these rockshelters had only scanty notions of hygiene. The diet was heavy in vegetable foods, some of which came from domesticated plants. Earliest of all is the bottle gourd; this appeared by about 6500 BC. It is even older in the Archaic period of Oaxaca and is thus with squash the most ancient cultigen of the New World. The history of the bottle gourd, usable only as a container since the meat is inedible, is puzzling. It is believed by botanists to be of Old World origin, probably with an initial center of domestication in Africa. Tests have shown that the seeds are viable after the dried gourd has been immersed for several years in sea water. Accordingly, the likelihood is that the plant floated from Africa to the New World to land on some eastern shore. How, then, did the American Indians adopt it as their own? It is remotely possible that some beachcomber of a distant era came across the gourd by accident, carried it back to the camp and sowed the seeds. One hardly needs to stress that this reconstruction is pure fantasy, but we are not prepared to adopt the alternative explanation, namely that African voyagers carried the gourd with them on a sea trip to the west at this early date.

Other plants occur in the Tamaulipas sequence at somewhat later dates, including pumpkin, scarlet runner beans, chile peppers, common beans, and squashes, in that order. There was no wild maize in MacNeish's excavations, but the cobs of a tiny-eared pop corn with many pod corn characteristics appear between 3000 and 2200 BC. This suggested to MacNeish that he should be looking further south for the origins of maize.

Santa Marta rockshelter

As one travels west from the Grijalva Basin, the Chiapas highlands grow increasingly arid. Santa Marta rockshelter lies in this dry zone, near the town of Ocozocoautla on the Pan American Highway, and was tested by MacNeish and Fredrick Peterson in 1959. Five successive Archaic occupations in the cave were directly overlain by pottery-bearing deposits ascribable to the Early Preclassic horizon. Radiocarbon dates for the Archaic levels indicate a span from at least 6700 BC through an extremely dry period (after 5000 BC). The complex of tool and point types duplicates that of Tamaulipas, and includes dart points, gouges, scraper planes, pebble manos and boulder querns, etc. Four burials were found together, three of them flexed in fetal posture and one extended above, all the dead having been covered as a group with metates. Burials of this sort occur in Desert Culture contexts as far north as Wyoming.

Maize pollen makes its appearance only in the Early Preclassic occupation, both pollens and other maize plant parts being completely absent from the pre-pottery levels. So, we might draw the conclusion that in the search for maize origins, Chiapas, on the southeastern periphery of Mexico, is perhaps too far south, just as Tamaulipas appears to be too much to the north.

The Tehuacan Valley

One of the most exciting discoveries in Mexican archaeology in recent decades has been of actual remains of wild maize, found in archaeological deposits in highland Mexico. In 1960, MacNeish turned his attention to the Tehuacan Valley in southeastern Puebla, some 130 miles (200 km) southeast of Mexico City. Lying in the rain shadow of the Sierra Madre range that protects it on the east, the Valley is an arid cactus- and thorn-scrub-covered desert not unlike southern Arizona. So dry is it that effective agriculture capable of supporting a large population is only possible with irrigation, a technique that goes back here to the first millennium BC. MacNeish's prelim-

14 View of the Tehuacan Valley, looking out from Coxcatlan Cave.

15 Cob of wild maize from the Coxcatlan phase, Tehuacan Valley.

inary reconnaissance of the bone-dry caves and rockshelters which border the Valley led to a four-season project which uncovered, at long last, cobs of wild maize as well as of the earliest cultivated variety.

It will be remembered that the Ajuereado phase, an Early Hunters occupation of the Valley, ended about 7000 BC. During the succeeding El Riego phase (c. 7000–5000 BC), two significant changes had come about. The first is that the climate turned warmer, perhaps resulting (with human help) in the disappearance of "big game." The second is that by the end of the phase, the Tehuacan people had begun interfering with the evolution of certain plants: surely domesticated were the avocado, chile peppers, amaranth (this remained a grain of secondary importance in the highlands right through the Spanish Conquest), and walnut squash. As in Tamaulipas, the preponderance of vegetable food, both wild and domesticated, in the diet is reflected by numerous mortars and pestles, and by milling stones and pebble manos; large plano-convex scrapers and choppers were probably used for pulping various plant materials. Chipped projectile points for atlatl-propelled darts are present, used in hunting deer and other relatively small game.

There are some surprising features in El Riego. Two bolls of domestic cotton were recovered, apparently the world's first. Some quite elaborate burials from the phase were found in caves, the bodies being wrapped in blankets and nets, and the heads sometimes removed, ceremonially smashed, and deposited in baskets; in a burial group of two children, the head of the older was found in a basket resting on the chest of the younger. Possibly we are confronted here with a very early case of human sacrifice.

While population size had increased, the El Riego people remained seasonally nomadic. During the dry season, camps were occupied by microbands which lived mainly by hunting. In the spring, these moved into the slopes of the Valley, collecting seeds, and in the summer "wet season" they were able to pick fruit. Perhaps when there was more rain than usual, they were able to coalesce into macrobands. In the fall, with a diminution of food supplies, they moved back to their winter abodes.

One of the great transition points in New World prehistory is to be seen in the Coxcatlan phase (*c.* 5000–3400 BC). The economy and settlement pattern in the Valley remained much the same, but to the list of domesticates were added the bottle gourd, common bean, black sapote, and warty squash – the evidence is now quite clear that these and other plants were domesticated in different places and at different times. Most important is the appearance of maize for the first time anywhere in the New World, although dates early in this period are now under re-evaluation. Maize here proved to be of two types, a wild variety and an early domesticated one which was probably planted, like already existing cultigens, when microbands came together in the spring. The minuscule cobs of wild maize so closely approached the reconstructed ancestor of maize, that Mangelsdorf was confident that the ancestor of corn had been found. In particular, they exhibited the extended glumes, the tiny kernel size, and the bearing of the male tassel on the female ear of the hypothetical progenitor, as well as showing no variation among themselves, a wild characteristic. But, as proponents of the *teosinte* theory of maize origins have pointed out, they also looked distressingly like *teosinte*! Further, as we have seen, a botanist has been able to reproduce plants similar to the Tehuacan examples by crossing tripsacum and a certain strain of *teosinte*. The controversy, nevertheless, may be of more interest to plant geneticists than to students of ancient Mexican culture, for the important point to remember is that the world's most productive domesticated plant had now come under human control; the process of domestication, in Mac-Neish's present way of thinking, took place somewhere in the Puebla-Oaxaca region during the 7000 to 5000 BC time period. While current research agrees with this time frame, it is not certain that the area of domestication was the Puebla-Oaxaca region.

The succeeding Abejas phase (*c.* 3400–2300 BC) saw a distinct change in the Tehuacan settlement pattern, with small hamlets of five to ten pithouses down on the Valley floor. Domestic plants newly added to the cuisine were tepary beans, perhaps the pumpkin, and hybrid maize showing introgression ("capture" of genes by backcrossing) with *teosinte*. While a study by the late Eric Callen of Abejas coprolites reveals that 70 percent of the diet was still based on wild plants and animals, the increasing cultivation of crops for storage in specially made caches and pits was associated with longer and longer stays in band encampments. The result was the possibility of staying in one place all year; sedentism was gradually replacing nomadism.

It will be seen in the next chapter that Early Preclassic pottery centers on the neckless jar or *tecomate*, and the flat-bottomed bowl with outslanting sides. It is probably significant that in Abejas these same shapes are seen in beautifully made ground-stone vessels, perhaps prototypes for later ceramics.

In fact, during the final Archaic phase in the Valley, the poorly known Purrón (*c.* 2300–1500 BC), crude, gravel-tempered pottery makes its appearance – late in the sequence, but certainly by 1650 BC. The so-called "Pox pot-tery," found by Charles and Ellen Brush in middens on the coast of Guerrero, is close in appearance to the Purrón ceramics and has similarly early radiocarbon dates. In the hot, fertile Soconusco coast of southeastern Chiapas, on the border between Mexico and the Maya area, the people of the Barra culture were already crafting highly sophisticated ceramics that are at least in part contemporary with Purrón, and may be the source from which most of the pottery traditions of the Mesoamerican Preclassic stem. Nonetheless, it is quite unlikely that pottery – that index fossil of fully seden-tary life – was independently developed in Mesoamerica, for agricultural villages with well-developed ceramics have a far greater antiquity along the Caribbean and Pacific coasts of northern South America, and many archaeologists believe that the idea of firing clay to make vessels spread from there to Mexico.

Other Archaic sites

In the Valley of Oaxaca, Kent Flannery and his associates have uncovered a long preceramic sequence paralleling that of Tehuacan in some respects, but adding new and sometimes contradictory data. Most of Flannery's sites are caves, such as Guilá Naquitz cited above, but the open-air site of Gheo-Shih was particularly interesting as it showed evidence of activity features, such as a possible dance-floor (or ball court) area, some 65 ft (20 m) long and 23 ft (7 m) wide, bordered with stones. As for food plants, there are pollen grains of the genus *Zea* in 7400–6700 BC levels, which apparently represent wild maize. Rinds of bottle gourds and seeds and peduncles of pumpkins are also this early, and so predate their appearance in Tehuacan.

The role of the lowlands, plagued by poor archaeological preservation, is relatively unknown, although current research is certainly enlarging the role it will play in future accounts of the Archaic. It is probable that maize is a seed crop of highland origin, but lowland root crops like manioc leave little if any archaeological evidence. A single manioc pollen grain was found in Tabasco, associated with maize cultivation, and dated to 4600 BC, but pollen evidence cannot identify species, leaving the question of domestication open. Thus, while there are good data on hunting, gathering, and fishing for an extensive Archaic village found by Jeffrey Wilkerson at Santa Luisa, on the coast of northern Veracruz, the absence of manos and metates need not necessarily mean an absence of cultivation, since manioc preparation does not require these. Similarly, pre-pottery levels in shell middens at Puerto Marquez and Islona de Chantuto on the Pacific Coast may well be manifesta-tions of an otherwise unknown "incipient agricultural" way of life.

One of the most important Archaic discoveries has been at Tlapacoya, once an isolated island in the southern part of the Valley of Mexico; circular houses like those of the Abejas phase have been uncovered, along with an extremely crude female figurine of pottery, date 2300 BC±100, the oldest discovered in Mesoamerica and apparently the beginning of a tradition that was to flourish in the Preclassic.

The Archaic period and the origins of settled life

The idea that the invention and adoption of food production led to a "revolution" in the advancement of mankind was elaborated by V. Gordon Childe and has influenced the way of thinking of almost all who deal with this point in human history. At the time that Childe wrote (1925–56), almost nothing was known of the transition between the hunting and gathering and the food-producing way of life, either in the Old World or in the New. The mere absence of the evidence made the jump seem almost more sudden than subsequent work has shown it actually to have been. Now, for both Peru and Mexico, we have evidence of a very slow progress toward fully settled life: the alleged "revolution" was seemingly more in the nature of a leisurely evolution. Yet, it cannot be denied that the consequences of food production were in the long run of the greatest importance. Deevey has demonstrated that the density of population of peoples on the Neolithic (or Preclassic) level of food-getting is 25 times greater than the figure for primitive hunters and gatherers – the domestication of plants and animals obviously resulted in a quantum increase in the world's population, no matter how long the process took.

In Mexico, and probably in Mesoamerica in general, the development of plant cultivation took place during the Archaic period in a context which is almost indistinguishable from that of the Desert Culture, known so well in the Great Basin country of the American West. Back in this remote time, the ancestors of the mighty Aztecs and other civilized peoples of Mexico probably closely resembled the simple but resourceful "Digger Indians" of Nevada and California, so despised by Mark Twain and other western travelers of the Victorian era. Semi-nomadic bands were forced into a seasonal cycle of hunting and collecting by the poverty of the relatively rainless Mexican environment. As the Hypsithermal wore on, however, their efficiency at collecting plant foods began to outweigh their hunting prowess, with an increasing amount of settling down – seasonal camps took on the appearance of tiny villages. As the result of systematic exploitation of certain kinds of plants, especially of wild grasses like maize, vegetable foods and their energy were tamed and captured. According to present evidence, the process began with the bottle gourd, which may have been an accidental introduction, and squash, followed by beans and chile peppers. Maize was most likely domesticated before 5000 BC, although at that time it hardly resembled the giant hybrid plants of modern Iowa cornfields. Other domesticated food plants are much later and a few, like the peanut, were probably disseminated to Mexico from South America in post-Archaic times.

By the time of the first village-farming cultures, at the onset of the Preclassic, there were already present many of the features of settled life: all the important domesticates, the milling stones and manos on which maize was prepared, baskets, nets, cordage, mats, and apparently even wattle-and-daub houses. With the elaboration of pottery, almost certainly introduced from the lowland regions of South America, and with the yet mysterious improvement of maize at this great transition, the stage is set for a way of life that has remained unaltered to this day in the peaceful backwaters of Mexico.

4 · The Preclassic Period: Early Villagers

In the late nineteenth century, there was really no idea at all of the sequence of development in pre-Spanish Mexico. Of course, everyone knew perfectly well that the Aztecs were quite late, and that the Aztecs had spoken of an earlier people called the Toltecs. There was also a vague feeling that the great ruins of Teotihuacan were somehow the products of an even earlier people – but that was about all. Imagine the delight, then, of Mexican antiquarians when there began to appear in their collections little handmade clay figurines, of a naive and amusing style totally removed from that of the mold-made products of later peoples in the Valley of Mexico. Most astonishing was their obvious antiquity, for some had been recovered from deposits underlying the *Pedregal*, the lava covering much of the southwestern part of the Valley. Scholars, prone to labels, immediately named the culture which had produced the figurines and the very abundant pottery associated with it "Archaic," and in 1911 and 1912 Manuel Gamio demonstrated stratigraphically that the central Mexican sequence runs from earliest to latest: "Archaic," Teotihuacan, Aztec.

It was not very long before the "Archaic" or something like it was turning up all over Mexico and Central America, wherever, in fact, the archaeological spade went deep enough. Similar materials were found even in South America: in Peru, along the waterways of the Amazon basin, and on the Caribbean coast of Venezuela. On the basis of this distribution, Herbert J. Spinden in 1917 proposed that there was an "Archaic" basement underlying all the civilizations of the Western Hemisphere, a unitary culture which had originated with the supposed first domestication of maize in the Valley of Mexico and which had spread with that plant everywhere, bearing along the little figurines as a hallmark. Quite naturally, this idea – based on incomplete and faulty evidence – met with very determined opposition, especially by those whose subsequent delvings into "Archaic" remains had shown them the considerable diversity within this allegedly monolithic culture.

Today the old "Archaic" is known as the Preclassic or Formative period. Let us for the moment define the Preclassic as that epoch when farming based on maize, beans, and squash really became effective – effective in the sense that villages, and hamlets had sprung up everywhere in Mexico. As such, the Preclassic period is quite comparable to the Neolithic of the Old World, and almost all the Neolithic arts, with the exception of animal husbandry, were present: the construction of compact settlements, pottery, loom weaving, working of stone by grinding as well as chipping, and the modeling of female figurines in clay.

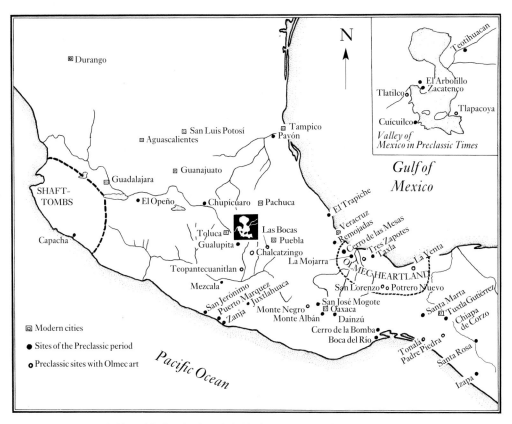

16 Sites of the Preclassic period. The inset shows the distribution of Preclassic centers in the Valley of Mexico.

Villages mean more people, and more people are, broadly speaking, the result of a greatly increased supply of food. What had happened to bring this about? As outlined in the previous chapter, the plants involved had already been domesticated for several millennia prior to the Preclassic. We may be seeing the result of a hasty improvement in the size and number of kernels of the maize ear through increased introgression of *teosinte*. A resulting population spiral of the most Malthusian sort could have suddenly filled all of central and southern Mexico, and indeed all of Mesoamerica, with land-hungry farmers, and camps and hamlets might have become permanently settled villages in almost a few generations.

When did all this take place? Somewhat arbitrarily, it must be admitted, we set the lower limits of the Preclassic at the first appearance of pottery in abundance, about 1800 BC according to recent radiocarbon dates. The upper boundary of this period is more problematical. In the lowland Maya area, the first carved monuments appear *c.* AD 250, and this is usually taken as the beginning of the Classic throughout Mesoamerica. However, in central Mexico, the Classic is initiated *c.* AD 150, when the great city of Teotihuacan took its present shape; we shall thus adopt the latter date as the termination of the Preclassic. These dates therefore span some nineteen-and-a-half centuries.

It might also be reasonably asked why it took so long for the Mexicans to cross the threshold to village-farming life. In the Old World this event first occurred, along the hilly flanks of Mesopotamia, as early as the tenth millennium before Christ, not very much later than the first experimentation with plant and animal domestication. In Mexico, where the American Indian originally took this step, the process of domestication took at least three millennia; was this delay caused by the lack of domesticable animals, by the nature of the plants domesticated, by the cultural milieu of Mexico, or by some other factor? We do not yet know the answer, but a handicap of this kind is the real reason why sixteenth-century Mexico was the technological inferior of Europe, for once past the frontier into peasant life, ancient Mexican culture unfolded at the same rate as did that of the Old World. Given this late start, the civilization that Cortés destroyed should be compared not to Renaissance Europe, but to the Bronze Age of the Near East and China.

Archaeologists are generally agreed that the Preclassic development can be divided into three parts: Early, from 1800 to 1200 BC; Middle, from 1200 to 400 BC; and Late, from 400 BC to AD 150. It is also increasingly apparent, as we shall see, that both simple village cultures and more complex societies can be detected in all three subperiods. The emerging picture is far more intricate than could have been imagined fifty or even thirty years ago.

The Early Preclassic in Chiapas

Knowledge of the Early Preclassic in Chiapas is relatively recent; it began in the 1950s with the interest of the New World Archaeological Foundation (NWAF) in Chiapa de Corzo. Excavations conducted at that site, lying in the center of the dry Grijalva Depression of Chiapas, have disclosed no fewer than eighteen successive occupations from the earliest times to the present. For much of its history, the Grijalva drainage basin seems to have been little more than a buffer state between the Maya to the east and an assortment of lesser nations to the west, south, and north. However, in the Preclassic period each of several distinctive cultures was linked to other more distant village cultures, chiefdoms, and even states in southeastern Mexico and the Maya area.

More recently, the NWAF, under the direction of John Clark, has turned its attention to the Soconusco region, the broad, Pacific coastal plain of southeastern Chiapas and neighboring Guatemala, where the oldest Preclassic cultures of all have been revealed by the excavator's spade, beginning with the Barra culture, and continuing through the complex and sophisticated Ocós culture (these have been treated separately in *The Maya*). We now know that the Early Preclassic occupation of Chiapa de Corzo is an extension of developments by the probably Mixe-Zoquean-speaking inhabitants of Soconusco.

As reconstructed from debris recovered deep in a test pit at Chiapa de   17
Corzo, the Chiapa I, or Cotorra, phase presents us with a good example of Early Preclassic culture, with a total span estimated to be about 1400 to

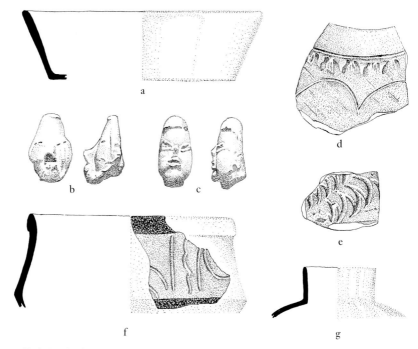

17 Early Preclassic ceramics, Chiapa I phase (1400–1000 BC), from Chiapa de Corzo. *a*, dish; *b–c*, figurine heads; *d, e, f*, rim fragments from neckless jars; *g*, fragment of necked jar. Various scales.

1200 BC. Admittedly we have only a fragmentary picture of the first farmers at Chiapa de Corzo, but they prepared their maize on simple milling stones that are heavily worn and thus must have been rare, and they manufactured solid, handmade clay figurines. Their pottery was advanced in technique and quite sophisticated in form and decoration. Most of it consists of a hard, monochrome white or two-color red-and-white ware, in the shape of dishes and large storage jars that might be either simple globular or else necked. Of some interest is the plastic decoration found on the rims of otherwise plain neckless jars: brushing with a handful of vegetable fibers, rows of gouges effected with the thumbnail, dimples popped out from the vessel interior, and plain rocker-stamping. Now, rocker-stamping is a most peculiar way to alter the surface of a jar or dish. The trick is to "walk" the edge of a crescentic implement held in the hand across the damp clay in such a way that curved, zigzag patterns are produced. Rocker-stamping is found on pots of the allied and coeval Ocós culture, where the tool used was the crinkly edge of a cardium shell; and, in fact, the technique was known to Preclassic (or Formative) peoples all the way from the Valley of Mexico to Peru. Whatever its point of origin, rocker-stamping is thought to have spread through the advanced regions of the New World at a fairly early date.

Vestiges of a culture much like Chiapa I lie just above the latest Archaic occupation of Santa Marta cave, further west in Chiapas (see Chapter 3), and are accompanied by the pollen of maize and other plants indicating a very wet phase. Quite certainly, the farmers of the Early Preclassic enjoyed a climate which contrasted with the rainless conditions of the preceding Archaic.

Early Preclassic villagers in Oaxaca

The Valley of Oaxaca, the homeland of the Zapotec people and the locus of the remarkable Monte Albán culture of later periods, is three-armed and shaped like an inverted Y. It was once thought that prior to 500 BC, the Valley was completely filled with a lake, and that therefore no earlier cultural remains would ever be found. This has been totally disproved by the large-scale University of Michigan archaeological-ecological project, directed by Kent V. Flannery, which has shown that there was always a river valley here, and never a lake. Furthermore, the Flannery group has uncovered a cultural sequence extending all the way from the earliest preceramic Archaic, right up through Monte Albán I, the latter dated to 500–150 BC.

Survey and excavations carried out by the Michigan archaeologists have identified seventeen permanent settlements of the Tierras Largas phase (1650–1350 BC), but almost all of these are little more than hamlets of ten or fewer households; the largest settlement in the Valley of Oaxaca at that time was San José Mogote, which ranked as a small village of about 150 persons, sharing a lime-plastered public building. The villagers grew maize and cultivated avocados, collected wild plant foods, and hunted deer, cottontail rabbits, and other game.

By the following San José phase (1350–950 BC), San José Mogote, located in the Etla arm of the Valley $6\frac{1}{4}$ miles (10 km) northnorthwest of Monte Albán, had grown into a village of 80 to 120 households covering about 50 acres (20 hectares), with an estimated population of 400 to 600 persons. Carbonized seeds recovered by the flotation method show that a number of crops were raised, probably on the high alluvium: maize, chile peppers, squashes, and possibly the avocado (although this may have been traded in from the lowlands). Our old friend *teosinte* grew in cornfields and crossed with local maize, either by accident or design.

Food storage was probably the main function of the bell-shaped pits which here, as elsewhere in Preclassic Mesoamerica, are associated with household clusters. Many could have held a metric ton of maize, and if capped with a flat rock, might have inhibited insect growth through lack of oxygen. As they "soured" or otherwise lost their usefulness for preservation of grain, they were employed for other purposes, such as the preservation of household items and implements, or for refuse disposal, or even as burial places.

The only domestic animals eaten were dogs – the principal source of meat for much of Preclassic Mesoamerica – and turkeys – understandably rare because that familiar bird consumes very large quantities of corn and is thus expensive to raise. Wild animals in the San José Mogote diet were cottontail rabbits, and deer and peccary which were hunted on the mountain slopes, an area which also produced acorns and black walnuts.

Houses were rectangular and about 20 ft (6 m) long, with slightly sunken floors of clay covered with river sand. The sides were of vertical canes held between wooden posts, and were daubed with mud, then white-washed; roofs were thatched. Sleeping arrangements were typically Mesoamerican: the people slept on mats rolled out on the floor. The Michigan project found that there was a division of labor between and within households. Some houses, for instance, specialized in the manufacture of small, flat mirrors made of magnetite, an iron ore that takes a high polish. Within houses, clear signs of an area mainly used by women consisted of concentrations of bone needles, deer bone cornhuskers, and spindle whorls made from potsherds. Men's place in households was indicated by chipped stone debris and by stone burins and drills used in the manufacture of shell and mica ornaments.

Not all households were alike in status, either, and the concentration of magnetite mirrors – an item rich in symbolic prestige since it was connected, as we shall see, with the burgeoning and contemporary Olmec civilization of the Gulf Coast – was unequal across the village. Furthermore, there was a marked degree of social differentiation in the goods accompanying burials: high-status individuals tended to have burial offerings like mirrors, cut shell, jade labrets and earspools, and above all gray or white pottery vessels with Olmec designs. This was no egalitarian society, and bore a marked Olmec imprint, a state of affairs which we shall find repeated for Tlatilco, in the Valley of Mexico.

The site of Tlatilco

The simple picture of myriad "Neolithic"-looking villages such as that at Chiapa de Corzo scattered over the Mexican countryside without any great social differentiation among them is an over-simplification, as the Oaxaca data suggest. Evidence from excavations in the Valley of Mexico makes clear that some settlements had already taken precedence over others in both social rank and in economic advantage. The key site for the Early Preclassic in the Valley is Tlatilco, which came to light in 1936 during excavations carried out by brickworkers digging for clay, not, alas, by archaeologists. The visitor to the site today will find nothing but a series of huge holes in the ground, surrounded by factories. In actuality, only a tiny fraction of Tlatilco was ever cleared under scientific conditions.

Settled by about 1300 BC, Tlatilco was a very large village (or small town) sprawling over about 160 acres (65 hectares). Located to the west of the great lake on a small stream, it was not very far removed from the lakeshore where fishing and the snaring of birds could be pursued. In the Tlatilco refuse are the bones of deer and waterfowl, while represented in the potter's art are armadillo, opossum, wild turkey, bears, frogs, rabbits, fish, ducks, and turtles. Conspicuously present in those parts of the site actually excavated by archaeologists were the outlines of underground, bell-shaped pits. They were filled with dark earth, charcoal, ashes, figurine and pottery fragments, animal bones, and lumps of burned clay from the walls of pole-and-thatch houses; as in Oaxaca, they must have served originally for the storage of grain belonging to various households.

18 Sub-floor burials with offerings of pottery bottles, bowls, dishes, and figurines at Tlatilco, Early Preclassic period, 1500–1200 BC.

No fewer than 340 burials were uncovered by archaeologists at Tlatilco, but there must have been many hundreds more destroyed by brickworkers 18 (sometimes at the instigation of unscrupulous collectors). All these were extended skeletons accompanied by the most lavish offerings, especially by figurines which only rarely appear as burial furniture in Preclassic Mexico.

There are two sorts of figurines: one that is large and hollow, and painted 19 red, and the other small, solid, and of incredibly delicate and sophisticated workmanship. The latter usually represent girls with little more to wear than paint applied in patterns (probably with the clay roller stamps which have 20, 21 been found in the excavations), although some are attired in what would seem to be grass skirts. Here we encounter males as well, clothed in a simple breechclout. What an extraordinary glimpse of the life of these Preclassic aristocrats is provided in their figurines! We see women affectionately

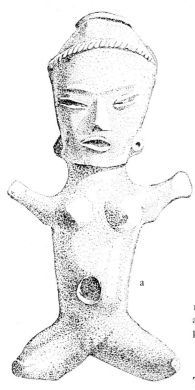

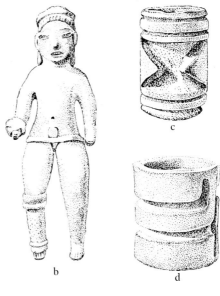

19 Pottery figurines and roller stamps from Tlatilco. *a* is hollow and bears traces of red, yellow, and white paint; *b* is hollow, was painted red and yellow, and represents a ball player. 3/8.

Tlatilco figurines and pottery

20, 21 Pottery figurines of two dancers, Tlatilco, Valley of Mexico. Early Preclassic period. Hts 11.4 cm and 12 cm respectively.

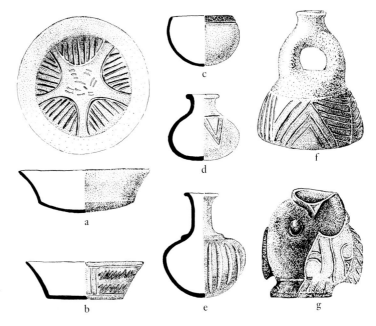

22 Representative pottery vessels from Tlatilco, Early Preclassic period. *a*, polished brown bowl with "sunburst" striations on the interior; *b*, rocker-stamped dish; *c*, red-rimmed bowl; *d–e*, necked jars; *f*, black stirrup-spout jar; *g*, black effigy in the shape of a fish, polished in zones. 1/5.

carrying children or dogs; dancers, some with rattles around the legs; acrobats and contortionists; and matrimonial couples on couches. While no ball courts are known for this period, it nevertheless is certain that the ball game was played, for many figurines show players with the protection for the hand and knee required by that sport.

A distinctly macabre streak appears in the art of the inhabitants of Tlatilco, possessed by a psychological bent that delighted in monstrosities. To illustrate this point, one might mention such representations as two-headed persons, or heads with three eyes, two noses and two mouths; hunchbacks; idiots; horribly ugly and sometimes masked individuals who may be shamans; and many other outrageous deformities. Several actual clay masks have been found, of the most sinister appearance; a few of these are oddly split vertically into two distinct faces, one of which might be a skull, for instance, and the other half an idiot with protruding tongue. Let it be noted here that dualism, the unity of basically opposed principles such as life and death, constitutes the very basis of the later religions of Mexico, no matter how great their complexity. Here we see the origin of the concept.

The pottery of Tlatilco bears a vague relation to the later peasant wares of El Arbolillo and Zacatenco, but there the resemblance ends. Within the bounds of the Preclassic tradition of plastic decoration and the restrained use of color, the potters of this village made ceramics that are among the most aesthetically satisfying ever produced in ancient Mexico. Forms include bowls, neckless jars, long-necked bottles, little spouted trays (possibly for libations), bowls and jars with three tall feet, and, most peculiarly, jars with spouts that resemble stirrups. One or two colors of slip such as red and white are sometimes applied; colors and all kinds of roughening of the

22

surface are confined to definite areas of the vessel by broad, grooved outlines. Particularly favored were contrasting zones of matt and polished surfaces, as well as zoned rocker-stamping. Designs such as stylized jaguar paws were carried out by cutting away part of the surface, the deep areas often filled with bright red pigment after firing.

There was great excitement in archaeological circles when the Tlatilco complex came to light, for something resembling it was already known elsewhere – thousands of miles to the south, in Peru. There also, in the very earliest civilization of the South American continent, the Chavín culture (c. 900–200 BC), were found such odd pottery shapes as stirrup spouts and long-necked bottles, associated with unusual techniques like rocker stamping and red-filled excising, as well as roller seals, figurines of Mexican appearance and split-face dualism. A chance resemblance or not?

Early editions of this book leaned heavily toward the idea, reminiscent of the old Spinden hypothesis, that such resemblances were the result of Mexican intrusion on the north coast of Peru, but this now seems unlikely. There is an overwhelming body of evidence which points to an independent evolution of ceremonial architecture, art, and therefore civilization in Peru. Further, if there *were* intercontinental diffusion at such an early time, it might well have been cultural spread to both areas from the lowland Pacific coastal area of Ecuador, where such indications of settled life as large villages, ceramics, and maize agriculture extend back beyond 3000 BC. Two finds in western Mexico suggest that such was the case. At the site of Capacha, in Colima, Isabel Kelly unearthed grave goods dating to about 450 BC which emphasize pottery bottles and stirrup spouts, and which unmistakably point to an Ecuadorian origin; and an elaborate tomb in El Opeño, in Michoacan, has very similar ceramics with a radiocarbon date of about 1300 BC.

On the other hand, it is certain that domestic maize was transmitted to Peru from the north, and only a few South American specialists are opposed to the idea that Early Formative (Preclassic) iconography – focused upon the awesome images of the jaguar, cayman, and harpy eagle – was shared through diffusion between the two areas. It must be admitted, however, that the conclusive evidence bearing on this most important problem of long-range diffusion in the hemisphere has yet to be gathered.

No mention has yet been made of another curious element in the burial offerings of Tlatilco, namely, the very distinct presence of a strange art style known to have originated at the same time in the swampy jungles of the Gulf Coast. This style, called "Olmec," was produced by the first civilization of Mesoamerica, and its weird iconography that often combined the lineaments of a snarling jaguar with that of a baby is unmistakably apparent in many of the figurines and in much of the pottery. The great expert on the pre-Spanish art of Mexico, Miguel Covarrubias, reasoned that the obviously greater wealth and social superiority of the Tlatilco people over their more simple contemporaries in the Valley of Mexico were the result of an influx of Olmec aristocrats from the eastern lowlands. This may possibly have been so, but it is equally likely that these villagers were a favorably placed people under heavy influence from "missionaries" spreading the Olmec faith, without a necessary movement of populations. But more about the Olmecs in the next chapter.

Established villages of the Middle Preclassic

Let us turn now from the Early Preclassic to the somewhat incomplete information which is at hand for the villages girdling the Valley of Mexico during the middle range (*c.* 1200–400 BC) of that period. A word of caution, however – because of our first knowledge of these sites, the impression has been given that the Valley had more ancient Preclassic beginnings than elsewhere. On the contrary, that isolated basin was probably a laggard in cultural development until the Classic period, when it became and stayed the flower of Mexican civilization. Notwithstanding its later glory, the Valley was then a prosperous but provincial backwater, which occasionally received new items developed elsewhere.

These Middle Preclassic villages fringed the placid waters of the great lake, once more fully expanded. Their remains are now swallowed up by the urban sprawl of Mexico City. From the reed-covered marshes, abounding in waterfowl, across the rich, soft soils in the bottomlands of the Valley, to the forested hills populous with deer, this was an environment favorable in the extreme. Perhaps the surroundings were too bountiful for the stimulation that a people seem to need in order to make real progress: no challenge, and therefore no response, in the scheme propounded by Arnold Toynbee in his overview of world civilizations, *A Study of History*.

The first phase at the site of El Arbolillo seems to mark the initial Middle Preclassic occupation of the Valley. This little village was established directly on the sands of a beach fronting an arm of the great lake. Protected from the chill winds of winter by the slopes of a nearby hill, the farmers drew sustenance from the products of their fields and from the lake. That the village was occupied for many centuries is indicated by the more than 23 ft (7 m) of accumulated midden deposits cut into by the excavator, consisting of refuse, casts of maize leaves, and burned daub fallen from the walls of pole-and-thatch huts.

Zacatenco, another site similarly placed on the edge of the lake, provides further evidence for the intensity of the village-farming life in the Valley. So much refuse was deposited in the Early Zacatenco phase (which follows on the heels of El Arbolillo I), that the villagers were forced to level it from time to time as terraces along which they built their wattle-and-daub houses.

Farmers they were, but the chase also provided much food for the villagers, as is well documented in the immense quantities of bones from deer and aquatic birds in the refuse. They hunted with small lance points chipped from obsidian, a hard, black volcanic glass worked with ease. Deer provided not only meat but also hides, which were cleaned of fat with little obsidian scrapers, and bones from which were fashioned awls and bodkins for working baskets and skins. Within each house, the farmer's wife ground the soaked maize on the familiar quern, although for some reason this was absent at

El Arbolillo. For cooking and storage, they had a pleasant but undistinguished pottery, usually reddish brown in color and finely burnished; a somewhat better type was produced at El Arbolillo, little three-legged bowls, smoked black, with red paint rubbed into geometric designs incised on the surface.

At these two sites and elsewhere in the Valley the midden deposits are literally stuffed with thousands of fragments of clay figurines, all female, providing a lively view of the costume of the day, or its lack. Although nudity was apparently the rule, these little ladies have elaborate face and body painting in black, white, and red; headdresses and coiffures as shown were very fancy, wraparound turbans being most common. The technique of manufacture was about like that with which gingerbread men are made, features being indicated by a combination of punching and filleting. Significantly, no recognizable depictions of gods or goddesses have ever been identified in these villages, suggesting the possibility that the only cult was that of the figurines, which may have been objects of household devotion like the Roman *lares*, perhaps concerned with the fertility of the crops.

The dead were buried under the floors of houses, the usual fashion in Mesoamerica, but also occasionally together in cemeteries. With knees drawn up against the chest and wrapped in the mat upon which he or she had slept in life, the deceased was placed in a simple grave dug in the sand, although sometimes this was outlined and covered by stone slabs. A few pots or implements dropped in the grave, and a jade bead occasionally placed in the mouth (a symbol of life here and in China), tell something of a belief in an existence after death. Child mortality was high, as a good percentage of the skeletons found are of immature individuals.

Late Preclassic cultures of the central highlands

The isolation of the Valley of Mexico from what was happening in the rest of Mesoamerica became even more pronounced in the period from 400 BC to AD 150. The mainstream of higher culture in that period was running through the lowlands of eastern Mexico and up the river valleys into the southern highlands and southeastern part of the Republic, ignoring the Valley. This isolation holds true for much of the central highland region, except where direct Olmec intrusions had taken place.

Bright colors and an increase in the size and length of vessel feet were the concern of the potter in Late Preclassic times. The predilection toward the use of two or more colors in ceramic decoration is well illustrated by Chupícuaro, the burial ground of a village which lay above the Lerma River in the state of Guanajuato, about 80 miles (130 km) northwest of the Valley of Mexico. While the Chupícuaro complex is widespread in the region, until recent excavations it was known, like Tlatilco, only from commercial pot-hunting. The skeletons of 390 individuals were found, almost all of whom had been laid on their backs in simple graves with abundant offerings of pottery, figurines, jade, and various clay objects. The later Mexicans believed that the owner's dog would help his soul across their equivalent of

23 Polychrome tripod jar, Chupícuaro culture, Guanajuato. Late Preclassic period. Ht 14 cm.

24 Pottery figurine of the "pretty lady" type, Chupícuaro culture, Guanajuato. Late Preclassic period. Ht about 10 cm.

the Styx, and we find at Chupícuaro that dogs were also interred, many of them with great care. The pottery vessels found in the cemetery are in both shape and decoration quite exuberant. In form one encounters bowls with all sorts of supports: short tripods, very long and attenuated tripods, swollen feet in the shape of breasts, pedestal bases. There are a few stirrup-spout jars, the last time this odd type is seen in Mexico, although it continued to enjoy great popularity in Peru until Colonial days. Vessel painting is lively, the slips used most often being red on buff, red and black on buff, or red and brown on buff, in finely proportioned, abstract designs which appear to have been derived from textiles. Little handmade, clay figurines of the "pretty lady" type were likewise dropped into the graves; these are charming and quite nude, with slanting eyes and fancy coiffures that were built up from clay strips.

The most notable advance in the Late Preclassic of central Mexico was the appearance of the temple-pyramid. The earliest temples of the highlands were thatch-roof, perishable structures not unlike the houses of the common people, erected within the community on low earthen platforms faced with sun-hardened clay. There are a few slight indications that some such platforms once existed at Tlatilco. By the Late Preclassic, however, they had become almost universal, as the nuclei of enlarged villages and even towns. Toward the end of the period, clay facings for the platforms were occasionally replaced by retaining-walls of undressed stones coated with a thick layer of stucco, and the substructures themselves had become greatly enlarged, sometimes rising in several stages or tiers. Here we have, then, a definite progression from small villages of farmers with but household figurine cults, to hierarchical societies with rulers who could call the populace to build and maintain sizeable religious establishments.

25 View west of a portion of the circular temple platform at Cuicuilco, Valley of Mexico. Late Preclassic period.

How grandiose some of these substructures were can be seen at Cuicuilco, located to the south of Mexico City near the National University, in an area covered by the *Pedregal* – a grim landscape of broken, soot-black lava with a sparse flora eking out its existence in rocky crevices. The principal feature of Cuicuilco is a round platform, 387 ft (118 m) in diameter and rising in four inwardly sloping tiers to a present height of 75 ft (23 m). Two ramps placed on either side of the platform provide access to the summit, which was crowned at one time by a cone-like construction which brought the total height to about 90 ft (27 m). Faced with volcanic rocks, the interior of the surviving structure is filled with sand and rubble, with a total volume of over 2 million cubic ft (60,000 cubic m).

It is little wonder that Cuicuilco was once thought to be of hoary antiquity, for the main structure, excavated many years ago, is surrounded and partly covered by lava which had flowed down from Xictli volcano, looming on the western horizon above the Valley floor. Estimates varying anywhere from 8,500 to 30,000 years were made for the age of the flow by competent authorities. But this was in the pre-radiocarbon era, and long prior to George Vaillant's careful work on the cultural stratigraphy of the Valley.

On the grounds of the associated ceramics and figurines, quantities of which are found beneath the *Pedregal*, Cuicuilco is clearly Late Preclassic, as confirmed by radiocarbon dates. The doom of Cuicuilco was set some time around AD 100, an end which must have been spectacular. The young Xictli first sent out dust and ashes that fell in quantity on the site, then the great eruptions themselves began, molten lava pouring out over the southwestern margin of the Valley. All must have fled in panic from the region. Did the inhabitants have any premonitions of the final cataclysm? One might think so, for prominent among the remains of their culture are clay incense burners in the form of Xiuhtecuhtli, who was Fire God and lord of the volcanoes among the ancient Mexicans.

In lieu of extensive excavations underneath the lava, it is difficult to be precise about the size and function of a regional center like Cuicuilco. On the basis of his unrivaled knowledge of the Valley of Mexico, however, William Sanders ascribes to it a population of 20,000, the chief center of a total Valley population of perhaps 140,000 souls. Regardless of the uncertainty about Cuicuilco, it surely presaged the great Teotihuacan civilization of the Classic period (Chapter 6).

Thanks to another volcanic event, we have a spectacularly preserved Late Preclassic village at Tetimpa, Puebla, on the northeastern flank of the Popocatepetl volcano. Unlike Cuicuilco, which was buried under a lava flow, Tetimpa was encased in ash falls, preserving much of what the villagers left in haste as Popocatepetl erupted around AD 100. Archaeologists Patricia Plunket and Gabriela Uruñuela discovered the still-furrowed corn fields under the ash, as well as the house mounds and domestic artifacts of the farmers who tilled these fields. The house compounds consist of two or three small structures, carefully set at right angles to each other around a central patio. An altar was often placed in the center of the patio, with a volcano effigy, crudely carved figure, or plain andesite stela on the summit. The buildings themselves consist of wattle-and-daub structures built on a stone platform. Most importantly, the platforms use the *talud-tablero* form, consisting of a sloping wall surmounted by a horizontal panel, which later becomes an architectural marker of the Classic metropolis, Teotihuacan.

The Mezcala puzzle

Although a rich source for portable jade objects in Olmec style, the rather dry basin of the upper Balsas or Mezcala River, in the state of Guerrero, is one of the archaeologically least-known regions in Mexico. During the Middle and Late Preclassic, and perhaps developing out of an Olmec substratum, appears the style called Mezcala, known largely from carved pieces of andesite and serpentine recovered by illegal excavations. These objects are highly abstract, usually representations of human figures recalling in pose and technique the simpler small productions of Teotihuacan, which they may foreshadow. As well as these, miniature facades of colonnaded temples are also known, and a few effigies of natural objects like conch shells.

26

27

The exact dating and cultural context of Mezcala art have long been unknown, since the overwhelming majority of Mezcala objects come from large-scale looting by the local population; in fact, this practice is known to go all the way back to the Aztecs, as many objects in this style were recovered in

The Mezcala style

26, 27 (*left*) Standing figure of stone. Ht 32 cm. (*Right*) Stone model of a temple. Ht 12 cm. Both Late Preclassic period.

dedicatory caches found in recent investigations of the Great Temple of Tenochtitlan, as we shall see in Chapter 10. This chronological puzzle has at last been solved, through the field project carried out by Louise Paradis of the University of Montreal; during the 1989–90 digging season, she excavated an *in situ* cache of Mezcala objects at the site of Ahuinahuac, just north of the Mezcala River, in a context radiocarbon-dated to 500–200 BC.

The shaft-tomb art of western Mexico and the Teuchitlan Tradition

The marshy highland area of Jalisco was a rich one for the development of civilization, with significant mineral riches (obsidian, greenstone, and salt) and a fertile agricultural area covering several interlocking lake basins. By 1500 BC we find shaft tombs with offerings at nearby El Opeño in northwest Michoacan. By 300 BC, this same burial type is associated with a specific circular architecture, in which a central circular altar is ringed by platforms surmounted by residential or temple structures. The widespread looting of archaeological sites in this area left us woefully ignorant of the cultural and historical context of this culture, now called the Teuchitlan tradition, until recently. Three decades of work by Phil Weigand and his associates have found monumental circles distributed around the Volcano of Tequila in the state of Jalisco, which forms the heartland of the Teuchitlan tradition. These monumental concentric circles are found illustrated in the tomb offerings, where the circles form the stage for elaborate feasting ceremonies and other rituals. The actual circles are often associated with monumental ball courts,

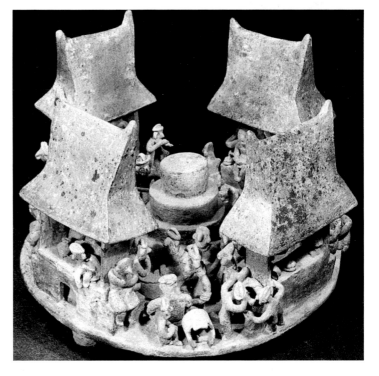

28 Pottery house group from Ixtlan del Río, Nayarit. The circular "floor" has a diameter of 53 cm. The exact chronological placement of this, like almost all western Mexican hand-modeled figures and groups, is unknown but is probably Late Preclassic. Here we see four thatch-roof houses on platforms arranged around a plaza, in the center of which is a four-tiered, circular temple-pyramid. Among the fifty figures are musicians playing trumpets and rasps, a pair of lovers, water carriers, children, dogs, and five men attempting to seduce a woman.

the latter also illustrated in the ceramic sculptures, in some of the most life-like renderings of the athletic ceremony to come out of Mesoamerica. It is also during this period that a remarkably vivid tradition of portraiture develops in the region, often showing rulers and venerated ancestors in seated postures with accoutrements of rank and ritual.

An earlier school of thought held that this shaft-tomb sculpture was little more than a kind of genre art: realistic, anecdotal, and with no more religious meaning than a Dutch interior. This view has been vigorously challenged by the ethnologist Peter Furst, who has worked closely with the contemporary Huichol Indians of Nayarit, almost certainly the descendants of the people who made the tomb figures. Among the Huichol and their close relatives, the Cora, religious practitioners are always shamans, powerful specialists who effect cures and maintain the well-being of their people by battling against demons and evil shamans. Furst noted that the warriors with clubs from Nayarit and Jalisco tombs are down on one knee, the typical fighting stance of the shaman. The Nayarit house models are interpreted by   28
him not just as two-story village dwellings, but as chthonic dwellings of the dead: above would be the house of the living, below is the house of the dead. Such a belief is consonant not only with Huichol ideas about death and the soul, but also with the supernatural concepts of Southwestern Indians like the Hopi. It also agrees with the archaeological evidence, for these "houses" may be identified as the funerary structures ringing the monumental circular architecture.

Nayarit, Jalisco and Colima

29 (*above*) Pottery figure of a man striking a turtle-shell with a deer antler, from Nayarit. The face and body have been decorated with polychrome paints. Percussion instruments of this sort are still in use in remote villages of Mexico. Probably Late Preclassic period. Ht 38 cm.

30 (*above, right*) Seated person holding a dish, pottery, from Jalisco, western Mexico. Probably Late Preclassic period. Ht 51 cm.

31 (*right*) Pottery dog wearing a mask with a human face, from Colima, western Mexico. Late Preclassic period. Ht 20.9 cm.

The Furst hypothesis that the symbolism of shaft-tomb art "conforms closely to characteristically shamanistic initiatory, funerary, and death-and-rebirth beliefs and rituals" is entirely logical considering the funerary context of this sculpture. Dogs, as we have seen with Chupícuaro, had a special mortuary significance in ancient Mexico, and one fine Colima example even wears a human mask – perhaps the face of his master! At the same time, Mark Miller Graham has argued that many of these figures are rulers, and not exclusively shamanistic practitioners. Miller Graham is certainly right to call our attention to the political meanings of these figures, for they can no longer be conceived as products of a village culture with little political hierarchy, as they were thirty years ago.

Recently a monumental shaft tomb was scientifically excavated by Lorenza López Mestas Camberos and Jorge Ramos de la Vega at Huitzilapa, Jalisco, the first of its kind to be so explored. The shaft cut down 21 ft (7.6 m)

31

32

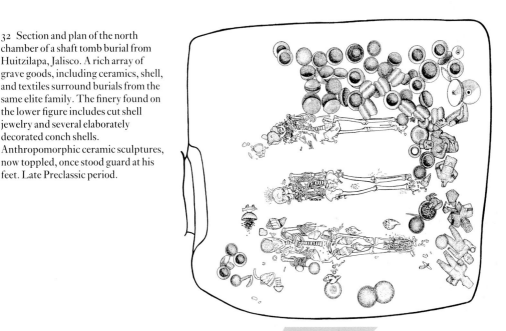

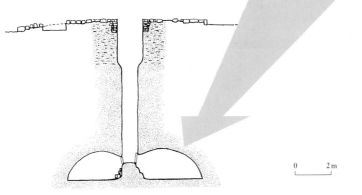

32 Section and plan of the north chamber of a shaft tomb burial from Huitzilapa, Jalisco. A rich array of grave goods, including ceramics, shell, and textiles surround burials from the same elite family. The finery found on the lower figure includes cut shell jewelry and several elaborately decorated conch shells. Anthropomorphic ceramic sculptures, now toppled, once stood guard at his feet. Late Preclassic period.

0   2 m

through the center of an elite residential structure. At the bottom of the shaft were two chambers, each containing three individuals and a rich array of offerings. Five of the six individuals exhibited a congenital hereditary defect (the fusion of cervical vertebrae), indicating a close kinship relationship. One of the members of this lineage group, a forty-five-year-old male, was treated with more deference, however, as witnessed by the presence of more exotics, especially conch shells from both the Caribbean and Pacific Coasts, along with numerous other objects of shell, greenstone, and quartz. Given that this was the only shaft tomb constructed at Huitzilapa, and that this figure was obviously of higher rank than his kin, he was surely a ruler of the site. All the other individuals, two adult females and three adult males, appear to have died earlier and were prepared and preserved as funerary bundles until the death of the ruler, at which time all six figures were deposited into the shaft tomb.

Outside the heartland, in the states of Jalisco, Colima, and Nayarit, only much smaller shaft tombs and simple pit burials are found, also with ceramic sculpture and other offerings, suggesting that there was a regional hierarchy centered on the Volcano of Tequila region. A massive relocation of much of the population to the central area occurred around AD 200, at the dawn of the Classic period. After this concentration of settlement around the Volcano of Tequila, the shaft tombs become much smaller and simpler, with more emphasis placed on the monumental circular architecture as a sign of power and prestige. By the Teuchitlan I phase (AD 400–700), an advanced Classic-period culture is now emerging from the archaeological record, one in which 10 sq. miles (24 sq. km) of ritual and residential precincts covered the central area, alongside over 115 sq. miles (300 sq. km) of intensive agricultural modifications, including extensive terraces and *chinampas*. Between AD 700 and 900 the Teuchitlan tradition went into decline, signalled by the cessation of circular building and the introduction, on the edges of the old sacred precincts, of a new architecture based on the square and rectangle. Metallurgy was introduced into West Mexico by AD 600 and from there to the rest of Mesoamerica. Given the specific technologies used by the West Mexicans, it is almost certain that knowledge of metalworking arose from long-distance contact with much older Central and South American traditions, and it may be the social disruption signalled by these new exotics, along with environmental stress, that eventually led to the collapse of a millennial tradition.

5 · The Preclassic Period: Early Civilizations

Background of civilized life

The advance in the arts and technology that is implied by the word "civilization" is usually bound up with the idea of urbanism. Nonetheless, the evidence is equivocal or negative for the presence of true cities among some Old and New World civilizations. One learns to one's surprise that cities were apparently missing among the Khmer of Cambodia and the Mycenaean Greeks. On the other hand, the great Classic Maya sites that were once relegated to the status of near-empty "ceremonial centers" are now considered by many to have been truly urban. Given such theoretical fluctuations, Mesoamerican archaeologists have looked to other criteria for "civilization."

V. Gordon Childe, among others, held writing to be a critical touchstone of civilized life, but of course it should be remembered that the large and complex Inca empire had no writing at all, relying as it did on the *quipu*, or knot record, for administrative purposes. However, most, if not all, the peoples of Mesoamerica eventually developed systems of writing; the Maya took this trait to its highest degree of development, with a mixed semantic-phonetic script in which they apparently could write anything they wished. As we shall see, Mesoamerican writing has very early origins, appearing in a few areas by the middle or end of the Preclassic period.

"By their works ye shall know them," and archaeologists tend to judge cultures as civilizations by the presence of great public works and unified, evolved, monumental art styles. Life became organized under the direction of an elite class, usually strengthened by writing and other techniques of bureaucratic administration. Early civilizations were qualitatively different from the village cultures which preceded them, and with which in some cases they co-existed. The kind of art produced by them reveals the sort of compulsive force which held together these first civilized societies, namely, a state religion in which the political leaders were the intermediaries between gods and humans. The monumental sculpture of these ancient peoples therefore tends to be loaded with religious symbolism, calculated to strike awe in the breast of the beholder.

Unless the written record is extraordinarily explicit, which it seldom is in Mesoamerica except for the Classic Maya and the Late Post-Classic peoples of central Mexico, it is extremely difficult to detect the first appearance of the state from archaeological evidence alone. A state is characterized not only by a centralized bureaucratic apparatus in the hands of an elite class, but also by the element of coercion: a standing army and usually a police force.

Mesoamerican archaeology provides plentiful data on the emergence of elite, high-status groups, but not very much on warfare or internal control, although both were surely present for over 2,000 years prior to the arrival of the Spaniards. Thus, in the absence of extensive written records, the argument over whether peoples like the Olmec had true states may never be resolved.

There was considerable variation in the extent of urbanism among the later cultures of Mesoamerica, from ones in which an elite center was served by a population living in villages scattered through the countryside, to ones with vast cities comparable to those of Europe and China. But all of them had administrative hierarchies, and rulers who could call on the peasantry as corvée labor to build and maintain the temples and palaces, and for food to support the non-farming specialists, whether kings, priests, or artisans. In conjunction with an elaborate ritual and civic calendar, writing sprang up early to ensure the proper operation of this process, and to celebrate great events in the life of the elite. Furthermore, in these centers were held at regular intervals the markets in which all sorts of food and manufactures of hinterland and center changed hands. This is the basic Mesoamerican pattern, established in the Preclassic, and persisting until Conquest times in many areas.

The Olmec civilization

The most ancient Mexican civilization is that called "Olmec." For many years, archaeologists had known about small jade sculptures and other

33 Jade effigy ax, known as the "Kunz" ax. The combination of carving, drilling, and incising seen on this piece is characteristic of the Olmec style. Olmec culture. Middle Preclassic period, provenience unknown. Ht 28 cm.

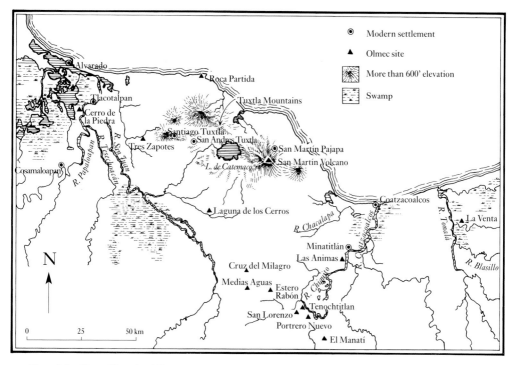

34 Map of the Olmec "heartland."

objects in a distinct and powerful style that emphasized human infants with 33
snarling, jaguar-like features. Most of these could be traced to the sweltering
Gulf Coast plain, the region of southern Veracruz and neighboring Tabasco,
just west of the Maya area. George Vaillant recognized the fundamental
unity of all these works, and assigned them to the "Olmeca," the mysterious
"rubber people" described by Sahagún and his Aztec informants as inhabiting jungle country of the Gulf Coast; thus the name became established.

Actually, nothing is known of the real people who produced Olmec art,
neither the name by which they called themselves nor from where they came.
Old poems in Nahuatl, recorded after the Conquest, speak of a legendary
land called Tamoanchan, on the eastern sea, settled long before the founding
of Teotihuacan

> In a certain era
> which no one can reckon
> which no one can remember,

where

> there was a government for a long time.[1]

This tradition is intriguing, for Tamoanchan is not a good Nahuatl name
but Mayan, meaning "Land of Rain or Mist." It will be recalled that an
isolated Mayan language, Huaxtec, is still spoken in northern Veracruz.

One possibility is that there was an unbroken band of Mayan speech extending along the Gulf Coast all the way from the Maya area proper to the Huaxteca, and that the region in which the Olmec civilization was established could have been in those distant times Mayan-speaking. This would suggest that the Olmec homeland was the real Tamoanchan, and that the original "Olmecs" spoke a Mayan tongue.

In contradiction to this hypothesis, some compelling evidence has been advanced by the linguists Lyle Campbell and Terence Kaufman strongly suggesting that the Olmecs spoke an ancestral form of Mixe-Zoquean. There are a large number of Mixe-Zoquean loan words in other Mesoamerican languages, including Mayan. Most of these are words, such as *pom* ("copal incense"), associated with high-status activities and ritual typical of early civilization. Although the dominant language of the Olmec area was until recently a form of Nahua, this is generally believed to be a relatively late arrival; on the other hand, Popoloca, a member of the Mixe-Zoquean family, is still spoken along the eastern slopes of the Tuxtla Mountains, in the very region from which the Olmec obtained the basalt for their monuments. Since the Olmec were the great, early, culture-bearing force in Mesoamerica, the case for Mixe-Zoquean is very strong.

There has been much controversy about the dating of the Olmec civilization. Its discoverer, Matthew Stirling, consistently held that it predated the Classic Maya civilization, a position which was vehemently opposed by such Mayanists as Sir Eric Thompson. Stirling was backed by the great Mexican scholars Alfonso Caso and Miguel Covarrubias, who held for a placement in the Preclassic period, largely on the grounds that Olmec traits had appeared in sites of that period in the Valley of Mexico and in the state of Morelos. Time has fully borne out Stirling and the Mexican school. A long series of radiocarbon dates from the important Olmec site of La Venta spans the centuries from 1200 to 400 BC, placing the major development of this center entirely within the Middle Preclassic. Another set of dates shows that the site of San Lorenzo is even older, falling within the Early Preclassic (1800–1200 BC), making it contemporary with Tlatilco and other highland sites in which influence from San Lorenzo can be detected. There is now little doubt that all later civilizations in Mesoamerica, whether Mexican or Maya, ultimately rest on an Olmec base.

The hallmark of Olmec civilization is the art style. Its most unusual aspect is the iconography on which it is based, through which we glimpse a religion of the strangest sort. The Olmecs evidently believed that at some distant time in the past, a woman had cohabited with a jaguar, this union giving rise to a race of were-jaguars, combining the lineaments of felines and men. These monsters are usually shown in Olmec art as somewhat infantile throughout life, with the puffy features of small, fat babies, snarling mouths, toothless gums or long, curved fangs, and even claws. The heads are cleft at the top, perhaps representing some congenital abnormality, but certainly symbolizing the place where corn emerges. Were-jaguars are always quite sexless, with the obesity of eunuchs. In one way or another, the concept of the were-jaguar is at the heart of the Olmec civilization. What were these creatures in function?

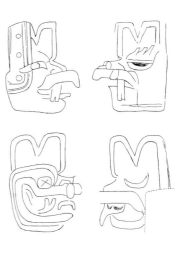

35, 36 Greenstone figure from Las Limas, Veracruz (*left*). A young man or adolescent boy holds the figure of an infant were-jaguar deity in his arms, while his shoulders and knees are incised with the heads of four other deities (see drawings, *above*). Olmec culture, Middle Preclassic period. Ht 55 cm.

Covarrubias, an artist-archaeologist with a profound feeling for Meso-american art styles, developed an ingenious scheme purporting to show that all the various rain gods of the Classic and Post-Classic cultures could be derived from an Olmec were-jaguar prototype, a somewhat implausible hypothesis since the Olmec area is one of the rainiest in Mexico and could have had little need for such a supreme deity. The chance find of a large greenstone figure near the village of Las Limas, Veracruz, shows that Olmec iconography was far more complex. This figure represents an adolescent boy or young man, holding in his arms a were-jaguar baby, a theme also to be seen on some Olmec "altars." Incised on both shoulders and both knees are the profile heads of four Olmec gods; each of them has distinctive iconographic features, although all four have cleft heads.

Following the lead of the Las Limas figure, David Joralemon has been able to show that the Olmec worshipped a variety of deities, only a few of whom exhibit the features of the jaguar. Just as prominent in their pantheon were such awesome lowland creatures as the cayman and harpy eagle, and fearsome sea creatures like the shark. These were combined in a multitude of forms that bewilder the modern beholder.

Given its odd content, Olmec art is nevertheless "realistic" and shows a great mastery of form. On the great basalt monuments of the Olmec heartland and in other sculptures, scenes which include what are apparently

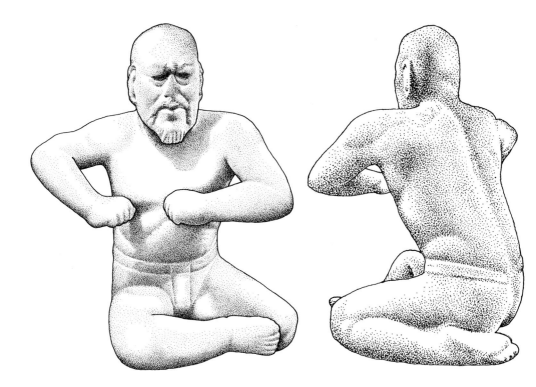

37 (*above*) Basalt figure of a bearded man, the so-called "Wrestler." Olmec culture, Early or Middle Preclassic period, Arroyo Sonso, Veracruz. Ht 66 cm.

38 (*left*) Small stone figure of a woman and child, provenience unknown. Olmec culture, Middle Preclassic period. Ht 11.4 cm.

39 (*right*) Wooden mask, encrusted with jade, supposedly from a cave near Iguala, Guerrero. Olmec culture, Middle Preclassic period. Ht 19 cm.

portraits of real persons are present; many of these are bearded, some with aquiline features. Olmec bas-reliefs are notable in the use of empty space in compositions. The combination of tension in space and the slow rhythm of the lines, which are always curved, produces the overwhelmingly monumental character of the style, no matter how small the object.

The Olmec were above all carvers of stone, from the really gigantic Colossal Heads, stelae, and altars of the Veracruz-Tabasco region, to finely carved jade celts, figurines, and pendants. Typical is a combination of carving, drilling (using a reed and wet sand), and delicate incising. Olmec sculptures are usually three-dimensional, to be seen from all sides, not just from the front. Very small sculptures and figurines of a beautiful blue-green jade and of serpentine were, of course, portable, so that we are not always sure of the place of origin of many of these pieces. Olmec objects of small size have been found all over Mexico, especially in the state of Guerrero in the western part of the Republic, but most of these could have been carried thence by aboriginal trade or even by Olmec missionaries. Among these are magnificent effigy axes of jade, basalt, or other stone, some of which are so thin and completely useless as axes that they must have had a ritual purpose. The were-jaguar is on many of these, sometimes inclining towards the feline, sometimes more anthropomorphic, along with other Olmec deities. The Olmec style was also represented in pottery bowls and figurines, and even in wood (in a miraculously preserved mask with jade incrustations from a cave in Guerrero and in the recently discovered offerings at El Manatí: see below).

34   The region of southern Veracruz and neighboring Tabasco has been justi-fiably called the Olmec "heartland." Here is where the greatest Olmec sites and the largest number of Olmec monuments are concentrated, and here is where the myth represented in Olmec art appears in its most elaborate form. There is hardly any question that the civilization had its roots and its highest development in that zone, which is little more than 125 miles long by about 50 miles wide (200 × 80 km). The heartland is characterized by a very high annual rainfall (about 120 in or 300 cm) and, before the advent of the white man, by a very high, tropical forest cover, interspersed with savannahs. Much of it is alluvial lowland, formed by the many rivers that meet the Gulf of Mexico near by. The so-called "dry season" of the heartland is hardly that, for during the winters cold, wet northers sweep down from the north, keep-ing the soil moist for year-round cultivation. It was in this seemingly inhospitable environment that Mesoamerica's first civilization was produced.

The San Lorenzo Olmec

Credit for the discovery of the Olmec civilization goes to Matthew Stirling, who explored and excavated Tres Zapotes, La Venta, and San Lorenzo during the 1930s and 1940s. In 1945, he and his wife Marion were led to the site of San Lorenzo by a report of a stone eye looking up from a trail. They realized that this belonged to one of the Colossal Heads typical of Olmec culture, and excavated the site through two field seasons, during which they discovered a wealth of sculpture, much of it lying in or near the ravines that surround San Lorenzo. However, they were able to date neither the sculpture nor the site itself.

Convinced that San Lorenzo might hold the key to the origin of Olmec civilization, Michael D. Coe directed a Yale archaeological-ecological project there from 1966 to 1968. San Lorenzo is the most important of a cluster of three sites lying near the flat bottoms of the Coatzacoalcos River, not very far from the center of the heartland. When we had mapped it, it turned out to be a kind of plateau rising about 150 ft (45 m) above the surrounding lowlands; about three-quarters of a mile (1.2 km) long in a north–south direction, exca-vations proved it to be artificial down to a depth of 23 ft (7 m), with long ridges jutting out on its northwest, west, and south sides. Mirror symmetry is characteristic of San Lorenzo, so that a particular feature on one ridge is mimicked on its counterpart. It is difficult to imagine what the Olmec meant by this gigantic construction of earth, clay, and other materials brought up on the backs of the peasantry, but it is possible that they intended this to be a huge animal effigy, possibly a bird flying east, but never completed because of the destruction of the site.

San Lorenzo had first been settled about 1700 BC, perhaps by Mixe-Zoqueans from Soconusco, but by 1500 BC had become thoroughly Olmec. For the next 300 years San Lorenzo was several times larger than any other settlement in Mesoamerica – there was in fact nothing quite like it before or
40   during its apogee. Some of the most magnificent and awe-inspiring sculp-tures ever discovered in Mexico were fashioned without the benefit of metal

San Lorenzo and Potrero Nuevo

40, 41 Monuments 17 (*left*) and 4 (*right*), San Lorenzo, Veracruz, shortly after excavation. Monument 17 is one of the smaller Colossal Heads, wearing the typical "football helmet." The nearest source of the basalt from which this was carved lies more than 50 miles (80 km) to the north. Olmec culture, Middle Preclassic period. Hts 1.67 m and 1.78 m respectively.

42 (*below*) Monument 2, Potrero Nuevo (subsidiary site of San Lorenzo), Veracruz. Two atlantean dwarfs support the top of this basalt "altar," which probably served as a throne. Olmec culture, Early Preclassic period. Ht 94 cm.

tools; petrographic analysis showed this to be basalt which had been quarried from boulders on the volcanic Cerro Cintepec, in the Tuxtla Mountains, a straight-line distance away of 50 miles (80 km). Presumably the stones were dragged down to navigable streams and loaded on great balsa rafts, then floated first down to the coast of the Gulf of Mexico, then up the Coatzacoalcos River, whence they would have had to be dragged, probably with rollers, up to the San Lorenzo plateau. The amount of labor that must have been involved staggers the imagination.

The Early Preclassic sculptures of San Lorenzo include ten Colossal Heads of great distinction. These are up to 9 ft 4 in (2.85 m) in height and weigh many tons; it is believed that they are all portraits of mighty Olmec rulers, with flat-faced, thick-lipped features. They wear headgear rather like American football helmets that probably served as protection in both war and in the ceremonial game played with a rubber ball throughout Mesomerica. Indeed, we found not only figurines of ball players at San Lorenzo, but also a simple, earthen court constructed for the game. Also typical are the so-called "altars": large basalt blocks with flat tops that may weigh up to 40 metric tons. The fronts of these "altars" have niches in which sits the figure of a ruler, either holding a were-jaguar baby in his arms (probably the theme of royal descent) or holding a rope which binds captives (the theme of the warfare and conquest), depicted in relief on the sides. Rather than actually serving as altars, David Grove has demonstrated that they must have been thrones. One of San Lorenzo's finest "altars" was found near the satellite site of Potrero Nuevo, and depicts two pot-bellied, atlantean dwarfs supporting the "altar" top with their upraised hands.

Sculptures could be related in elaborate tableau, such as the four-piece ensemble recently uncovered at El Azuzul. Here two stunningly carved young male figures are shown kneeling before two seated jaguars. While the jaguars are slightly different in size and treatment, the two human figures resemble each other closely. Stories of twins and jaguars abound in the heroic literature of Mesoamerica, suggesting that basic elements of mythology, as well as fundamental rites like the ball game, crystallized earliest at San Lorenzo.

In his work at San Lorenzo, Stirling had encountered trough-shaped basalt stones which he hypothesized were fitted end-to-end to form a kind of aqueduct. In 1967, we actually came across and excavated such a system *in situ*. This deeply buried drain line was in the southwestern portion of the site, and consisted of 560 ft (170 m) of laboriously pecked-out stone troughs fitted with basalt covers; three subsidiary lines met it from above at intervals. We have reason to believe that a drain system symmetrical to this exists on the southeastern side of San Lorenzo, and that both served periodically to remove the water from ceremonial pools on the surface of the plateau. Evidence for drains has been found at other Olmec centers, such as La Venta and Laguna de los Cerros, and must have been a feature of Olmec ritual life.

Large quantities of household debris came from our San Lorenzo phase levels, including pottery bowls and dishes carved with Olmec designs, beautiful Olmec figurines and fragments of white-ware were-jaguar "babies," and small mirrors, some of them convex, polished from iron-ore nodes, which

43 (*above left*) Two stone sculptures of young males which face two seated jaguar sculptures in a tableau from El Azuzul. The site functioned as a main entry on to the central plateau of San Lorenzo. Olmec culture, Early Preclassic period.

44 (*above right*) Part of a deeply buried drain line, formed of U-shaped troughs placed end-to-end and fitted with covers. The entire line is made of basalt brought in from the Tuxtla Mountains. Olmec culture, San Lorenzo, Early Preclassic period.

had perhaps been traded in from distant areas like highland Oaxaca. We recovered thousands of obsidian artifacts, mostly razor-like blades but also dart-points and bone-working tools; there is no natural obsidian in the Gulf Coast heartland, but trace-element analysis showed this material to have been imported from many sources in highland Mexico and Guatemala, testifying to immense trade networks then controlled by the rising Olmec state.

We found no preserved plant remains, but occasional pockets of midden contained mammal, fish, and amphibian remains. The San Lorenzo Olmec were only slightly interested in hunting deer and peccary. The mainstays of their diet were fish such as the snook, and domestic dog. Human bones showing butchering and burn marks were also plentiful, an indication of their cannibalistic propensities. There were also a high number of bones from the marine toad (*Bufo marinus*), a creature that is inedible because of the poison in its skin, but perhaps utilized for its production of bufotenine, a known hallucinogen.

From our ecological studies, we discovered a great deal about the economic basis of early Olmec civilization along the middle Coatzacoalcos. The bulk of the people were maize farmers, raising two crops a year on the more upland soils where rainy-season inundations do not reach; today, these lands are held communally. In contrast, the Olmec elite must have seized for themselves the rich river levees, where bumper crops are secured after the summer floods have subsided. The rise of the first Mesoamerican state, dominated by a hereditary elite class with judicial, military, and religious power, seems to have been the result of two factors: first, an environment with very high agricultural potential due to year-round rains and wet-season inundations of the river margins, along with abundant fish resources; and second, differential access to the best land by crystallizing social groups. The parallel with ancient Egypt – the "gift of the Nile" – is obvious.

There was nothing egalitarian about San Lorenzo society, as the Colossal Heads testify. While the elite lived in palatial structures at the summit of the site, large numbers of more humble houses were found on the terraced sides of the plateau. The latter were only recently uncovered when Roberto Lunagómez led a careful survey of the region. One particularly important elite residence on the summit, the "Red Temple," was fitted with basalt drains and columns, a sign of the highest prestige in this region which lacked stone resources. Attached to the residence were the chief stone sculpture workshops, where the scarce material was turned into public monuments. Ann Cyphers has shown that one of these workshops specialized in recarving stone monuments. Around 1200 BC, this workshop ceased to function, but not before the sculptors or others had deposited the partially finished works in a line near the shop itself. At the same time the entire site experienced a significant decline in activity and population. Although the specific causes are still unclear, San Lorenzo was never to regain its position as Olmec capital. The shifting rivercourse now bypassed the plateau, possibly causing an upheaval in the distribution systems so important to the San Lorenzo elites. Perhaps there was an uprising from below or outside, although the evidence for this is not as abundant as once thought.

El Manatí

Archaeologists working in the Olmec "heartland" have long lamented the lack of preservation in their sites – the carved wood, the textiles, and almost every other organic material have perished without a trace. There was high excitement, then, when the site of El Manatí, only 10 miles (16 km) southeast of San Lorenzo, came to light. It was discovered in 1988 when locals were digging out a pond for pisciculture, at the foot of the western slope of one of the few hills in the region. The site is thoroughly waterlogged, being bathed by strong springs, with highly complex stratigraphy caused in part by modern disturbances.

The waterlogging has resulted in extraordinary preservation of otherwise perishable Olmec materials, belonging to virtually all phases of San Lorenzo's development, from 1600 to 1200 BC. An archaeological team directed by Ponciano Ortiz of the University of Veracruz has found eighteen wooden figures *in situ*, all "baby-faced" just like Olmec hollow clay figurines,

45 Wooden busts emerge from the spring at El Manatí near San Lorenzo. Jades, rubber balls, and other precious items were also delivered as offerings to the spring. The preservation of wooden sculpture from any period is extremely rare in the tropical lowlands. Olmec culture, Early Preclassic period.

and each just under 20 in (50 cm) high; all were little more than limbless torsos, and most had been carefully wrapped in mats and tied up, before being placed with heads pointing in the direction of the hill's summit and covered with a small rock mound. All the wooden busts were discovered in the most recent levels of the site, and one has been radiocarbon-dated to *c.* 1200 BC. Other objects included polished stone axes, jade and serpentine beads, a wooden staff with a bird's head on one end and a shark's tooth (surely a bloodletter) on the other, and an obsidian knife with an asphalt handle. The jade offerings were evident from the earliest levels, thus placing complex Olmec ceremonialism earlier than previously thought. The order and placement of offerings became more complex and prescriptive as time went on, so that earlier rituals that included jade objects thrown into the spring were replaced after 1500 BC with carefully placed bundles of jade axes or other materials, ending finally in the spectacular series of wooden busts. Most surprisingly, the archaeologists turned up seven rubber balls, two of which are from the very earliest activity at the springs; measuring from 3 to 10 in (8–25 cm) in diameter, these are the only examples to have survived from pre-Conquest Mesoamerica of what must have been a very common artifact. They confirm that the ball game is at least as old as the Olmec civilization.

The Olmec of La Venta

After the downfall of San Lorenzo, its power passed to La Venta, Tabasco, one of the greatest of all Olmec sites, although now largely demolished by oil operations. It is located on an island in a sea-level coastal swamp near the Tonalá River, about 18 miles (29 km) inland from the Gulf. The island has slightly more than 2 sq. miles (5 sq. km) of dry land. The main part of the site

73

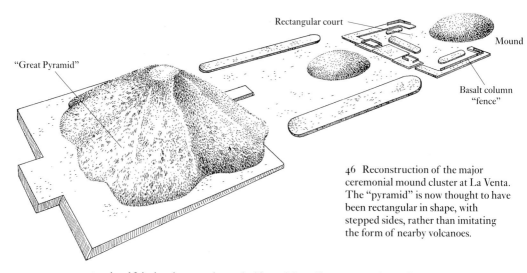

"Great Pyramid"

Rectangular court

Mound

Basalt column "fence"

46 Reconstruction of the major ceremonial mound cluster at La Venta. The "pyramid" is now thought to have been rectangular in shape, with stepped sides, rather than imitating the form of nearby volcanoes.

46   itself is in the northern half, and is a linear complex of clay constructions stretched out for 12 miles (19 km) in a north–south direction; it has been extensively excavated, before its desecration by air strips, bulldozers, and parking lots, first by Matthew Stirling of the Smithsonian Institution and later by the University of California. The major feature at La Venta is a huge pyramid of clay, 110 ft (34 m) high. While the building was once thought to have imitated the form of volcanoes nearby, recent work on its south side by Rebecca Gonzaléz-Lauck has shown that it was in fact a rectangular pyramid, with stepped sides and inset corners. The idea behind such enormous mounds is of interest here, for this is the largest of its period in Mexico. It is almost as though people were struggling to get closer to the gods, to raise their temples to the sky. This cannot have been their only function, however, for inside many Mesoamerican pyramids have been found elaborate tombs, made during construction of the pyramids themselves, so that it is likely that the temple-pyramid was an outgrowth of the ancient idea of a burial mound or funerary monument. Whether this is so in the case of the La Venta pyramid we do not know, for although still extant it has never been penetrated.

To the north of the Great Pyramid are two long, low mounds on either side of the center-line, and a low mound in the center between these. Then, one comes to a broad, rectangular court or plaza which was once surrounded by a fence of basalt columns, each about 7 ft (over 2 m) tall, set side by side in the top of a low wall made of adobe blocks. Finally, along the center-line, is a large, terraced clay mound. There are some who believe that the layout of the main portion of the site represents a gigantic, abstract jaguar mask.

Robert Heizer calculated that this elite center must have been supported by a hinterland population of at least 18,000 people; the main pyramid alone probably took some 800,000 person-days to construct. Heizer and his colleague Philip Drucker once wrote that the nearest arable land was an area between the Coatzacoalcos and Tonalá Rivers, and that it was on this that the rulers of La Venta depended for food and labor. This land, however, is relatively poor and eroded, making the proposition unlikely. From our own work at San Lorenzo, it would seem far more plausible that the agricultural support area consisted of the rich, natural levees of the tangle of rivers that once flowed in the region of La Venta. This has been borne out by a survey and excavation project directed by William Rust of the University of Pennsylvania, who has demonstrated that there was a dense occupation of the levee zone beginning at 1750 BC, and other work has shown incipient agriculture in the region may date to as far back as the fifth millennium BC. Concurrently, survey and testing of the La Venta "island" itself makes it clear that this was no empty ceremonial center, but rather a town of some size.

In its heyday, the site must have been vastly impressive, for different colored clays were used for floors, and the sides of platforms were painted in solid colors of red, yellow, and purple. Scattered in the plazas fronting these rainbow-hued structures were a large number of monuments sculptured from basalt. Outstanding among these are the Colossal Heads, of which four were found at La Venta. Large stelae (tall, flat monuments) of the same material were also present. Particularly outstanding is Stela 3, dubbed "Uncle Sam" by archaeologists. On it, two elaborately garbed men face each other, both wearing fantastic headdresses. The figure on the right has a long, aquiline nose and a goatee. Over the two float chubby were-jaguars brandishing war clubs. Also typical are the so-called "altars." The finest is Altar 5, on   47

47 North end of Altar 5 at La Venta. The two adult figures carry were-jaguar babies with cleft heads. Overall height of the monument 94 cm.

48 (*above left*) Mosaic pavement of serpentine blocks, representing an abstract jaguar mask, one of three known at La Venta. The pavement was covered over with a layer of mottled pink clay and a platform of adobe bricks.

49 (*above right*) Tomb constructed of basalt pillars at La Venta. The tomb contained several burials accompanied by jade offerings and was covered with an earthen mound.

which the central figure emerges from the niche holding a jaguar baby in his arms; on the sides, four subsidiary adult figures hold other little were-jaguars, who are squalling and gesticulating in a lively manner. As usual, their heads are cleft, and mouths drawn down in the Olmec snarl.

A number of buried offerings, perhaps dedicatory, were encountered by the excavators at the site. These usually include quantities of jade or serpentine celts laid carefully in rows; many of these were finely incised with pl. II were-jaguar and other figures. A particularly spectacular offering comprised a group of six celts and sixteen standing figurines of serpentine and jade arranged upright in a sort of scene. In some offerings were found finely polished ear flares of jade with attached jade pendants in the outline of jaguar teeth. Certain Olmec sculptures and figurines show persons wearing pec- pl. IV torals of concave shape around the neck, and such have actually come to light in offerings. These turned out to be concave mirrors of magnetite and ilmenite, the reflecting surfaces polished to optical specifications. What were they used for? Experiments have shown that they can not only start fires, but also throw images on flat surfaces like a *camera lucida*. They were pierced for suspension, and one can imagine the hocus-pocus which some mighty Olmec priest was able to perform with one of these.

48 Three rectangular pavements, each *c.* 15 ft × 20 ft (4.5 × 6 m), are known at La Venta, each of about 485 blocks of serpentine, laid in the form of a highly abstract jaguar mask. Certain details were left open and emphasized by filling with colored clays. Strange as it may seem, these were offerings, as they were covered up with many feet of clay and adobe layers soon after construction.

In the acid soil of La Venta (as at San Lorenzo), bones disappear quickly, and very few burials have been discovered. Of those found, however, the most outstanding was the tomb in Mound A-2, which was surrounded and roofed with basalt columns. On a floor made of flat limestone slabs were laid the remains of two juveniles, badly rotted when discovered, each wrapped up in a bundle and heavily coated with vermilion paint. With them had been placed an offering of fine jade figurines, beads, a jade pendant in the shape of a clam shell, a sting-ray spine of the same substance, and other objects. Outside the tomb a sandstone "sarcophagus" with a cover had been left, but other than some jade objects on the bottom, nothing was found within but clay fill. It could be that the children or infants in the tomb were monstrosities who to the Olmecs may have resembled were-jaguars and thus merited such treatment.

49

Like the earlier San Lorenzo, La Venta was deliberately destroyed in ancient times. Its fall was certainly violent, as twenty-four out of forty sculptured monuments were intentionally mutilated. This probably occurred at the end of Middle Preclassic times, around 400–300 BC, for subsequently, following its abandonment as a center, offerings were made with pottery of Late Preclassic cast. As a matter of fact, La Venta may never have lost its significance as a cult center, for among the very latest caches found was a Spanish olive jar of the early Colonial period, and Heizer suspected that offerings may have been made in modern times as well.

Tres Zapotes and the Long Count calendar

In its day, La Venta was undoubtedly the most powerful and holy place in the Olmec heartland, sacred because of its very inaccessibility; but other great Olmec centers also flourished in the Middle Preclassic. About 100 miles (160 km) northwest of La Venta lies Tres Zapotes, in a setting of low hills above the swampy basin formed by the Papaloapan and San Juan Rivers. It comprises about fifty earthen mounds stretched out along the bank of a stream for 2 miles (3.2 km) with little marked hierarchy among the architectural groups, suggesting to excavator Christopher Pool that the site was controlled by several powerful lineages of equal rank. Pottery and clay figurines recovered from stratigraphic excavations have revealed an early occupation of Tres Zapotes which was apparently contemporaneous with La Venta, but it was during the Late Preclassic that the site reached its zenith, according to the recent excavations. Belonging to this earlier, purely Olmec, horizon are two Colossal Heads like those of La Venta. But the importance of Tres Zapotes lies in its Late Preclassic stela, discussed below.

Thus far we have said nothing about writing and the calendar in the Olmec heartland. Actually, no inscriptions or written dates have come to light at La Venta itself. Nonetheless, several fine jade objects in the Olmec style, now in public and private collections but of unknown provenience, are incised with hieroglyphs. Although unreadable to us, some of them appear to be ancestral to certain Maya glyphs. If they can be assigned to the Middle Preclassic horizon – and there seems to be no valid reason not to consider them of that age –

then these inscriptions mark the very beginnings of writing in Mexico; but the evidence for this is weak.

It has already been said that Tres Zapotes flourished in the Late Preclassic, after La Venta had been overthrown. Tres Zapotes has produced one of the oldest dated monuments of the New World, Stela C, a fragmentary basalt monument which had been re-used in later times. On one side is a very abstract were-jaguar mask in a style which is derivative from Olmec, but not in the true canon. The reverse side bears a date in the Long Count.

The Long Count system of calculating dates needs some explanation. In Chapter 1, it was mentioned that all the Mesoamerican peoples had a calendar that entailed the meshing of the days of a 260-day "Almanac Year" with those of the 365-day solar year. A day in one would not meet a day in the other for 52 years; consequently, any date could be placed within a single 52-year cycle by this means. This is the Calendar Round system, but it obviously is not much help when more than 52 years is involved (just as a Maori would not necessarily know what revolution occurred in '76, or a Choctaw what happened to an English king in '88), for it would require special knowledge to know in which century the event happened. A more exact way of expressing dates would be a system that counted days elapsed from a definite starting point, such as the founding of Rome or the birth of Christ. This is the role that was fulfilled by the Long Count, confined to the lowland peoples of Mesoamerica and taken to its greatest refinement by the Classic Maya. For reasons unknown to us, the starting date was 13 August 3114 BC (Gregorian), and dates are presented in terms of the numbers of periods of varying length that have elapsed since the mechanism was set in motion. For instance, the largest period was one of 144,000 days, the next of 7,200 days, then 360 days, followed by 20 days and one day. Coefficients were expressed in terms of bar-and-dot numerals, the bars having the value of five and the dots, one. Thus, a bar and two dots stand for "seven."

In Stela C, the coefficient accompanying the great first period was missing when the stone was discovered by Matthew Stirling, but he reconstructed it as seven. He read the entire date as (7).16.6.16.18, or 3 September 32 BC in terms of our calendar, raising a storm of protests from Mayanists who felt sure that a monument outside Maya territory could not be this old. Stirling was vindicated in 1969 when a Tres Zapotes farmer accidentally turned up the missing top part of the stela, complete with its coefficient of seven. Another date, this time with a fairly long, unread text, is inscribed on a small jade figure in epi-Olmec style, a duck-billed, winged figure with human features. This is the Tuxtla Statuette (of which more below), discovered many years ago in the Olmec area, with the Long Count date of 8.6.2.4.17 (14 March AD 162). Since both dates fall in the Late Preclassic and were found within the Olmec heartland, it is not unlikely that Olmec literati invented the Long Count and perhaps also developed certain astronomical observations with which the Maya are usually credited.

However, the earliest Long Count date of all turned up on a reused slab at the site of Chiapa de Corzo, in the Grijalva Depression of Chiapas, outside the heartland proper. It bears a date which can be reconstructed as

50

51

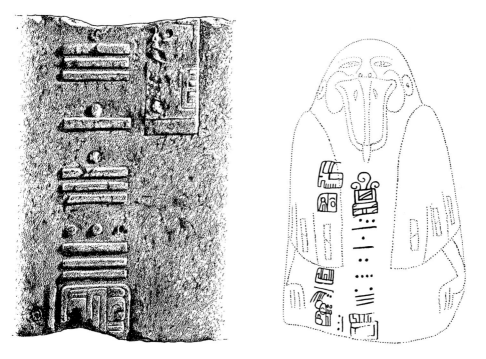

50 (*above, left*) Lower part of Long Count date on Stela C, Tres Zapotes.

51 (*above, right*) The Tuxtla Statuette, with Long Count date and other hieroglyphs. Ht 15 cm.

(7.16).3.2.13 or 8 December 36 BC, some four years earlier than Stela C. Quite possibly, we have not yet discovered the answer to where, when, and why the Long Count was invented.

The Olmecs beyond the heartland

Notwithstanding their intellectual and artistic achievements, the Olmecs were by no means a peaceful people. Their monuments show that they fought battles with war clubs, and some individuals carry what seems to be a kind of cestus or knuckle-duster. Whether the indubitable Olmec presence in highland Mexico represents actual invasion from the heartland is still under vigorous debate. The Olmecs of sites like San Lorenzo and La Venta certainly needed substances, often of a prestigious nature, which were unobtainable in their homeland – obsidian, iron-ore for mirrors, serpentine, and (by Middle Preclassic times) jade – and they probably set up trade networks over much of Mexico to get these items. Thus, according to one hypothesis, the frontier Olmec sites could have been trading stations. Kent Flannery has put forth the idea that the Olmec element in places like the Valley of Oaxaca could have been the result of emulation by less advanced peoples who had trade and perhaps even marriage ties with the

52 Relief 1, Chalcatzingo, Morelos. A woman ruler is seated within a cave or stylized monster mouth which gives off smoke or steam, while raindrops fall from clouds above. Olmec culture, Middle Preclassic period. Ht 3.2 m.

Olmec elite. And finally, the occurrence of iconography based on the Olmec pantheon over a wide area of Mesoamerica suggests the possibility of missionary efforts on the part of the heartland Olmecs.

pl. V   Among the sites in central Mexico which have produced Early Preclassic Olmec objects, principally figurines and ceramics, are Tlatilco and Tlapacoya in the Valley of Mexico, and Las Bocas in Puebla; from the latter have come bowls, bottles, and effigy vases, along with fine, white kaolin Olmec babies and human effigies. Many of these items might have been manufactured at San Lorenzo itself.

Although it is still in the highlands, the state of Morelos, to the south of the Valley of Mexico, is warm and even subtropical, and might well have proved attractive for the Olmec. Chalcatzingo is the most important highland Olmec site, and lies in the Amatzinac Valley of eastern Morelos. There, three isolated, igneous intrusions rise over 985 ft (300 m) above the valley floor, and must have been considered sacred in ancient times, as they were by the Aztecs and even the modern villagers. At the juncture of the talus slope and the sheer rock cliff of the central mountain has been found a series of Olmec bas-52   reliefs carved on boulders. The most elaborate of these depicts a woman holding a ceremonial bar in her arms, seated upon a throne.

I This sensitively carved, massive sculpture was found deeply buried in Early Preclassic deposits at the great Olmec site of San Lorenzo, Veracruz, and is unusually well preserved. Like all other Colossal Heads, it is probably a portrait of a ruler, with helmet-like headgear.

II (*above*) Offering 4 at La Venta, Tabasco, consists of a number of figurines and celts of jade and serpentine, arranged in a kind of assembly scene. The bald, deformed heads are typical of Olmec culture. Middle Preclassic period.

III (*left*) This flat, jade celt from Tomb E at La Venta was carved to represent an important Olmec deity, whose flame-like eyebrows invoke the crest feathers of harpy eagles. Cinnabar has been applied to highlight the relief. Middle Preclassic period.

IV (*right*) Their appearance in art suggests that women played an important role in Olmec society. This small, jade figurine (also coated in cinnabar) was found in Tomb A at La Venta, and depicts a woman seated tailor fashion; on her breast she wears a small piece of hematite, representing the polished concave mirrors of high-ranking individuals.

V (*below, left*) "The Acrobat," a hollow, white-ware Olmec figure from Burial 154 at Tlatilco. Representations of this sort may symbolize the "doubling over" of ripe maize ears at the end of the growing season. Early Preclassic period.

VI (*below, right*) The iconography of the Olmec pantheon of gods is not well understood, but this hollow clay figure from Atlihuayan, Morelos, is probably a deity, wearing the head and skin of a fantastic caiman and with harpy-eagle brows. Early Preclassic period.

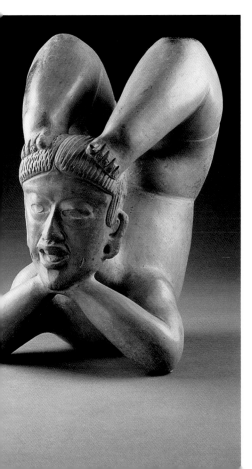

VII (*left*) In its day, Teotihuacan was the largest city in the Western Hemisphere. Here we see the Pyramid of the Moon, lying at the northern terminus of the Avenue of the Dead. The *talud-tablero* structures in front of it are considerably later than the pyramid itself.

VIII (*below*) While this stone mask is in the Teotihuacan style of the Early Classic, the shell-inlaid eyes, the applied turquoise mosaic, and the bead necklace were probably added a millennium later by an Aztec craftsman.

IX (*left*) A corner in the patio of the Quetzalpapalotl ("Quetzal-Butterfly") Palace, Teotihuacan. The great city had many luxurious apartment compounds, but most had painted mural decoration, rather than the carvings we see here. The devices on the roof are year symbols.

X (*overleaf*)The Great Plaza of Monte Albán, Oaxaca, the hilltop capital of the Zapotec nation, looking south from the North Platform. Most of the buildings seen in this view belong to the Late Classic Monte Albán IIIB period.

XI Many hundreds of gray-ware effigy urns have been discovered in tombs of the Classic Monte Albán civilization, usually placed in groups surrounding the corpse. This fine effigy depicts an officiant wearing a headdress in the form of a feline god.

The scene itself takes place within the open, profile mouth of the Olmec earth monster, as though within a cave, which emits smoke or mist. Above this tableau are three stylized rain clouds, from which fall phallic rain drops. The woman must have been a ruler of Chalcatzingo, and the theme is one of power and fertility.

Other sculptures at Chalcatzingo include a relief showing three Olmec warriors brandishing clubs above an ithyphallic captive, and a scene of two rampant felines, each attacking a human. The Feathered Serpent, one of the most important deities of Mesoamerica, makes an appearance on another boulder, with a man disappearing into its open mouth.

In the 1970s, David C. Grove and Jorge Angulo directed a University of Illinois project at Chalcatzingo, which cleared up many of the mysteries posed by the site. The site itself, which consists of platform mounds and terraces below the central mountain, was founded by about 1500 BC, but reached its height during the Middle Preclassic Cantera phase, from 700 to 500 BC, at which time the carvings were apparently made. They are therefore coeval with the apogee of La Venta, which surely was the center from which Olmec influence emanated to Morelos. The Illinois project discovered a table-top "altar" with a relief of the earth monster's mouth; a child, probably a human sacrifice, had been buried within the "altar." The Chalcatzingo elite received elaborate crypt burials, one being accompanied by a greenstone figure in the purest La Venta style; jade earspools, pendants, and necklaces were also present.

Although this part of Morelos is somewhat arid, the Cantera-phase farmers did little irrigation, but planted their crops on artificial terraces. Deer and cottontail were hunted, but the most prominent food animal, as in most Preclassic sites, was the dog.

Grove, like Flannery, is skeptical about whether a frontier site like Chalcatzingo actually represents an invasion or takeover by Gulf Coast people, and he too favors the idea of Olmec influence coming in through long-distance trade and marriage alliances. In his view, the monuments, many of which depict the Chalcatzingo rulers, have no local antecedents and may well have been carved by artists imported from the heartland to explain the Olmec belief system to the local people.

Guerrero is a mountainous, extremely dry state lying south of Morelos, on the way to the Pacific Coast. Many of the most beautiful blue-green Olmec jades have come from this unpromising region, leading Covarrubias to the often-revived but poorly founded claim that this is where the Olmec must have originated. Three extraordinary sites show that the Olmec were here, however. Juxtlahuaca Cave had been known for many years; it lies east of the Guerrero capital, Chilpancingo, near the village of Colotlipa, in one of the most arid parts of the state. The cave, whose importance was first revealed by the Princeton art historian Gillett Griffin and by Carlo Gay, a retired Italian businessman, is a deep cavern. Almost a mile in from the entrance is a series of extraordinary Olmec paintings in polychrome on the cave walls. One of these shows a tall, bearded figure in a red-and-yellow striped tunic, his limbs clad in jaguar pelts and claws; he brandishes a trident-shaped object over

53

53 Polychrome painting on the walls of Juxtlahuaca Cave, Guerrero. A bearded ruler with striped tunic, wearing jaguar arm coverings and jaguar leggings, brandishes a trident-like instrument before a black-faced figure cowering on the lower left. Olmec culture, Early or Middle Preclassic period.

a lesser, black-faced figure, probably a captive. Nearby is the undulating form of a red Feathered Serpent, with a panache of green plumes on its head. Deep caves and caverns were traditionally held to be entrances to the Underworld in Mesoamerica, and Juxtlahuaca must have had a connection with secret and chthonic rites celebrated by the frontier Olmec.

Shortly after the Juxtlahuaca paintings were brought to light, David Grove discovered the cave murals of Oxtotitlan, not very far north of Juxtlahuaca. These paintings are in a shallow rockshelter rather than a cavern, and are dominated by a polychrome representation of an Olmec ruler wearing the mask and feathers of a bird representing an owl, the traditional messenger of the lords of the Underworld. He is seated upon an earth monster throne closely resembling the "altars" of La Venta. It is extremely difficult to date rock art, but it is possible that Juxtlahuaca may be contemporary with San Lorenzo, and Oxtotitlan with La Venta.

The third site was being sacked by looters in the early 1980s before archaeologists from the National Institute of Anthropology and History moved in to excavate it properly. Given the name Teopantecuanitlan ("The Place of the Temple of Jaguars") by the director of the team, Guadalupe Martínez Donjuan, it lies near the confluence of the Amacuzac and Balsas Rivers in the extreme northeast of Guerrero, in a region of dry hills with sparse vegetation. The site consists of three groups of ceremonial constructions spread out over 395 acres (160 hectares). Group A is the most important of these;

construction began here with a sunken court of yellow clay, reached by two pairs of stairways on its south side. Each pair of stairs shares a stone tablet decorated with a stylized jaguar face. According to preliminary accounts, this phase has been dated to 1400 BC, leading some Guerrero enthusiasts to revive the Covarrubias hypothesis of Olmec origins.

Phase 2 of Group A at Teopantecuanitlan, dated to 900 BC, sees the substitution of construction in yellow clay by travertine blocks; overlooking the sunken court at this time were four stone monoliths with indubitable Olmec bas-reliefs in straightforward Olmec style. Associated with this phase is the building of a reservoir and canal system, but whether this was for mundane irrigation purposes or more religious and ceremonial – along the lines of the San Lorenzo and La Venta stone drains – is yet unclear.

Sites with Olmec carvings and stelae have been found along the Pacific coastal plain of southeastern Mesoamerica. Perhaps these were founded by warrior-traders interested in new sources of precious stones like jade, for Olmec jades are known in Costa Rica, which may well have had outcrops of this substance, and Costa Rica jades have turned up in Guerrero. Such sites are known for Chiapas; the Guatemalan south coast; and as far southeast as Chalchuapa, El Salvador, around 500 miles (800 km) from the Olmec heartland, where a boulder is carved with warlike figures in their characteristic style.

So few Olmec sites have been excavated – and even fewer fully published – that it remains difficult to be very precise about the nature of the Olmec presence beyond the Gulf Coast. In fact, some modern revisionists have questioned the reality of an Olmec civilization, and have downgraded the Veracruz-Tabasco "heartland" as the *fons et origo* of the culture. Basing themselves upon Teopantecuanitlan, there are even those who claim that the Olmec pattern of life began in Guerrero, a position contradicted by the severe environmental constraints posed by that region. Disagreements like this are compounded by the fact that we have no real written documents for the Olmec, leaving the subject wide open to different interpretations and even unfounded speculation.

Yet whatever we call it, it can hardly be denied that during the Early and Middle Preclassic, there was a powerful, unitary religion that had manifested itself in an all-pervading art style; and that this was the official ideology of the first complex society or societies to be seen in this part of the New World. Its rapid spread has been variously likened to that of Christianity under the Roman Empire, or to that of westernization (or "modernization") in today's world. Wherever Olmec influence or the Olmecs themselves went, so did civilized life.

Early Zapotec civilization

San José Mogote, mentioned in the previous chapter in connection with early Preclassic life, remained the most important regional center in the Valley of Oaxaca until the end of the Middle Preclassic. By that time, it had full-fledged masonry buildings of a public nature; in a corridor connecting two of these, Kent Flannery and Joyce Marcus found a bas-relief threshold stone

54

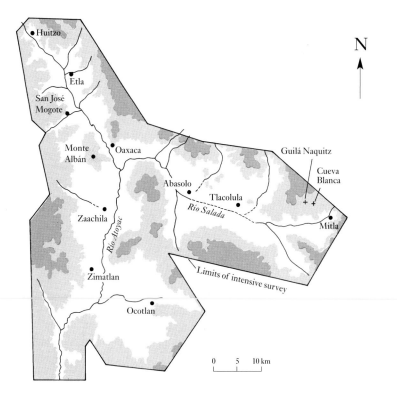

54 The Y-shaped Valley of Oaxaca, homeland of the Zapotecs: major sites within the area intensively surveyed by Kent Flannery and his colleagues.

showing a dead captive with stylized blood flowing from his chest, so placed that anyone entering or leaving the corridor would have to tread on him. Between his legs is a glyphic group possibly representing his name, "1 Eye" in the 260-day ritual calendar. This may be a precursor of the famous *Danzantes* of Monte Albán, and is one of the oldest examples of writing in Mesoamerica.

Toward the close of the Middle Preclassic, the Zapotec of the Valley were practicing several forms of irrigation. At Hierve el Agua, in the mountains east of the Valley, there has been found an artificially terraced hillside, irrigated by canals coming from permanent springs charged with calcareous waters that have in effect created a fossilized record from their deposits.

pl. X   Monte Albán is the greatest of all Zapotec sites, and was constructed on a series of eminences about 1,300 ft (400 m) above the Valley floor, near the close of the Middle Preclassic, about 500-450 BC, when it replaced San José Mogote as the Valley's most powerful center. The founding of the city took place in a rapid, deliberate episode, suggesting that people were resettled in the formerly sparsely inhabited area. The choice to settle here was probably due to the strategic hilltop location at the juncture of the Valley's three arms. It lies in the heart of the region still occupied by the Zapotec peoples; since there is no evidence for any major population displacement in central Oaxaca until the beginning of the Post-Classic, about AD 900, archaeologists feel reasonably certain that the inhabitants of the site were always speakers of that language.

Most of the constructions that meet the eye at Monte Albán are of the Classic period. However, in the southwestern corner of the main plaza, which is laid out on a north–south axis, excavations have disclosed the Temple of the *Danzantes*, a stone-faced platform contemporary with the first occupation of the site, Monte Albán I. The so-called *Danzantes* (i.e. "dancers") are bas-relief figures on large stone slabs set into the outside of the platform. Nude men with slightly Olmecoid features (i.e. the down-turned mouth), the *Danzantes* are shown in strange, rubbery postures as though they were swimming or dancing in viscous fluid. Some are represented as old, bearded individuals with toothless gums or with only a single protuberant incisor. About 300 of these strange yet powerful figures are known at Monte Albán, and it might be reasonably asked exactly what their function was, or what they depict. The distorted pose of the limbs, the open mouth, and closed eyes indicate that these are corpses, undoubtedly chiefs or kings slain by the earliest rulers of Monte Albán. In several individuals the genitals are clearly delineated, usually the stigma laid on captives in Mesoamerica where nudity was considered scandalous. Furthermore, there are cases of sexual mutilation depicted on some *Danzantes*, blood streaming in flowery patterns from the severed part. Evidence to corroborate such violence comes from one *Danzante*, which is nothing more than a severed head.

Whereas we have little evidence for writing and the calendar in the Olmec area, there is abundant testimony of both these in Monte Albán I, whence come our first true literary texts in Mexico. These are carved in low relief on the *Danzantes* themselves and on other slabs. Numbers were symbolized by bars and dots, although a finger could substitute for a dot in the numbers 1 and 2. Alfonso Caso has deduced that the glyphs for the days of the 260-day Almanac Year (based on a permutation of 20 named days with 13 numbers) were in use, as well as those for the "months" of the solar year. Thus, these ancient people already had the 52-year cycle, the Calendar Round. However, the Long Count was definitely absent. A fair number of other hieroglyphs, unaccompanied by numerals, also occur, and these probably were symbols in a script which had both phonetic and semantic elements, often combined; some are so placed on the *Danzante* monuments as to attest to their function as proper names, but none can be read. The ancient Zapotec script will be more fully examined in Chapter 6.

The pottery of Monte Albán I is known from tombs at this site and in others affiliated with it, such as Monte Negro in the Mixteca Alta of western Oaxaca. It is of a fine gray clay, a characteristic maintained throughout much of the development of Monte Albán. The usual shapes are vases with bridged spouts and bowls with large, hollow tripod supports – typical of the end of the Middle Preclassic and most of the Late Preclassic. Probably the phase does not begin until about 500 BC and ends about 150 BC. Some of the vessels bear modeled and incised figures like the *Danzantes*, confirming the association.

Bas-reliefs at Monte Albán I

55 Bas-relief figure of a so-called *Danzante* or "dancer." This is a portrait of a slain enemy, whose name glyph appears in front of his mouth.

56 Bas-relief figure of a bearded *Danzante*.

Monte Albán was surely the capital of a burgeoning state during this Late Preclassic period. The city was able to do several things associated with later Mesoamerican states: to develop a distinctive art style along with a script, both associated with the necessary proclamations of power and sacrality, and to gather a large population around the urban center. Two recent investigators, Richard Blanton and Stephen Kowalewski, give its population as 10,000 to 20,000, and the first Monte Albán palaces seem to appear at this time to meet the administrative needs of the local and Valley-wide citizenry.

The development from the first phase of the site to Monte Albán II, which is terminal Preclassic and therefore dates from about 150 BC to AD 150, was

57 (*right*) Hieroglyphic inscription on large stone slab. Monte Albán I, Middle to Late Preclassic period.

58 (*above*) Fragment of an effigy whistling jar, provenience unknown. The vessel originally consisted of two connected chambers, and when liquid was poured out, air was forced through a whistle in the head. Monte Albán I culture, Middle to Late Preclassic period.

59 (*right*) Funerary urn from Cuilapan, Oaxaca, probably representing a young god. The incised hieroglyphs may be the days 13 Water and 13 Flint. Monte Albán II culture, Late Preclassic period.

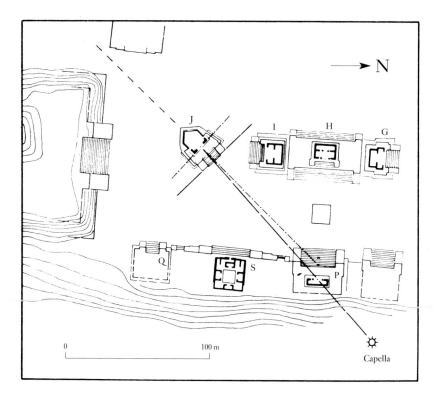

Building J
at Monte Albán

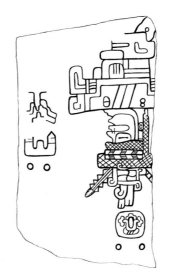

60, 61 Building J at Monte Albán (*left, below*), a stone-faced structure in the form of a great arrowhead pointing southwest. The astronomer Anthony Aveni has identified an alignment of Building J (*left*) with the bright star Capella. Monte Albán II culture, Late Preclassic period.

62 (*right*) Hieroglyphs representing a conquered town, from Building J at Monte Albán.

gradual. Near the southern end of the main plaza of the site was erected Building J, a stone-faced construction in the form of a great arrowhead pointing southwest. The peculiar orientation of this building has been examined by the astronomer Anthony Aveni and the architect Horst Hartung, who have pointed out important alignments with the bright star Capella. The exterior of the building is set with over forty inscribed stone slabs all bearing a very similar text. These Monte Albán II inscriptions generally consist of an upside-down head with closed eyes and elaborate headdress, below a stepped glyph for "mountain" or "town"; over this is the name of the place, seemingly given phonetically in rebus fashion (like the "I saw Aunt Rose" puzzles of youth). In its most complete form, the text is accompanied by the symbols for year, month, and day. There are also various yet-untranslated glyphs. Such inscriptions were correctly interpreted by Alfonso Caso as records of town conquests, the inverted heads being the defeated kings. It is certain that all are in the Zapotec language.

60, 61

62

This obsession with the recording of victories over enemies is one characterizing early civilizations the world over, and the rising Preclassic states of Mexico were no exception. It speaks for a time when state polities were relatively small and engaged in mutual warfare, when no ruler could extend his sway over a territory large enough to be called an empire.

Dainzú, an important site of Late Preclassic and Classic date lying some 12½ miles (20 km) southeast of Oaxaca City, has a large Monte Albán II platform *c.* 150 ft (45 m) long; the 1966 investigations of Ignacio Bernal showed that its base was faced with fifty stones carved in low relief, somewhat reminiscent of the *Danzantes*. Most of the figures are ball players wearing elaborate protective gear, including barred helmets like those of the medieval knights, knee guards, and gauntlets, and each figure has a small ball in the hand. It is a measure of our ignorance of the early Mesoamerican mind that we are not sure whether these represent the victors or the vanquished!

Izapan civilization

Another culture of the Preclassic period upon which we will touch is of high significance. This is the civilization centered on the site of Izapa, located in the southeastern part of the state of Chiapas on a tributary stream of the Suchiate River, which divides Mexico from Guatemala. We are here in the broad, Pacific Coast plain, one of the most unbearably hot, but at the same time incredibly fertile, regions of Mexico. Izapa is a very large site, with numbers of earthen mounds faced with river cobbles, all forming a maze of courts and plazas in which the stone monuments are located. There is possibly a ball court, formed by two long, earth embankments. Samples of pottery taken from Izapa show it to have been founded in the Early Preclassic, and to have reached its height in the Late Preclassic, persisting into the Proto-Classic period.

The art style as expressed in bas-reliefs is highly distinctive. Although obviously derived from the Olmecs, it differs in its use of large, cluttered, baroque compositions with several figures, as opposed to the Olmec focus on

63 Stela 1, Izapa, Chiapas. At the top is a stylized mouth representing the sky. Below, a god with reptile-head feet is dipping fish from the water with a net; he carries a bottle-shaped creel strapped to his back. Izapan style, Late Preclassic period. Ht 1.93 m.

the single figure of the ruler. Several of these multi-figure Izapan compositions are concerned with the sacred stories of Mesoamerican divine heroes;
many of these stories were still in use when the Spanish arrived almost 2,000
years later. Izapan style appears on stone stelae that often are associated with
"altars" placed in front, the latter crudely carved to represent giant toads,
symbols of rain. The principal gods are metamorphoses of the old gods of
the Olmec, the upper lip of the deity now tremendously extended to the
degree that it resembles the trunk of a tapir. Most scenes on Izapan stelae
take place under a sky band in the form of stylized monster teeth, from which
may descend a winged figure on a background of swirling clouds. On Stela 1,   63
a "Long-lipped God" – prototype of the Maya rain god Chac – is depicted
with feet in the form of reptile heads, walking on water from which he dips
fish to be placed in a basketry creel on his back, while on Stela 3, a serpent-
footed deity brandishes a club. Most interesting of all is Stela 21, on which a
warrior holds the head of a decapitated enemy; in the background, an important person is carried in a sedan chair, the roof of which is embellished with a
crouching jaguar.

The real importance of the Izapan civilization is that it is the connecting
link in time and space between the earlier Olmec civilization and the later
Classic Maya. Izapan monuments are found scattered down the Pacific
Coast of Guatemala and up into the highlands in the vicinity of Guatemala
City. On the other side of the highlands, in the lowland jungle of northern
Guatemala, the very earliest Maya monuments appear to be derived from
Izapan prototypes. Moreover, not only the stela-and-altar complex, the
"Long-lipped Gods," and the baroque style itself were adopted from the Iza-
pan culture by the Maya, but the priority of Izapa in the very important
adoption of the Long Count is quite clear-cut: the most ancient dated Maya
monument reads AD 292, while a stela in Izapan style at El Baúl, Guatemala,
bears a Long Count date 256 years earlier.

La Mojarra and the Isthmian script

Chance finds can often lead archaeologists in new directions. Such has been
the case with the La Mojarra stela, accidentally discovered in November
1986 beneath the waters of the Acula River, in the Veracruz lowlands about
half way between Tres Zapotes and the Classic site of Cerro de las Mesas.
This 4-ton monument is of fine-grained basalt, and depicts an imposing,
standing figure, richly attired in Izapan style, with a towering headdress
formed of multiple masks of a bird-monster known for the Maya Late Preclassic, topped by a fish creature which has been identified as a shark.

But it is the accompanying hieroglyphic text which caused a sensation
among Mesoamerican epigraphers: arranged in 21 beautifully drawn
columns are about 400 signs, the longest inscribed text known thus far for
Mesoamerica. The script is clearly the same as that inscribed on the Tuxtla
Statuette, but otherwise unknown, and has been dubbed "Isthmian" by specialists. Intensive study by John Justeson and Terence Kaufman has resulted
in a proposed decipherment of Isthmian, in which the script is identified as a

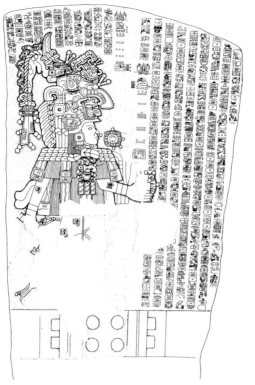

64 Stela 1, La Mojarra, Veracruz. End of Late Preclassic period.

mixed, partly logographic (semantic), partly phonetic system which reproduces the proto-Zoquean language – which would fit in with the known distribution of the Mixe-Zoquean linguistic family in this area. However, this decipherment has not received general acceptance, a situation that will continue until a larger body of "Isthmian" texts comes to light.

64   There are two Long Count dates on the La Mojarra stela: 8.5.3.3.5 and 8.5.16.9.7, corresponding respectively to 21 May AD 143 and 13 July AD 156 (the latter only 6 years earlier than the Tuxtla Statuette), placing the stela, and the Isthmian script, toward the end of the Late Preclassic. There are obvious connections here with both the Izapan civilization of the Pacific Coast and the Guatemalan highlands, and with the early Maya civilization then taking form in the Petén-Yucatan lowlands, but until further Isthmian texts are found and studied, the script will remain mostly undeciphered and its external relationships will continue to be a mystery.

6 · The Classic Period

Rise of the great civilizations

By any criteria, the period from about AD 150 to 650 was the most remarkable in the whole development of ancient Mexico. This era of florescence is called the Classic, and it is at this time that the peoples of Mexico built civilizations that can bear comparison with those of other parts of the globe. With justification, the Classic is thought of as the Golden Age, when the seeds that were planted during the Preclassic reached their fruition.

The Classic era began at other times in other areas of Mesoamerica. The Classic span is given in most books as AD 250–900, based upon the period during which the lowland Maya were inscribing Long Count dates on their stone monuments. However, central Mexico began the Classic in the second century AD and possibly even earlier, when urban construction began at the great city of Teotihuacan. And Teotihuacan itself had fallen into ruins long before the last Classic Maya city was abandoned.

By the Classic period, literacy may have been pan-Mesoamerican, although probably only the Maya and to a lesser extent the Zapotecs had fully developed hieroglyphic scripts – that is, writing systems which recorded the spoken language. Although no books have survived from the Classic into our day, we have every reason to believe that many peoples possessed them. Dates were generally recorded in terms of the 52-year Calendar Round, but in the Gulf Coast the Long Count was used. What for, if not to write their own history?

From their genesis in the Olmec period the gods of Mexico had finally revealed themselves in all their bewildering variety. There had now crystallized a complete pantheon, one that was shared by all Mexicans, and probably, in somewhat altered form, even by the Maya. The most ubiquitous of these deities were the Rain God, perhaps metamorphosed from one of the Olmec were-jaguars; his consort, the Water Goddess; a creator divinity, viewed as an aged Fire God, or as an old man and an old woman; the Sun God; the Moon Goddess; and the Feathered Serpent, known to the later Aztecs as Quetzalcoatl.

On the basis of older and now out-dated notions about what the Classic Maya were supposed to be like, it used to be thought that the Classic throughout Mesoamerica was a time of general peace and tranquility, without the obsession with warfare and human sacrifice considered typical of the Post-Classic. That idea is probably a delusion stemming from the fact that we have a tremendous amount of post-Conquest documentation on the late peoples of Mexico, and none at all on the Classic. It is true that not many fortified

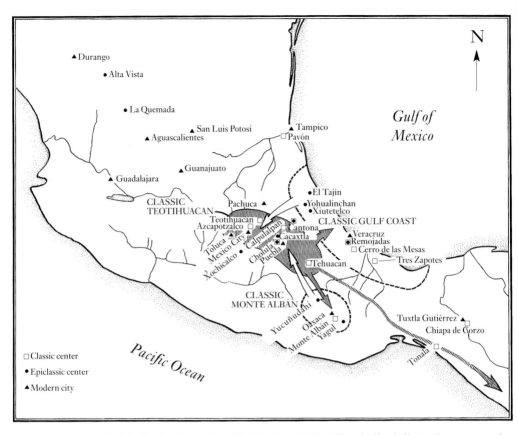

65 Distribution of Classic and Epiclassic period sites. The shading indicates the area covered by the Classic Teotihuacan civilization and its extensions in Mexico.

sites are known from the Classic, but it should be stressed that all temple clusters and compounds in Mesoamerica were defensible, and that many peoples of this era were careful to place their civic-ceremonial centers on hilltops. In reality, there has never been a people who did not indulge in warfare, including the Classic Maya. In this connection, the sudden spread of the art styles and products of some Classic civilizations has quite justly been interpreted as the result of conquest. Furthermore, in at least one area, the Gulf Coast, human sacrifice was probably as common as it was among the later Aztecs.

There must have been many more people in Mexico during the Classic than formerly. Ruins are everywhere in central and southeastern Mexico, and most of them are Classic. In the Valley of Mexico alone, the monumental survey carried out by William Sanders and his associates has shown that by the end of the Early Classic, there were forty times as many inhabitants of the area than in the Middle Preclassic.

On the basis of a technology that was essentially Neolithic – for metals were unknown until after AD 800 – the Mexicans raised fantastic numbers of buildings, decorated them with beautiful polychrome murals, produced pottery and figurines in unbelievable quantity, and covered everything with sculptures. Even mass production was introduced, with the invention (or importation from South America) of the clay mold for making figurines and incense burners. Behind this abundance was the same economic theme that had been emphasized by their predecessors: simple farming of maize, beans, squash, and chile peppers, reflected in the continued importance of nature gods in their pantheon. Some authors have claimed that the Classic achievement could only have resulted from utilization of some form of irrigation, but this was of primary importance only in the drier regions of Mexico, such as the Tehuacan Valley and the Valley of Oaxaca.

Very clearly, the Classic florescence saw the intensification of sharp social cleavages throughout Mexico, and the consolidation of elite classes. It was long assumed on *a priori* grounds that the mode of government was theocratic, with a priestly group exercising temporal power. Evidence from both the imagery and archaeology at Teotihuacan indicate a more complex picture, with warriors also playing key roles. Below these groups that held the political reins was a peasantry which had hardly changed an iota from Preclassic times. Apart from the post-Conquest introduction of animal husbandry and steel tools, the old village-farming way of life has hardly been altered until today.

How extensive was the sway of each state over surrounding territory may never be known; we have this kind of information only for the fully literate Maya. It is probable that most administrative centers held less land and directed far fewer people than the great urban state that then had its capital in the Valley of Mexico. For the Classic period, Teotihuacan had no rival in the extent of its influence or the intensity of its contacts with the rest of Mesoamerica. Only the Post-Classic Aztec capital of Tenochtitlan would rival the size and reach of the great Classic city.

The urban civilization of Teotihuacan

Planned cities of the order of those in the Old World were rare anywhere in the Mesoamerican Classic. Of the few that did exist, the greatest of all was ancient Teotihuacan, the most important site in the whole of Mexico – even 66 Motecuhzoma Xocoyotzin himself made frequent pilgrimages on foot to its ruins during late Aztec times. Memories of its greatness persisted in Aztec myths recorded after the Conquest, for it was then thought that the civilization that had begun at Tamoanchan had been transferred to Teotihuacan. There the gods met to decide who was to sacrifice himself so as to become the new, the fifth, sun and bring light again to the world:

> Even though it was night,
> even though it was not day,
> even though there was no light
> they gathered,
> the gods convened
> there in Teotihuacan.[2]

66 Oblique airview of Teotihuacan from the northwest. In the lower left is the Pyramid of the Moon. The Pyramid of the Sun lies at left center. The furthest visible group is the Ciudadela ("Citadel"), connected to the Pyramid of the Moon by the Avenue of the Dead. The city was laid out on a grid plan, and present-day field boundaries correspond roughly to old foundation walls.

67 View south along the Avenue of the Dead from the Pyramid of the Moon. The Pyramid of the Sun is visible on the left, echoing the shape of the mountain behind.

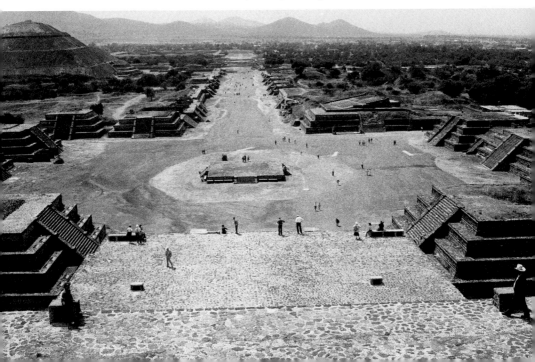

The city of Teotihuacan

68 (*left*) Life-size stone mask in Classic Teotihuacan style. Early Classic period.

69 (*below*) Plan of the central core of Teotihuacan, showing some of the numerous smaller structures around the major monuments revealed by René Millon's great mapping project.

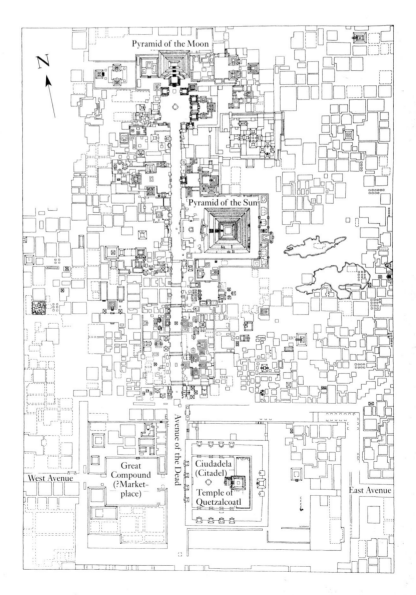

The most humble of them all, Nanahuatzin, the "Purulent One," cast himself into the flames and became the sun. But the heavenly bodies did not move, so all the gods sacrificed themselves for mankind. Finally, government was established there; the lords of Teotihuacan were "wise men, knowers of occult things, possessors of the traditions." When they died, pyramids were built above them. The largest of the pyramids, those of the Sun and Moon, were said by tradition to have been built by the giants which existed in those days (thus the legend naively says, "It is not unbelievable that they were made by hand").

The Teotihuacan Valley is actually a side pocket of the Valley of Mexico, comprising about 190 sq. miles (490 sq. km) of bottom land lying to the northeast of the Valley proper and surrounded by hills. Of this about one half is suitable for farming. Springs produce copious water that could have been used by the Teotihuacanos for farming, and there is some evidence for irrigation. These natural resources do not explain, however, the movement of most cultivators from throughout the Valley of Mexico to Teotihuacan between 150 BC and AD 200. For this we must turn to evidence from the city itself.

69   The detailed mapping project carried out by René Millon of the University of Rochester gives an idea of the gigantic size of this metropolis, the largest city of the Pre-Columbian New World. It covered over 8 sq. miles (20 sq. km) and was fully urbanized. Teotihuacan was laid out shortly after the time of Christ on a grid plan that is consistently oriented to 15 degrees 25 minutes east of true north, arguing that the planners must have been sophisticated surveyors as well. Various astronomical explanations have been advanced for this alignment, none of them completely convincing. Perhaps the strangest fact regarding this great city plan is that there is absolutely no precedent for it anywhere in the New World.

Teotihuacan's major axis is the Avenue of the Dead, which used to be thought to end at the so-called Ciudadela ("Citadel") in the south, a distance of 2 miles (3.2 km) from its northern terminus at the Pyramid of the Moon. It is now known that the avenue is *twice* this length, and that it is bisected in front of the Ciudadela by an east–west avenue of equal length, so that the city, like the much later Aztec capital, was laid out in quarters. Everything built at Teotihuacan conformed to the orientation of the main axis. The three monumental structures that anchor these sacred ways, and indeed all of Teotihuacan, are the Pyramids of the Sun and of the Moon and the Temple of Quetzalcoatl, the latter the centerpiece of the huge Ciudadela complex.

The great pyramids

67   The Pyramids of the Sun and of the Moon are explicitly named in old legends, and there is no reason to doubt that they were dedicated to those divinities. The former lies to the east of the Avenue of the Dead and not far from it. Its sides 700 ft (215 m) long and about 200 ft (60 m) high, it towers above the surrounding mounds and other ruins. Within it, at the base, are the remains of an earlier pyramid almost as large as the final version. The Pyramid of the Sun was raised in stages during the Tzacualli phase at the site, near the close of the Late Preclassic. The interior fill is formed entirely of

more than 41,000,000 cu. ft (1,175,000 cu. m) of sun-dried brick and rubble. A stone stairway, in part bifurcated, led to a now-destroyed temple on its lofty summit. The Pyramid of the Moon, which contains six earlier versions inside its massive bulk, was broadly similar, although smaller, and was built during the next phase, Miccaotli, at the beginning of the Classic. Both structures attest the immense power of the early Teotihuacan hierarchy to call up corvée labor from the villages of the territory over which it ruled. It has been pointed out that in the absence of advanced technology, a powerful state must rely on the work of such "human ants."

Discovered by accident in 1971, an extraordinary cave underneath the 70 Pyramid of the Sun throws light on why the pyramid was constructed, and perhaps even on why Teotihuacan itself was built where it was. The cave is actually a natural lava tube enlarged and elaborated in ancient times; it runs 330 ft (100 m) in an easterly direction 20 ft (6 m) beneath the Pyramid, in from the stairway on its main axis, reaching a multi-chambered terminus shaped something like a four-leafed clover. It will be recalled that Aztec tradition placed the creation of the Sun and Moon, and even the present universe, at Teotihuacan. The ancient use of the cave predates the pyramid, and it remained as a cult center after its construction. Unfortunately, official excavations carried out in it were never published, but scholars such as Doris Heyden and René Millon note that in pre-Conquest Mexico such caverns were symbolic wombs from which gods like the Sun and the Moon, and the ancestors of mankind, emerged in the mythological past. While there is no spring within the cave (a combination highly sacred to Mesoamericans), there were U-shaped drains (recalling Olmec prototypes) that certainly channeled water into the interior of the cave. This immensely holy spot was eventually looted of its contents and sealed off, but the memory of its location may have persisted into Aztec times.

The Pyramid of the Moon contained no such cave or other outstanding pl. VII feature in its interior. It does, however, echo the form of the sacred Cerro Gordo, the major mountain to the north, and may have been conceived by

70 The Pyramid of the Sun at Teotihuacan covered an already sacred cave which was greatly modified for symbolic and ceremonial purposes. Beginning of the Classic period.

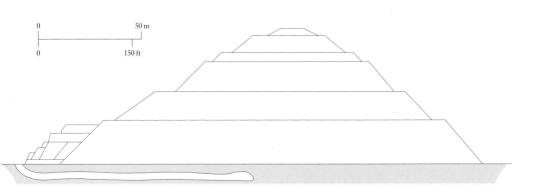

the Teotihuacanos as a replica of that natural feature. Recent work by Rubén Cabrera Castro and Saburo Sugiyama has detailed six previous constructions and three dedicatory offerings in the interior of the Moon Pyramid. The building began as a small platform in the last century BC, but by the completion of the Pyramid of the Sun 200 years later, the Moon was also a monumental pyramidal structure. To inaugurate this monumental phase, a sacrificial offering of felines, eagles, finely carved obsidian and greenstone, and one human victim was laid in the foundation. It is only at this point that the building was brought into line with what was to become the orientation of the city. The building was enlarged three more times, with two of these construction episodes marked by elaborate offerings and sacrifices. In the vicinity a monumental statue of a female deity was found. It may be that the pyramid was actually dedicated to the Moon deity, who was often considered female in Mesoamerica.

The third building in the triumvirate of Teotihuacan architecture, the 71 Temple of Quetzalcoatl, is considerably smaller than the two monumental pyramids discussed above. What it lacks in size, however, it makes up for with its central location, lavish offerings, and the wealth and importance of its facade decoration. The structure is a seven-tiered step-pyramid with typical *talud-tablero* facades (see below) located within the Ciudadela, at the very heart of the city, where the two main axes cross. The Temple of Quetzalcoatl was the last monumental public structure built at Teotihuacan, completed early in the third century AD. Around the tiers of *talud-tableros*, Feathered Serpents carry mosaic headdresses fashioned after another ophidian. Elsewhere at Teotihuacan this headdress is shown on warriors, and was probably specific to that office. Effigy seashells are sculpted in the background, suggesting that the scene is taking place in a watery environment. A legend from the Maya highlands suggests that we have here another version of the first moment of creation, with an opposed pair of serpents, one representing life, greenness, and peace, and the other heat, the desert regions, and war, cavorting or conversing in the primal ocean.

Excavations within and around the Quetzalcoatl pyramid by Rubén Cabrera Castro, Saburo Sugiyama, and George Cowgill revealed that it had been built in a single episode during which more than 200 individuals had been 72 sacrificed in elaborate dedicatory rites. Young warriors with their hands tied behind their backs had been dispatched in two groups of eighteen individuals (the number of 20-day months in the year), each group being interred in a large burial pit on the north and south sides of the pyramid. Other pits near these contained a smaller number of young females. More sacrificed warriors were interred on the east–west axis of the building. Investigations made in 1925 had shown that in addition to this great slaughter, a single slain captive had been placed at each of the pyramid's four corners. In the center of the

71 West facade of the Temple of Quetzalcoatl, Teotihuacan, transition between the Late Preclassic and Early Classic periods. On the left, Feathered Serpents peer out from the stairway flank; to the right, Serpent heads undulate on the sloping batters, while Fire Serpent heads alternate with Feathered Serpents within the entablatures.

72 Large numbers of warriors, indicated by the presence of back mirrors and dart points as in this burial, were sacrificed at the dedication of the Temple of Quetzalcoatl, Teotihuacan. Classic period.

pyramid was the richest offering of all, with twenty victims and thousands of pieces of jade, shell, and other materials. By using sacred numbers like 18 and 20 and by placing these offerings in each of the major world directions, the Teotihuacanos were mirroring the symbolism of Mesoamerican Creation epics.

The exact mode of sacrificial death has not yet been established, but in the absence of obvious signs of violence on the bones, strangulation or poisoning seems likely. The grim nature of this mass act, unique thus far in the archaeology of any Mesoamerican group, including the Aztecs, is highlighted by the macabre necklaces that many of the victims wear: strings of human jaws, upper and lower, sometimes real, sometimes crafted from shell. The warrior was celebrated throughout the building: on the facade with the headdress of the office, as well as in the interior through the identity of the sacrificial victims. This episode in the life of Teotihuacan is sure testimony that the Classic was definitely not a time of peace.

One of the more intriguing bits of evidence uncovered by the archaeologists was evidence of looting by the Teotihuacanos themselves: two burial pits near the center of the pyramid had been cleaned out, leaving only the slimmest of clues as to what was originally placed there. One of the groups was on the exact centerline of the structure and contained a feathered serpent baton, surely a signal of very high rank. This looting took place around AD 400, long before the decline of the city and the fall of its government.

Classic Teotihuacan architecture is based on a few simple principles. Interiors of small stones are faced with broken-up volcanic stones set in clay and covered with a smooth coat of lime plaster. The typical architectural motif is that known as *talud-tablero*: a rectangular panel with inset is placed over a sloping wall. Buildings from the humblest family shrine to large temples are decorated with this motif throughout the city. The panel area is often painted, and in the Temple of Quetzalcoatl it serves as the support for elabo-

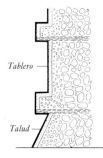

Tablero

Talud

73 Cross-section to show the typical *talud-tablero* building style at Teotihuacan

74 Representation of a temple on a Teotihuacan pottery vessel of the Early Classic period.

rate sculptural decoration. Interestingly, the *talud-tablero* form itself seems to be an import from the Puebla-Tlaxcala region, but is used to such an extent by Teotihuacanos that it becomes associated specifically with the metropolis.

Most of what we see today at Teotihuacan was built after the completion of these three great public structures by the early third century AD. By the early fourth century AD it had reached the height of its population, estimated by René Millon at a probable figure of 125,000, but possibly reaching 200,000 at its maximum.

Palaces and apartment compounds

A major finding of the Teotihuacan Mapping Project was that most of the city consisted of walled residential compounds divided internally into apartments. Most if not all apartment compounds were built after the completion of the monumental pyramids; we know little of how the already substantial population lived before the onset of apartment building. The few entrances to each compound suggest that access was carefully controlled. Compounds measure from 4,300 to 75,000 sq. ft (400–7,000 sq. m), although the majority fall near the middle of this range. The differences in construction, decoration, and room size indicate a rather large range of wealth and status. From analysis of excavated artifacts, it seems that the compounds were grouped into something like wards based upon kinship and/or commercial interests. The city was cosmopolitan: in its western part there was a Oaxaca ward, in which Zapotecs carried on their own customs and worshiped their own gods, while on the east there was one made up of people with strong connections to the lowland Veracruz and Maya areas.

Typical of the compound layout might be Tetitla, a 60 by 60 meter (196 ft) square complex of several dozen rooms and nine temple structures, all organized around courts. Each court was open to the sky, sometimes with a small altar in the center. Triadic temple arrangements, found at Tetitla and throughout the Classic city, consist of a single raised platform containing the central temple joined to two flanking temples at 90 degree angles. This form is found already at Late Preclassic Tetimpa, Puebla, as well as at the earliest occupations at Teotihuacan. While windows were lacking, several of the rooms had smaller sunken courts very much like the Roman *atria*, into which light and air were admitted through the roof, supported by surrounding piers. The rainwater in the sunken basins could be drained off when desired. All compounds known were one-storied affairs, with flat roofs built from beams and small sticks and twigs, overlain by earth and rubble. Doorways were rectangular and covered by a cloth.

It is estimated that the Tetitla compound would have housed 60 to 100 people. Each Teotihuacan compound must have been a rather tightly organized social group, given the specialization and planning essential to compound life. Males in the compound seem to have been more closely related to each other than the females. Most compounds had one or two rich burials, suggesting that founders or important family members were especially honored.

The sophistication and artistry of the Teotihuacanos can be seen in the magnificent murals, almost all of religious content, which adorn the walls of the palaces and apartment compounds. Many of these are highly repetitive, with rows of human figures whose bodies disappear under the elaborate description of their ritual attire. In the porticoes of one of the buildings in the White Patio at Atetelco are depicted processions of jaguars and coyotes, painted in various shades of red, and perhaps symbolizing the knightly orders of this warlike society. The larger and more richly decorated residences mainly found grouped around the Avenue of the Dead were surely the residences of the lords of the city. These qualify as true "palaces" in that they are significantly finer than the great majority of the other 2,000 compounds found throughout the city.

75, 76

pl. IX

75 Reconstruction of the White Patio, in a palace at Atetelco, Teotihuacan. Early Classic period. Width of floor between the stairways of the two flanking buildings 8.5 m.

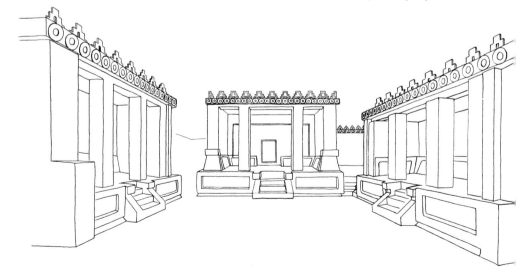

76 Prowling coyote from mural painting at Atetelco, Teotihuacan. The painting is done in subtly contrasting values of red. A "speech scroll" curves from the mouth of the beast, and below the mouth is apparently a symbol for the human heart, dripping blood. Early Classic period.

The most famous of the compound murals are those at Tepantitla; following their discovery, these were interpreted by Alfonso Caso as a depiction of the Paradise of the Rain God, or to use the Nahuatl term, Tlalocan. But the deity dominating the scene, once thought to be Tlaloc himself, is now universally accepted as a female, following the work of Esther Pasztory and others. Karl Taube of the University of California, Riverside, has further shown that this goddess has the mouth parts (fangs and palps) of a spider. In Taube's view, the Teotihuacan Spider Woman, as he calls this great goddess, was responsible for the creation of the present universe, and was the supreme deity of the Teotihuacanos. Very often in Teotihuacan art other individuals wear items associated with the goddess, thereby associating themselves with her power. For reasons yet unexplained, she bears a close relationship, if not identity, with the Spider Grandmother who plays such an important role in Pueblo and Navajo creation mythology in the American Southwest, as well as with the Spider Woman goddess of the Kogi of Colombia. While other Mesoamerican urban cultures certainly had female deities, few if any gave a female deity such a central role.

In this vein, then, the landscape accompanying the Spider Woman in the Tepantitla murals would depict a place or places in the origin myth of the Teotihuacano people themselves, including a magic mountain with gushing springs at its base – perhaps the Cerro Gordo which looms to the north of the city – near which little human figures sing, conduct rituals, and play games; butterflies and flowering trees add to the general gaiety of the scene.

Few if any of these palaces are of sufficient size to have been the abode of the supreme rulers of the city. Some years ago the late Pedro Armillas suggested that the Ciudadela, a huge square enclosure with sides over 1300 ft (400 m) long near the center of the city, was the royal palace itself. Recent investigations have, in fact, revealed two apartment complexes – one in the northern half of the enclosure and one in the southern – which probably were seats of royal authority (quite possibly there could have been dual rulership, which some have suggested for the later Aztecs). As we have seen, the adjoining Temple of Quetzalcoatl carries the imagery of Creation and sacred war. If the Ciudadela complex really was the royal palace, then the ruling family may have identified itself with the center of the universe, the very beginning of time, and the sacred foundation of Teotihuacan's military might, a combination of royal legitimacy seen throughout Mesoamerica.

If palaces alone had been built in ancient Teotihuacan, this would have been a peculiar sort of city. Some idea of the way more ordinary people lived is given by the compound called Tlajinga 33, in the far south of the city, studied by Rebecca Storey and Randolph Widmer. Although the general layout is comparable to the finer residences in the center, the builders used cheaper materials and did not decorate the residence with murals. Fairly humble artisans occupied this compound throughout its history, and it seems that as time progressed, they became poorer and had less control over their crafts. There must have been an immense multitude of traders, artisans, and other non-food producers living in quarters of this sort. Mexico was to see nothing like this again until the Aztecs built their capital Tenochtitlan.

The Teotihuacan pantheon

In Karl Taube's view, as we have seen, the presiding deity of the Teotihuacan pantheon was the Spider Woman, the patroness of our own world. Depictions of related female deities, or perhaps aspects of the goddess, include a colossal statue representing the Water Goddess (in Nahuatl, Chalchiuhtlicue, "Her Skirt Is of Jade"). An even larger statue, weighing almost 200 metric tons and now in front of the Museum of Anthropology in Mexico City, was found in an unfinished state on the slopes of Tlaloc Mountain. It is identified in the popular Mexican consciousness with that deity, but wears abstracted versions of the female garments seen on the Water Goddess. It is

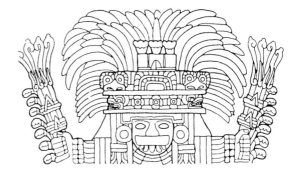

77 The goddess identified by Karl Taube as the Spider Woman, perhaps the presiding deity at Teotihuacan. She wears a fanged mask representing a spider's mouth parts. Detail from a Classic period sculpture at the site.

78 Giant statue of the Water Goddess, Chalchiuhtlicue, from Teotihuacan. Early Classic period. Ht 3 m.

79 (*below*) Tlaloc, God of Rain, from a mural painting on a palace at Zacuala, Teotihuacan.

likely that these and other supernatural females formed a closely related deity complex, much like the female deities of the Aztec. Many of the other gods of the complete Mexican pantheon are already clearly recognizable at Teotihuacan. Here were worshipped the Rain God ("Tlaloc" to the Aztecs) and the Feathered Serpent (the later "Quetzalcoatl"), as well as the Sun God, the Moon Goddess, and Xipe Totec (Nahuatl for "Our Lord the Flayed One"), the last-named being the symbol of the annual renewal of vegetation with the onset of the rainy season. Particularly common are incense burners of the Old Fire God, a creator divinity and the probable consort of the Spider Woman. At any rate, it should be noted that almost all the gods venerated in this great urban capital were intimately connected with the well-being of maize, with their staff of life.

79

Tradition holds that Teotihuacan was a sacred burial ground. Really important tombs have seemingly been discovered only by professional treasure hunters, but underneath the floors of the palaces and apartment buildings have been encountered a number of slab-lined graves and simple pit burials. The Teotihuacanos like the later Aztecs favored cremation of the dead, the body first being wrapped in a bundle. Around the remains were placed fine offerings of all sorts, particularly lovely and graceful vases, obsidian artifacts, and perishable things like textiles. Beliefs about the hereafter are recorded in a Nahuatl song:

> And they called it Teotihuacan
> because it was the place
> where the lords were buried.
> Thus they said:
> "When we die,
> truly we die not,
> because we will live, we will rise,
> we will continue living, we will awaken.
> This will make us happy."
> Thus the dead one was directed,
> when he died:
> "Awaken, already the sky is rosy,
> already sing the flame-colored guans,
> the fire-colored swallows,
> already the butterflies fly."
> Thus the old ones said
> that who had died has become a god,
> they said: "He has been made a god there,"
> meaning, "He has died."[3]

Arts, crafts, and trade

The Teotihuacan art style as revealed in frescoes, sculpture, pottery, and other productions could be tremendously elegant and refined, as well as highly stylized and ordered. Even when the artisans were less careful, there is a grave, minimal quality to the art, and the best work is monumental and still, no matter its size. Sculpture is best represented in the austere stone masks, fashioned from greenstone, basalt, jade, andesite and other materials, each of which once had inlaid eyes of mussel-shells or obsidian, as well as in a few very large-scale pieces such as the Water Goddess. Frescoes filled the walls of many of the more opulent apartment compounds, where they were applied in "true fresco," with the diluted pigments applied to a fresh coat of lime plaster. Often a silicate such as mica was added to the pigment dilution to increase the paint's sheen, and after drying the whole was carefully burnished.

The hallmark of Teotihuacan culture is the cylindrical pottery vase with three slab-shaped feet. Adapted in the fourth century AD, perhaps from earlier experiments on the Gulf Coast, this ceramic form became associated specifically with the metropolis. These vases usually have fitted lids on top with handles in the form of a bird. Other characteristic forms in clay include vessels shaped like flower vases. Decoration on these luxury items, found in graves and far away as trade pieces, may be plano-relief or painted on a thin coating of lime, the latter executed in the same manner as the wall frescoes.

68, pl. VIII

80

81

80 Ceramics from Early Classic burials at Teotihuacan, *a–b*, cylindrical tripods decorated in carved relief technique; *c, florero*; *d*, "cream pitcher"; *e*, jar with face of Tlaloc; *f–g, candeleros*; *h–i*, Thin Orange ware. 1/4.

81 Fragment of cylindrical tripod vessel with relief design of a blowgunner hunting quetzal birds in a cacao tree. From Teotihuacan, Early Classic period. Ht 11.4 cm.

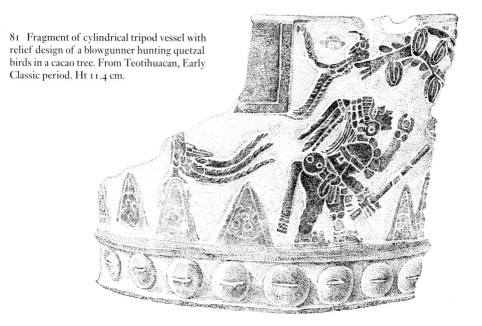

80   A fine ware known as Thin Orange was manufactured in southern Puebla, an area that may have been under Teotihuacan control, and appears as bowls with annular bases, boxes with lids, or effigies of little dogs.

Other objects of clay include large polychromed incense burners, built up of mold-made details, mold-made figurines of men and gods, and little two-holed *candeleros*, which might have been used to burn incense and contain the blood offered to the gods in an act of self-sacrifice. Clay pellets were carefully shaped for employment as blowgun missiles, and we know from a scene on a vase that this weapon was used in hunting birds.

82   Obsidian chipping reached new heights of elaboration, with the production of spear- and dart-points as well as little human effigies of that material. As usual, vast quantities of razor-like blades of obsidian are present. The Teotihuacan state controlled the great deposits of green obsidian near Pachuca, Hidalgo; and the 100 obsidian workshops known to have existed in the city were part of the thriving mercantile sector.

Bone needles and bodkins testify to the manufacture of clothing and basketry, and we have the charred remains of cotton cloth with weft pattern, coiled baskets, and twilled sleeping mats or *petates*. Paintings show that men wore a loincloth and/or kilt with sandals, and women the pull-over *huipilli* and underskirt.

Although none have survived, books must have been in both ritual and administrative use, for these people had writing, if only of a rudimentary sort. Teotihuacanos knew of the complex Maya writing system, but chose to limit their own writing mainly to dates, names, or locations accompanying an image. An exception is the fascinating glyphic patio found in the La Ventilla area, where clear Maya and Teotihuacan signs fill the floor in a regular grid pattern.

Cooking was done in kitchen areas within the compounds over clay, three-pronged braziers. Charred vegetal materials and animal bones give some idea of the citizens' diet: they subsisted on a small-cobbed maize, common and runner beans, squashes and pumpkins, husk tomatoes, prickly pear cactus, avocados, and amaranth, along with wild plant foods. The important food

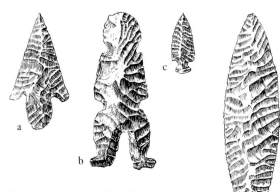

82 Chipped obsidian artifacts from the Early Classic period at Teotihuacan. *a*, *c*, and *d*, spear and dart points, 3/8; *b*, human effigy, 3/4.

animals were deer, dogs, cottontail rabbits and jackrabbits, turkeys, wild ducks and geese, and small fish. Much ink has been spilled over the problem of the agricultural base of Teotihuacan civilization. William Sanders is certain that there was a local irrigation system in the Valley itself. On the other hand, there is some evidence of *chinampa* or "floating garden" cultivation, for relict *chinampa* plots show up on the Millon map of the city, and it is suggestive that the well-known *chinampa* systems in the southern part of the Valley of Mexico, such as the one at Xochimilco, have the same orientation as Teotihuacan itself.

Yet it may be fruitless to look at the Valley of Teotihuacan alone for the secret of the capital's remarkable success, for the city that we have described held sway over most of the central highlands of Mexico during the Classic, and wielded significant influence over much of Mesoamerica. Like the later Aztec state, it may have depended as much on long-distance trade and tribute as upon local agricultural production. Elegant vases of pure Teotihuacan manufacture or showing pronounced Teotihuacan influence are found in the burials of nobles all over Mexico at this time, and the art of the Teotihua-canos catalyzed to some extent the styles of the other high civilizations of Mesoamerica. Especially interesting is the contact with the Maya on the other side of Mesoamerica. Some 650 miles (1,040 km) to the southeast, in the highlands of Guatemala on the outskirts of the modern capital of that republic, a little "city" has been found that is in all respects a miniature copy of Teotihuacan. The tombs of the chiefs of this center, Kaminaljuyu, are full of luxuries imitating those from Teotihuacan itself, while some pieces were imported directly from the metropolis.

A similar situation has been found at that colossus of Maya centers, Tikal, situated in the lowland jungle of northern Guatemala, where an Early Classic monument (Stela 31) shows a jade-bedecked ruler flanked by two views of his father garbed as a Teotihuacan warrior. Maya imagery and writing coexists with clear Teotihuacan symbolism on this and many other Tikal monuments and objects after the arrival of a Teotihuacan-related group in the late fourth century AD. Soon after the arrival of Teotihuacanos at Tikal, a kingdom was founded at Copán, near the border of Guatemala and Honduras, that was also based on the use of legitimating Teotihuacano symbolism. In all of these contact scenarios, Teotihuacan's donation is quickly folded into the local culture and made to signal the power of the local lords. The presence of Teotihuacan in an already complex Maya political landscape has yet to be fully understood, and only further work will help us solve this complex historical puzzle. What is certain is that the rulers of the great Classic cultures throughout Mesoamerica had a special reverence for the metropolis.

The rise and fall of a city

The question is, and it must be admitted that no definite answer can be given, who were the people of Teotihuacan? Who built this city, and whence did they come? The early Spanish historian Torquemada tells us that the Totonac claimed the honor, and in this light it is true that a few of the earliest Classic Teotihuacan buildings show a certain decorative influence from

Veracruz, the Totonac homeland. But there is little evidence that the Totonac were in Veracruz until much later, during the Epiclassic period. Some scholars claim an Otomí occupation of the city, others hold for the Popoloca. In view of the strong continuities between Teotihuacan on the one hand and the Toltecs and Aztecs on the other, in both sacred and secular features, the Nahua affinities of this civilization would appear to be the most probable. On this question we are little wiser than were the native peoples, who thought that Teotihuacan had been built by giants or gods.

The city met its end in the seventh century through deliberate destruction and burning by the hand of unknown invaders. It was mainly the heart of the city that suffered the torch, especially the palaces and temples on each side of the Avenue of the Dead, from the Pyramid of the Moon to the Ciudadela. Some internal crisis or long-term political and economic malaise, perhaps the disruption of its trade and tribute routes by a new polity such as the rising Xochicalco state, may have resulted in the downfall, and it may be significant that by AD 600 almost all Teotihuacan influence over the rest of Mesoamerica ceases.

Along with political and economic factors, stress on the physical environment could have played a role in the decline of the metropolis. George Vaillant proposed that the destruction of the surrounding forests necessary for the burning of the lime that went into the building of Teotihuacan resulted in a precocious erosion and desiccation of the region. A related factor might have been the increasing aridity of the climate all over Mexico during the Classic, which apparently was severest in the Valley of Mexico. The whole edifice of the Teotihuacan state may have perished through the ensuing agricultural debacle, opening civilized Mexico to peoples from the northern frontier.

Whatever the causes, the luxurious palaces of Teotihuacan were now in ruins, and its major temples abandoned. But away from the Avenue of the Dead, the city continued to live for another two centuries; this reduced occupation is called Coyotlatelco, from the simple red-on-buff pottery characteristic of the period. Through a probable combination of people leaving the city and natural decrease due to high infant and child mortality, the population of Teotihuacan had sunk to only a quarter of its former total. Atzcapotzalco, a Teotihuacan-related center west of the great lake, futilely carried on an epigonal version of their old culture.

The Great Pyramid of Cholula

As present-day travelers leave the Valley of Mexico and journey east-southeast across the mountains rimming the basin, they eventually drop down on to the plains of Puebla, the volcanic peaks of Iztaccihuatl and Popocatepetl rising on the right hand. Once on the plain itself, they see before them shining in the sun the yellow and green tiled domes of a Colonial period church that seems to rest on a very large hill. It comes as a shock to realize that this is not a hill at all, but a man-made pyramid, that of Cholula, one of the largest ancient structures in the New World.

83

83 View from the north of the Pyramid of Cholula, Puebla, crowned with a church of the Colonial period. This great adobe-brick platform, traditionally dedicated to Quetzalcoatl, rises 55 m above the surrounding plain and is one of the most massive structures in the Pre-Columbian New World.

The Great Pyramid, which was already in ruins when the Spaniards first arrived, is actually the result of four successive superpositions, the first two of which are Classic in date. The earliest pyramid exhibits the *talud-tablero* motif characteristic of the Puebla region and later of Teotihuacan, and is painted with insect-like designs in pure Classic Teotihuacan style. It was built at roughly the same time as the great pyramids of Teotihuacan. The second Great Pyramid, built directly over the first, no longer imitated local or Teotihuacan architectural forms. Here the architects created a radial pyramid, 590 ft (180m) on a side, with stairs covering all four sides, so that the summit could be approached from any direction.

A 165-ft (50-m) long polychrome mural with life-sized human figures has been discovered at Cholula and is said to be Classic in date; known as "the Drunkards," the scene is indubitably one of drinking and inebriation, but the liquid imbibed could have been a hallucinogenic potion derived from the powerful mushrooms of ancient Mexico, or even from peyote, rather than alcohol.

Cerro de las Mesas

Down on the Gulf Coast plain, new civilizations appeared in the Early Classic that in some respects reflect continuity from the old Olmec tradition of the lowlands, as well as intrusive elements ultimately derived from Teotihuacan. The site of Cerro de las Mesas lies in the middle of the former Olmec territory, in south-central Veracruz, approximately 15 miles (24 km) from the Bay of Alvarado, on a broad band of high land above the swamps of the Río Blanco. The site is the center of an area dotted with earthen mounds. Cerro de las Mesas was occupied from Middle Preclassic through Late Post-Classic times, but attained its apogee during the Classic.

A number of stelae encountered there by Stirling show features recalling both the Olmec and Izapan styles. One side of each monument is generally carved in low relief so as to depict a hieratically posed personage in rich attire, in profile with one leg stiffly outstretched before the other. The Olmec

84 Stela 6, Cerro de las Mesas, Veracruz. The vertical column on the left records the Long Count date 9.1.12.14.10 (AD 468). The headdress of the richly attired figure on the right is derived from an Olmec prototype.

were-jaguar appears in mask-like headdresses and on half-masks which are occasionally worn over the lower face. Two of the monuments record Long Count dates, one being 9.1.12.14.10 (AD 468) and the other 9.4.18.16.8 (AD 533), well within the Classic period. Other sculptures include a monstrous figure of a duck-billed human closely resembling the Tuxtla Statuette (see Chapter 5), which itself was found not very far from Cerro de las Mesas.

Excavations at the site brought to light a fantastically rich cache of carved jade. Altogether there were 782 pieces from several areas of Mesoamerica, buried together at some time during the Classic. While some are very much of the period, especially those in the local styles of the Maya highlands and of Oaxaca, a good number are purely Olmec, obviously heirlooms handed down from the ancient civilization that had once controlled this region. Was this cache left by some trafficker in fine jewelry? Does it represent the hoard of some local prince? Or, most plausible of all, is this an offering to the unknown gods of Cerro de las Mesas?

The Classic Veracruz civilization

A large number of fine stone objects found on the Gulf Coast plain are carved in a very distinct style that has become known as "Classic Veracruz." The majority of them are from the northern and central parts of that state, a zone in which are located several great elite centers that shared in the same art tradition. This style can be mistaken for no other in Mexico; on the

The Classic Veracruz style

85, 86 Carved slate back for a circular mirror (*left*) found in southern Querétaro. The reverse side was the reflecting surface, consisting of a consolidated mass of small pyrite crystals. Early Classic period. Diameter 15 cm. (*Right*) Thin human head of stone, with headdress in the shape of a crane, designed to fit the front of a stone "yoke." Late Classic period.

87, 88 Stone "yoke" in Classic Veracruz style (*left*), representing a stylized toad seen from above, covered with scrollwork patterns. Classic period, possibly beginning of Late Classic. Length about 46 cm. (*Right*) *Palma* stone in Classic Veracruz style. The double-strand interlace is highly unusual in this style. Late Classic period. Ht 51 cm.

contrary, its closest affinities seem to lie, for no apparent reason, across the Pacific with the Bronze and Iron Age cultures of China. It is a style in which all subject matter is secondary and bound to a complex ornamental motif, one of linked or intertwined scrolls with raised edges, perhaps the offspring of the cloud scrolls of the Izapan style.

86–88   The Classic Veracruz style commonly appears on a complex of enigmatic stone objects, the so-called "yokes," *palmas*, and *hachas* ("axes" or thin stone heads). Modern research has shown that all three are associated with the ritual ball game, as bas-reliefs and figurines depict them being worn in that connection. The "yokes," which are U-shaped and often intricately carved to represent stylized toads covered with convoluted scrolls and human faces, were stone replicas of the heavy protective belts worn by the players. They are found beginning in the Late Preclassic in central Veracruz, and continue to be made through the Epiclassic. As this sculptural tradition became more complex, the front of this ceremonial belt could be fitted with a *palma*, an elongated sculpture adapted for that purpose; *palmas* are often effigies of birds like turkeys, or are carved with realistic scenes. Their style is associated with late phases of the Classic Veracruz style, and several may be associated specifically with El Tajín, the Epiclassic culmination of this tradition. The thin stone heads probably were markers placed in the court to score the game, but they too could be worn on the yoke. In its formative phase, the style can best be seen in slate backs for circular mirrors of pyrite mosaic – these are certainly Classic in date, as are many of the "yokes."

The tribal name "Totonac" has often been inappropriately applied to these carvings; while it is true that the Totonacs now occupy most of the zone in which such remains are found, it may or may not have been they who made them. Archaeologists prefer caution in these matters. Nevertheless, Classic Veracruz influence is very perceptibly present in the beginnings of Classic Teotihuacan, and some are inclined to accept Torquemada's statement that these people built that city. On the other hand, reciprocal influence from the highlands is also present, here on the Gulf Coast.

Classic Monte Albán

The civilization of Monte Albán in the Valley of Oaxaca during Classic times was certainly the product of Zapotecan-speaking peoples. The changeover from the Late Preclassic appears to have been peaceful, with some new elements in the Proto-Classic Monte Albán II coming up from the Maya area as a kind of burial cult: potstands, painted stucco decoration of pottery, and so forth. But Maya influence stops with the commencement of the Classic proper, and a new series of cultural elements holds sway, with a particularly strong influence being exerted by Teotihuacan. There is no reason to think, however, of any major shift in population or of outside invasion. Furthermore, Oaxaca was sufficiently isolated to avoid some of the troubles visited upon Teotihuacan during the Classic period. Left to themselves to populate their own territory, the Zapotecs built site after site throughout the Valley of 89   Oaxaca, ruling the entire territory from the summit of Monte Albán.

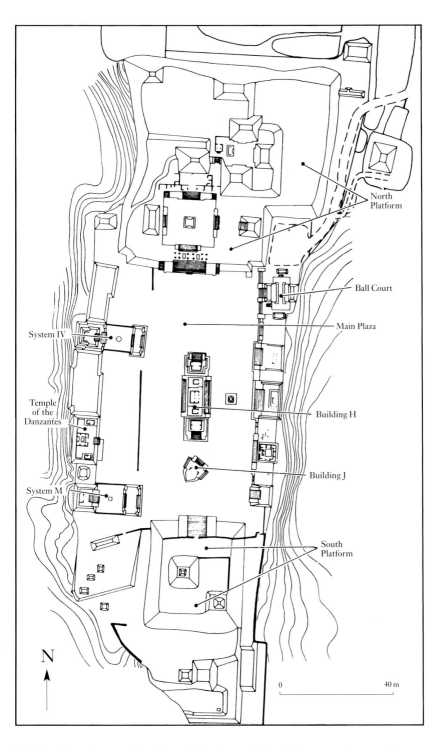

89 Plan of the main acropolis at Monte Albán, Oaxaca. Most of the constructions are of the Monte Albán III period.

90 View south across Monte Albán, with Building H in the center of the main plaza.

91 View of the Classic period ball court on the eastern edge of the acropolis at Monte Albán.

The slopes of the hill on which Classic Monte Albán stands are covered with hundreds of residential terraces containing an estimated population of 25,000 at its Classic apogee. A small number of strategically placed centers throughout the Valley were only slightly less populous than the capital, but the great majority of the over 1,000 Valley settlements were significantly smaller. Most of the Valley's inhabitants were farmers, irrigating the rich bottom lands for their crops, but they must also have farmed the piedmont zone above the Valley.

The Classic site as it now stands was developed around a very large and long plaza. Bigger constructions were raised on rock nuclei that remained after the hill was leveled off. Among the buildings of this epoch are stone-faced platforms, fronted by stairways with flanking balustrades. Something like the *talud-tablero* architecture of Teotihuacan is evident, but the panel is modified from its original form. These and other buildings were once completely stuccoed; some were given additional painted decoration. Also present is a magnificent masonry ball court with a ground plan like a capital "I," a form that was replicated at other important Valley centers, leading researchers to posit an "official" game that may have helped sort out conflicts among groups. Even more indicative of Monte Albán culture was the building form known as the Temple-Patio-Altar complex, which is found on the summit in Systems M and IV as well as on hilltops throughout the Valley where Monte Albán held sway.

Subterranean tombs – 170 of them – have been discovered all over the site, some of which were of great magnificence, testimony to the wealth of the lords of Monte Albán. The best are quite elaborate chambers, often with a corbeled vault, and have an antechamber. Fine murals were painted on the plastered walls. Tomb 104, in the northern part of the site, is certainly the most spectacular known thus far. Over the facade of the tomb is a niche with a pottery urn representing a person wearing the headdress of the Rain God. The door was a single great slab covered with hieroglyphs; within the

90, pl. X

91

92

92 Part of a painting on the walls of Tomb 104 at Monte Albán, Oaxaca. The Young Maize God appears on the right, holding an incense pouch. Early in Monte Albán III-B culture, *c.* AD 500. Ht of wall 1.6 m

93 A Zapotec lord is surrounded by richly painted walls and ceramic effigies. Elaborate funerary rites and offerings formed part of the Zapotec cult of deified ancestors. Tomb 104, Monte Albán, Classic period.

93 funerary chamber the skeleton was stretched out on the floor, surrounded by rich offerings including more clay urns. Lovely murals grace the walls, depicting a procession of figures with elaborate ritual dress advancing towards the rear of the tomb, interspaced with glyphs. While the organization of these tombs is typically Zapotec, the style of these and other Classic Monte Albán frescoes, down to the smallest details such as treatment of the feather ornamentation, is obviously derivative from Teotihuacan. Monte Albán had an enclave in Teotihuacan where they maintained Zapotec burial customs and scribal traditions, while at the same time cultivating an intimate relation to the techniques and traditions of the Teotihuacanos.

A large group of urn figures may be identified as representations of deified ancestors through their use of names culled from the sacred calendar. These were usually found in tombs, but could also be used as offerings placed in temples. This cult of deified ancestors was central to Classic Monte Albán culture, and accounts for the enormous amount of artistic capital spent shaping and decorating the numerous tombs. Tombs were re-entered time and time again during the Classic to place additional burials, or even to substitute new ones for old, with new paintings being applied over the old; thus, some of these murals, like those in Tomb 105 at Monte Albán, are virtual palimpsests.

Some, at least, of the gods of Monte Albán are shared with other Mexican peoples and can thus be identified. Their divinity finds abundant expression in the large numbers of the pottery urns placed with the dead, often in pl. XI groups. In these, the use of the mold is rare, much of the ornamentation being built up by sharply carved clay strips. Each god is generally shown as seated cross-legged, richly dressed with an elaborate headdress containing the symbol by which he is known. We have in an old dictionary the Zapotec names of some of these deities. The most important members of the pantheon were the Lightning God, *Cociyo*; the Maize God, *Pitao Cozobi*, often adorned with actual casts of maize ears; the Feathered Serpent; a Bat God; the Old Fire God; and, possibly, the Water Goddess.

The writing and calendric system of Classic Monte Albán was fully developed from the Preclassic base. Although there are no surviving codices, glyphs appear everywhere, both in sculptured relief, on the funerary urns, and painted on walls, at the principal site itself and at other Monte Albán centers. The numeration continues to be in the bar-and-dot system. Inscriptions typically open with a date in the 52-year Calendar Round. This is given by a Year Bearer: as Alfonso Caso and Javier Urcid have demonstrated, the year was named by one of four days in the 260-day count on which it could begin or end, along with the numerical coefficient of that day, and a Year Bearer-sign in the form of a royal headband. These Year Bearer days were in the 2nd, 7th, 12th, and 17th positions within the list of 20 named days. Unfortunately for Mesoamericanists, the Zapotecs never adopted the lowland Long Count, so that inscribed dates cannot be fixed within an absolute chronology. Another complicating factor, as Urcid has indicated, is that most Zapotec monuments have been reused and often moved from their original positions, with the result that texts which once made sense in the context of neighboring inscriptions no longer do so. And lastly, it now appears that many notations in the 260-day count, long interpreted as having chronological significance, are in reality the calendrical names of historical personages.

What kind of script was this? From its origins in the Monte Albán I period through the Classic and Epiclassic periods, there were always about 60 to 80 non-calendrical glyphs; this is far too high for a purely phonetic syllabary or alphabet, but within the range for known scripts of the logo–syllabic sort: ones in which there is a mixture of logographic (semantic) and syllabic (phonetic) signs. Thus far, it remains one of the very few undeciphered writing systems of the world, but progress in cracking it may be rapid once the proto–Zapotec language has been reconstructed by linguists, and also once the corpus of all Zapotec inscriptions now being compiled by Javier Urcid reaches completion.

While there are no signs of a conflagration, as at Teotihuacan, sometime before AD 800 the capital was largely abandoned and Monte Albán fell into ruins, as did many (but not all) other regional centers in the Valley. Later peoples like the Mixtecs used the old Zapotec sites as a kind of consecrated ground for their tombs, some of them as we shall see quite wonderful, perhaps in an attempt to establish their continuity with the native dynasties that had ruled here for over a thousand years.

The Classic downfall

The single most important fact that archaeologists have learned about the Classic period in Mexico is the supremacy of Teotihuacan, its impress being clearly recorded throughout this incredibly varied country and beyond, to other parts of Mesoamerica. As the urbanized center of Mexico, with high population and tremendous production, its power was imposed through political and cultural means not only in its native highland habitat, but also along the tropical coasts, reaching even into the Maya area. That this was a trading and tribute empire entirely comparable with the Aztec cannot be doubted. All other states were partly or entirely dependent upon it for whatever achievements they attained at this time, and any solution of the problem of why the Classic developed at all must be approached through the more central problem that Teotihuacan, without local antecedents, presents to puzzled archaeologists.

Perhaps agricultural collapse also had something to do with the Classic debacle, with the weary farmers of Mexico no longer willing to build pyramids and palaces for leaders who failed to provide the rains that would guarantee them full harvests. Also destabilizing were the internal pressures created by disaffected nobles. It is as if the pattern of Mesoamerican life, established with the first civilizations of the Preclassic, had become exhausted.

In short, the country was ripe for revolution as well as conquest from outside, and the two forces probably together produced the different way of life that we see in later periods.

7 · The Epiclassic Period

When Teotihuacan fell in the seventh century AD, the central unifying force in Mexico, and indeed in all of Mesoamerica, was gone. The largest city in Mesoamerica was now reduced to a quarter of its former population, which was still substantial in Pre-Columbian terms. It was never again a major political force, however, and the loss of that centralizing force left a large power vacuum in ancient Mexico. Into this vacuum stepped a number of smaller cities, each vying for power and prestige in the wake of the great capital's fall. Between AD 650 and 900, these competing cities developed new political and trade alliances and eclectic art styles, thus recreating the political, economic, and cultural systems of ancient Mexico after the loss of its imperial capital.

The Maya connection: Cacaxtla and Xochicalco

One of the more intriguing Epiclassic developments was the appearance of foreigners, almost certainly from the Gulf Coast lowlands and the Yucatan Peninsula, in the highlands of ancient Mexico. The interrelationship of the highland Mexicans and the Maya has been established by archaeology, but this was usually the domination by the former of the latter, such as the takeover of Kaminaljuyu by Teotihuacanos. During the Classic period, there must have been at least one enclave of Maya traders at Teotihuacan, and a fine Maya jade plaque in the British Museum is supposed to have been found at that site. The Maya, with their advanced knowledge of astronomy and sophisticated writing system, probably exerted considerable intellectual and religious influence over the rest of Mesoamerica, and there is some evidence that the dreaded Tezcatlipoca, the great god of war and the royal house in Post-Classic Mexico, was of Maya origin. Moreover, Maya civilization was experiencing its most active flowering during this period. Building activity at numerous Maya centers reached its zenith, as did the internecine strife brought on by the competition between the two great alliances in the area: that centered on Tikal, old ally of Teotihuacan during the Classic period, and that led by Kalak'mul, the metropolis to the north and heir to a kingdom even older than Tikal. Although we do not fully understand the dynamics, it seems that Maya rivalries and their concomitant search for alliances played a part in the repartitioning of ancient Mexico during the Epiclassic.

The site of Cacaxtla contains the most important evidence of powerful Maya groups in the heart of central Mexico. Cacaxtla is one of a number of hilltop sites in the Puebla-Tlaxcala border area, and lies only 15½ miles

(25 km) northnortheast of Cholula. The early chronicler Diego Muñoz Camargo tells us that it was a "seat and fortress" of the Olmeca-Xicallanca, whose capital was then Cholula. The name "Olmeca" (not to be confused with the archaeological Olmecs) means "people of the region of rubber," that is, of the southern Gulf Coast. "Xicallanca" is another Nahuatl name, referring to "the people of Xicallanco (or land of calabashes)." Xicallanco was an important trading town in southern Campeche controlled by the Putún, Mayan-speaking seafaring merchants whose commercial interests ranged from the Olmeca country, along the coast of the entire Yucatan Peninsula, as far as the Caribbean shore of Honduras. The late Sir Eric Thompson once referred to them as "the Phoenicians of the New World."

In November 1974, looters were discovered working at Cacaxtla; they had uncovered part of an extraordinary mural with colors so fresh that it seemed to have been painted only yesterday. Official excavations have now revealed a palace complex of the eighth and ninth centuries AD, with pilastered rooms arranged around patios and plazas. There is nothing Maya about its flat-roofed architecture, but there are similarities to the coeval palaces of Xochicalco and to the later Tula. The numerous murals appear on the stuccoed walls and jambs of Building A (or Building of the Paintings), on the *talud* or batter of the substructure of Building B, on a subterranean chamber called the Red Temple, and on two piers in the Venus Temple.

The North and South Murals flank a doorway, and are associated with unfired clay reliefs showing Maya dignitaries seated on monster-mask thrones. The North Mural depicts a man with jaguar feet and completely clad in jaguar skin, standing on an elongated jaguar recalling the bearskin

94 God L, the Maya god of merchants, from a mural at Cacaxtla, Tlaxcala. He is here given the non-Maya name "4 Dog." To the right is his *cacaxtli* or back-pack; attached to it is his headdress.

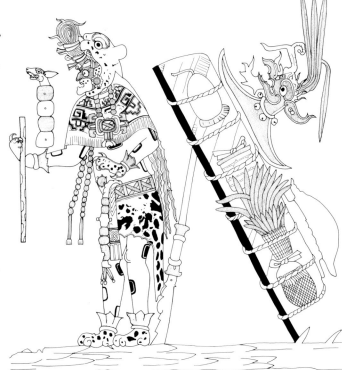

95 South Mural at Cacaxtla, Tlaxcala. The figure wears eagle costume and feet, and stands on a Feathered Serpent. Aquatic animals and stylized maize plants frame the scene. Epiclassic period.

rugs of a past generation. He holds an object suggesting the Maya "ceremonial bar" formed of tied-up spears from which drip blue drops of water; a nearby glyph in Teotihuacan style is to be read as 9 Reptile Eye. The frame is made up of symbols of water and fecundity. The jamb has another figure clothed in jaguar pelt, pouring water as plants emerge from his navel. In the South Mural, the personage wears an eagle costume and has eagle feet, and 95 he also holds a ceremonial bar in his arms; on the nearby jamb, a black-painted figure dances, carrying a large conch shell from which a distinctive red-haired figure emerges.

Both murals suggest some sort of opposition or juxtaposition between eagles and jaguars, perhaps symbolic of the knightly orders which we know from Post-Classic Mexico. Such an opposition is vividly depicted on the *talud* of Building B, on which is realistically painted a great battle in progress between jaguar-clad and feathered warriors. There is little doubt that the Cacaxtla artist had seen such conflict, for he depicts such grisly details as a dazed victim, seated on the ground holding his entrails in his hands. At the same time, the story is highly coded: the jaguar warriors are always victorious, while the defeated bird warriors are shown with heirloom costume elements reaching back to the Olmec period, as if they were symbolic of an older order. Art historian Mary Miller believes that such a battle had actually taken place, perhaps on the swampy plains of southwestern Campeche, but that it had been recast in supernatural terms, in that some of the contestants are improbably given the feet of eagles and jaguars.

On piers marking the entry to a ritual space called the Venus Temple are found two striking anthropomorphic supernaturals marked with the central Mexican star sign and embellished with scorpion tails – most probably the constellation Scorpio (known to the Mesoamericans as well as to ancient Europeans). But most breathtaking of all is a magnificent, polychrome wall painting flanking a stairway leading down to the subterranean Red Temple. Below, on the right of the scene, stands the Maya God L, lord of merchants; propped up beside him is his great carrying frame with his merchandise strapped to it. It is indeed probably no accident that the name of the site, Cacaxtla (or Cacaxtlan) means "Place of the Carrying-frame." In front of the god, as though hopping up the stairs, is the monstrous toad that symbolizes the 20-day period or *uinal* among the Maya, along with a cacao tree (emblematic of the Gulf Coast lowlands) and magic stalks of maize in which the ears have turned into heads of the Maya Maize God, but with the signature red hair found elsewhere at Cacaxtla. This may have been – in fact probably was – a cosmopolitan center controlling the old Teotihuacan trade routes, but the prestige symbolic language was now Maya, modulated to serve the needs of this cosmopolitan elite.

94

The Cacaxtla murals are thoroughly Maya in their style. Both the naturalistic body proportions and the organic, flowing profiles are diagnostic of the Epiclassic Maya painting tradition and contrast with the more blocky, geometric style of Teotihuacan and much of the rest of highland Mexico. Figural poses also strongly recall Maya models: particularly striking are the figures holding Maya-derived "ceremonial bars," either of whom might be at home on the reliefs of Seibal, an important center on the Río Pasión in the southern Maya lowlands which was deeply involved in Epiclassic disruptions of the political landscape. Also telling is the use of a vegetable binder to form the paint medium – a technique defined by art historian Diana Magaloni for Maya and Gulf Coast mural artists, but unknown in central Mexico, where pigments diluted with water were laid on fresh plaster in the true fresco technique. At the same time, the writing that accompanies these images is not Maya but a hybrid of earlier Teotihuacan and Oaxacan scripts along with innovative elements, the whole used mainly to designate the names of key figures. Certainly the main audience was not Maya lords, but central Mexican elites. Except for these important artistic characteristics, there is little in the cultural record of Cacaxtla that indicates a larger Maya presence, suggesting that these traits were imported by an intermediate group like the Olmeca-Xicallanca, who would have acquired such traits in their southern Gulf Coast homeland, immediately adjacent to the Maya area.

Equally intriguing is the presence of a large number of female figurines in an offering found in the nearby site of Xochitecatl, many of which share important elements with southern Gulf Coast female figures. Xochitecatl, which had an important Preclassic occupation, was reinhabited during the Epiclassic when the female figures were deposited and the entire pyramid aligned to the Cacaxtla palace. The group of figures with raised hands, filed teeth, and pronounced smiles share these traits with figures on the Gulf Coast, although the slab-like bodies at Xochitecatl follow local practices. Archaeologist Mari Carmen Serra and her team have identified numerous ritual and political offices for the female figures, which along with the female dress of several Cacaxtla battle figures point up the important role of females and gender symbolism at these closely related sites, a trait shared with Epiclassic southern Veracruz. Any description of the Olmeca–Xicallanca will lack precision, however, because we know so little of the Olmeca–Xicallanca homeland, and until we do this group will remain a cipher for Maya and Gulf Coast elements in the archaeological record, as well as a shadowy group of mobile conquerors in the historical documents.

Another regional center that reached importance with the twilight or disappearance of Teotihuacan's hegemony is Xochicalco, strategically placed 96 atop one of a string of defensively terraced hills in western Morelos. This cosmopolitan entrepôt has been mapped by Kenneth Hirth of Pennsylvania State University, who finds it to be the hub of a well-planned network of stone-surfaced causeways with access to the site via well-guarded ramps; this immediately brings to mind the causeways or *sacbeob* of Classic Maya centers such as Tikal. Founded before AD 700 and active throughout the Epiclassic, Xochicalco had extensive foreign contacts, especially with the Maya area, Zapotec and Mixtec Oaxaca, and Classic central Veracruz.

Its most striking structure, the Temple of the Feathered Serpent, is a 97 *talud-tablero* platform, but the *talud* element is very high compared with the

96 Oblique airview of the fortified hilltop town of Xochicalco, Morelos. This site reached its apogee during the Epiclassic.

97 Temple of the Feathered Serpent at Xochicalco. Figures in Maya style are seated within the serpent's undulations.

tablero. On the *talud* are sculpted reliefs of great, undulating Feathered Serpents covered with cut shell symbols, reminiscent of the Feathered Serpent floating in shells on the Temple of the Feathered Serpent, Teotihuacan. The folds of the serpents' bodies form a kind of protective shelter to the repeated figure of a man seated tailor-fashion with a headdress descended from the war serpent headdress of Teotihuacan, the latter again found on the Temple of the Feathered Serpent at that site. It is likely that the Xochicalco temple was an attempt to recreate that great central monument of Teotihuacan power, only now with seated lords also inhabiting the space. As far as we know, there is absolutely no prototype for these seated figures in highland Mexico: they are surely based upon seated rulers carved on Late Classic Maya jade plaques, although the raised edges of the bodies recall reliefs found at El Tajín, in the Gulf Coast lowlands. A monumental glyphic group is centered on all four sides of the *talud*, given Teotihuacan-style as 9 Reptile Eye surmounted by a house glyph with scrolls emanating from the top of the glyph; 9 Reptile Eye was also cited several times at Cacaxtla, and the great scholar Alfonso Caso believed this to be equivalent to "9 Wind," the name of the later culture hero, Quetzalcoatl. While other epigraphers are less certain of the "Wind" identity for Reptile Eye, it is clear that this name or date is important in the Epiclassic. Other dates or names based on the 260-day count are found elsewhere at Xochicalco, and, like those of Cacaxtla, these show resemblances to both Teotihuacan and Oaxaca. The elites of Xochicalco, like those of Cacaxtla, were drawn to the script and imagery of the illustrious past (Teotihuacan) as well as to that of the powers in the present (from Oaxaca, the Maya area, and the Gulf Coast) – a situation which led to the eclectic nature of Epiclassic styles and scripts.

There are numerous caves in the hill on which Xochicalco was built which could have been used for storage purposes by the local population, as Kenneth Hirth suggests. Directly adjacent to the main ceremonial plaza, and not far from the Temple of the Feathered Serpent, is a cave which has been transformed into an underground observatory: a man-made vertical tube leads up to the surface, and on the two days a year when the sun is at its zenith, or directly overhead, a beam of sunlight penetrates the shaft to the cave floor. This underground zenith observatory is the descendant of recently discovered underground chambers at Teotihuacan where the same celestial phenomena were marked.

Xochicalco – Maya-influenced and perhaps even Maya-directed but with important ties to the regional past – seems to form a kind of bridge between Classic and Post-Classic central Mexico. Xochicalco's main ball court, for instance, with its I-shaped layout, has exactly the same dimensions as the northern ball court at Tula of the Toltecs, which must be several centuries later.

98 Detail of personage on the Temple of the Feathered Serpent at Xochicalco.

Cholula

Following the withdrawal of Teotihuacan hegemony from central Mexico, the builders of Cholula incorporated prestige architectural elements from the now fallen center. For instance, beneath the west face of the Great Pyramid has been uncovered a stone-faced temple substructure with three superimposed *talud-tableros*, but here the *tableros* are embellished with a textile-like mosaic motif not seen at Teotihuacan. Relations with contemporary Gulf Coast peoples are evidenced by a patio with four stone altars, two of which are associated with slab-like stelae carved in relief with the interlaced motifs typical of the Classic Veracruz style. According to ethnohistoric accounts, Cholula was taken over by the Gulf Coast group known as the Olmeca-Xicallanca, who made it their capital, from which base they controlled the high plateau of Puebla and Tlaxcala. This is the same group we met at Cacaxtla. Both the stela format and the interlace scroll style seen first at Cholula during this period were also found in the probable homeland of the Olmeca-Xicallanca, as was a colorful Maya-influenced ceramic style, for it was under this group that the potters of Cholula began to develop the fine polychrome wares that were to become the most coveted containers in all of ancient Mexico.

The Olmeca-Xicallanca were overthrown by the Tolteca-Chichimeca – more commonly known as the Toltecs – sometime around 1200. These people left the Great Pyramid as a monumental ruin, moving the center of worship to the Temple of Quetzalcoatl, under the current town square. Finally, in AD 1359, the kingdom of Huexotzingo, which was in a state of perpetual war with the Aztecs, took over this, the holiest site in Mexico. But to all the Post-Classic Mexicans, the Great Pyramid – which in its final form covered an area of 25 acres (10 hectares) and reached a height of 180 ft (55 m) – was one of the wonders of their country.

Cantona

Cantona, like Cholula but unlike the rest of the Epiclassic powers, had an important Classic-period occupation. Angel García Cook, the chief archaeologist at this impressive but little-visited and little-known site north of the Oriental basin in the state of Puebla, describes the Classic-period city as founded on a volcanic flow which must have supplied much of the building material. This material was cut and then placed without the use of mortar. Cantona controlled the Oyameles-Zaragoza obsidian source only 6¼ miles (10 km) away, and trade in this product must have been a major resource for the site.

According to García Cook, suddenly around the year 600 the site filled with walled walkways leading to carefully delimited, walled residential compounds. These compounds are not the apartment buildings of Teotihuacan, but groups of house mounds that have been sealed and given one controlled point of entry. Access to the acropolis, where much of the sacred architecture was located, was carefully controlled through walkways and entry gates. The entire site became fortified and densely populated, and a moat was constructed at the most vulnerable point. The city was to remain a fortified center until its abandonment around AD 1000. Taken as a whole, the desire of the Epiclassic Cantona elite to keep enemies at bay was matched only by their desire to control circulation throughout the city itself.

At some point Cantona became a center for playing the rubber ball game on I-shaped masonry courts. To date some 24 ball courts have been found at the site, 18 of which the archaeologist believes were functioning at one time.

El Tajín

In accord with the importance of ball-court equipment in their art, there are no fewer than 17 ball courts at El Tajín, an elite center about 5 miles (8 km) southwest of Papantla, in the rich oil-producing zone of northern Veracruz. The surrounding land is highly fertile for maize, cacao, tobacco, and vanilla, all of which are still grown. The site derives its name from the belief of the modern Totonac that twelve old men called *Tajín* live in the ruins and are lords of the thunderstorm (and therefore the equivalent of the Rain God).

El Tajín was first occupied during the Classic, when it was a village among many others in the area. Recent work by Arturo Pascual Soto in several of these surrounding early sites has revealed a thriving Classic-period culture, with decoration of tripod cylinder vase supports that initially owes much to Teotihuacan. Morgadal Grande, the most important of these outliers, contains a Classic-period ball court with carved relief benches that prefigure El Tajín's central architectural form. Cerro Grande, another outlier, has produced a large Classic-period stela fragment, on which a figure in high relief is shown frontally, holding a feathered bag, with feet splayed to either side. Again, echoes of this style and format will appear in some of the earliest monumental art found at El Tajín itself. Sometime in the seventh or early eighth century, El Tajín began the systematic conquest and rebuilding of these important regional sites, and much of the evidence for the Classic culture is found in the fill of Tajín-style Epiclassic buildings.

Epiclassic El Tajín is very extensive, its nucleus covering about 146 acres (60 hectares), but subsidiary ruins are scattered over several thousand acres. The site is set among low hills, with a lower area dotted with pyramids and ball courts, and an upper area of elaborately decorated palaces and other structures for elite gatherings. The decorations in both paint and carved stone are done in the last major manifestation of Classic Veracruz style, as seen in the use of raised outlines and scroll forms throughout the site.

The central core of the site is defined by the Pyramid of the Niches, a 99 relatively small (only about 60 ft or 18 m high), four-sided structure of wonderful symmetry, faced with carved stone blocks, rising in six tiers to an upper sanctuary. A single stairway climbs to the top, flanked by balustrades embellished with a step-and-fret motif. The combination of niche surmounted by flying cornice, seen most strikingly in this building, was certainly emblematic of the site, appearing in other areas of northern Veracruz as Tajín extended its reach. The Pyramid of the Niches was

99 (*above*) Pyramid of the Nic[hes] at El Tajín, looking northwest. Epiclassic period. Ht about 18 m

100 (*left*) Relief panel from the northeast wall of the South Ball Court, El Tajín. The scene depicts the sacrifice of a ball player (the captain of the losing team?). The action takes place in a ball court, and all the figures wear the proper paraphernalia: "yokes," *palmas*, and knee pads. The Death God rises from a vase on the left to receive the sacrifice. Classic Veracruz style, Epiclassic period

101 (*right*) Relief panel from the South Ball Court, El Tajín. The rain god draws blood from his penis to replenish a pool of water. Agave plants can be seen on the left.

covered with a layer of stucco and painted red, as were most of El Tajín's structures (a few, however, were a vivid blue). War standards were raised on large rectangular bases at the foot of the structure, and just to the south the most important ball-court activities were held in the main ceremonial court.

Other stone buildings at El Tajín are very similar in their architectural design, the step-and-fret motif (a symbol of lightning in late pre-Conquest Mexico) being particularly common. Palace-like buildings with colonnaded doorways were roofed with massive concrete slabs (utilizing marine shell and sand cement mixed with pumice and wood fragments) poured over wooden scaffolds, rather an advanced construction technique for the day.

The Building of the Columns is the largest "palace" complex at the site. The drums of the columns are carved with narrative scenes from the ceremonial life of the city. The most interesting of these depicts a procession of victorious warriors bringing stripped captives to the enthroned ruler, a personage with the calendrical name 13 Rabbit; before him lies the corpse of a disembowelled victim. Similar names taken from the 260-day count are found here and elsewhere at El Tajín, but with the exception of a small number of texts on ceramic vessels, it was used exclusively for naming figures.

Above all, the inhabitants of El Tajín were obsessed with the ball game, human sacrifice, and death, three concepts closely interwoven in the Mesoamerican mind. The courts, which are up to 197 ft (60 m) long, are formed by two facing walls, with stone surfaces either vertical or battered. Interestingly, nowhere is the game itself depicted; instead there are references to the complex of rituals surrounding the game. Among these ball-court images, the six in the South Ball Court are the most elaborate, describing a series of rituals glimpsed only in parts elsewhere in Mesoamerica.

102 (*left*) Monument on the steps of Structure 5, El Tajín. The Death God emerges from a complex scrollwork design. Classic Veracruz style, Epiclassic period.

103 (*above*) Stela from Aparicio, Veracruz. Represented is a seated ball player; his head has been severed, and seven intertwined snakes sprout from the neck.

The sequence begins on a panel where two facing figures speak to each other, indicating their alliance. Later a figure is dressed for war and handed spears that appear to emerge from a celestial supernatural. Decapitation sacrifice in the ball court itself is depicted in a later panel, which could only happen if the raid had been successful in securing captives. On each panel, always nearest the center of the court, a skeletal figure rises from a jar floating in water. This probably refers to the place of the skull in the center of the court, which the later Aztecs conceived of as a spring that was the origin of agricultural fecundity. The central panels on either side of the court show the accession of the Tajín ruler and his control of this sacred spring at the behest of the gods.

El Tajín's destruction was by fire, traditionally by 1200, but perhaps by 1000 if recent evidence for post-Tajín squatter settlements around that date are taken into account.

Remojadas potters

An exuberant style in pottery sprang up during the Classic period in a zone of central Veracruz fronting the Gulf of Mexico near the modern port capital of the state. Named Remojadas from the site at which they are most abundant, tens of thousands of hollow clay figurines were fashioned in a naturalistic

style from which much ethnographic data can be drawn. The roots of the art 104
reach back to the Late Preclassic, but most production was during the Epiclassic, when Remojadas figurines have close kinship with those of the Maya
to the east and some interesting similarities to those of Xochitecatl to the
west. Features such as faces were generally cast from clay molds, and a black
asphalt paint was used to heighten details or to indicate face paint. The subjects are standing or seated humans, both male and female: curiously infantile
boys and girls with laughing faces and filed teeth; ball players; lovers or 105

104 Wheeled pottery toy depicting a deer or a dog.
Remojadas style, central Veracruz. The snout and
eyes are decorated with asphalt. These amusing toys
represent the only application of the principle of the
wheel in the New World.

105 Pottery figure of a smiling boy, Remojadas
style, central Veracruz. The upper teeth of this
individual are characteristically filed. Epiclassic
period. Ht 52 cm.

106 Pottery figure of a standing goddess with filed
teeth. Remojadas style, Epiclassic period. Ht 78 cm.

106 friends in swings; and warriors. The gods are also portrayed: Xipe Totec, as represented by a priest wearing the skin of a flayed captive; the Death God; and the Old Fire God, often shown as a wrinkled old man.

The most impressive of these hollow ceramic figures are near life-size and descend from the Classic tradition of monumental ceramic sculpture at Cerro de las Mesas. Thirteen of these hollow monumental figures, all females, were found in a single Epiclassic deposit at El Zapotal, near Cerro de las Mesas. The females were depicted both seated and standing, but all wear long skirts and serpent belts and have been identified as Cihuateteo, or the spirits of women who died in childbirth. Several of the sculptures were decapitated and all were smashed during deposition. Associated are numerous smiling figures and male warriors and ritual figures, but these are significantly smaller than the monumental females. Also associated is a mound of disarticulated human bone that included 82 skulls. This entire program is oriented to a sanctuary inside of which sits a striking, over-life-107 size seated Death God of uncooked clay, with remnants of the extensive painted decoration still adhering to the surface.

107 A seated life-size clay Death God forms the centerpiece of an elaborate deposit of ceramic figures at El Zapotal, Veracruz, Epiclassic period.

Valley of Oaxaca

The decline of Monte Albán appears more gradual than that of Teotihuacan, making a clear break with the Classic period in Oaxaca harder to define. Regional centers like Lambityeco and Suchilquitongo seem to have increased their power at the expense of declining Monte Albán, and the practice of writing on monumental art spread throughout Oaxaca. Elite tombs found in several of these centers contain carved panels which recount the genealogies and legitimating rituals of Epiclassic lords. An example is the Noriega Stone, where Javier Urcid has identified both early childhood rituals and the later accession to power of Lady 6 Owl, represented as the diminutive figure in the center of the upper register. The Ñuiñe style and script is another interesting cultural development that seems to have flowered late in the history of Monte Albán. Located to the west of the Oaxaca Valley, in the hot lowlands, these sites and monuments are related to Monte Albán style and script, but they also indicate connections with Xochicalco, the Pacific Coast of Guatemala, and the Gulf Coast. Farther west and south, sites on the Pacific Coast around the Río Verde drainage began erecting monuments obviously derived from the Monte Albán tradition but also evincing relationships with the central highlands. But what is perhaps most unusual in Oaxaca at this time is the presence of locally made pottery imitating Balancán Fine Orange, a ceramic associated with the Putún Maya of Tabasco and southern Campeche, and another group aping the "slate ware" of Maya sites like Uxmal and Kabah in the northern Yucatan Peninsula – the "Maya connection" again!

108

108 A low relief sculpture recounts the early years of Lady 6 Owl, an Epiclassic ruler in Oaxaca. In the middle register rituals are performed around the young girl, while in the top register she accedes to power. From Noriega, near Monte Albán.

Northwestern Mexico

While farmers had moved into the northwestern fringes of Mesoamerica by the beginning of our era, it was not until the Epiclassic that we see large settlements in this frontier zone formed by the modern states of Durango, Zacatecas, and Sinaloa. La Quemada, which flourished from AD 500 to 900, occupies a hilltop 820 ft (250 m) above the surrounding valley floor and is protected by strategically located defensive walls, behind which the bulk of the population lived. Ben Nelson's work at the site has shown that warfare was a central concern, indicated by the display of large quantities of disarticulated bones as trophies. This was true not only at La Quemada, but also at smaller centers in the area. One of the most important architectural innovations is the *tzompantli*, or skull rack; later this building type was important to Mesoamericans as the place to exhibit trophy heads related to ball game decapitation sacrifice. It is no surprise, then, that at La Quemada and other sites in the region we also find I-shaped ball courts. Other innovative architectural forms include the colonnaded hall, often with an adjoining sunken patio, and the soaring, steep-sided pyramid.

109 View from the air of La Quemada, a walled hilltop fortress in Zacatecas, north central Mexico. At the right of the picture is the Hall of Columns. La Quemada was one of the most northern outposts of civilization during the Epiclassic period.

110 Pyramid at La Quemada. The markedly steep sides and unbroken profiles are unusual in Mesoamerican architecture. A small temple may have been placed at the summit. Epiclassic period.

A series of roadways organize the immediate area into a set of linked settlements ruled, rather harshly it would seem, from La Quemada. The Huichol Indians of adjacent Jalisco recount that at one point an evil priest lived on a "great rock" which was also a fortress, protected by eagles and jaguars. This ruler-priest required tribute in peyote, and would not let the people acquire the items necessary to worship the gods: shells, feathers, and salt. The people appealed to the gods, who then destroyed the leader and his aides with twenty days of heat. This may be an indigenous account of the end of La Quemada, for the fortress was burned around AD 900 and never reoccupied.

Alta Vista, located 106 miles (170 km) northwest of La Quemada, was its contemporary, exhibiting much the same bellicose nature and several of the same architectural innovations. In addition, great quantities of turquoise have been found at the site, indicating the first large concentration of this precious stone destined to become important to later Mesoamericans. Turquoise had first appeared in the Preclassic period, mainly in West Mexico, and always in small amounts. In Alta Vista there was large-scale processing of the ore into regular tesserae for turquoise mosaic objects, at which stage it could be traded to the rest of Mesoamerica. Large amounts of turquoise mosaic objects were also laid into elite graves at Alta Vista itself.

Although Alta Vista was the center of a vast mining industry centering largely on malachite, azurite, ocher, cinnabar, and weathered chert, there are no high-quality turquoise deposits in the area. Trace element analysis, carried out through neutron activation by Garman Harbottle at the Brookhaven National Laboratory, has shown that much of the raw turquoise came from mines in the American Southwest, especially from New Mexico. It is fairly clear that the northwestern frontier was instrumental in the transmission of Mesoamerican traits into the American Southwest, in particular the colonnaded masonry building and the platform pyramid; the ball court and the game played in it; the organization of settlements into a linked hierarchy with roads; copper bells; and perhaps even the taste for turquoise-encrusted objects. It is also clear that these traits ran along a trading route, a "Turquoise Road," so to speak, analogous to the famous Silk Road of the Old World that bound civilized and "barbarian" alike into a single cultural whole.

The end of the Epiclassic

Around the year AD 900, many of the cities that had forged a post-Teotihuacan order went into their own decline and eclipse. Much of the West Mexican area, including the mining area around Alta Vista and the Teuchitlan Tradition heartland had collapsed by this date. Certainly the two sites with substantial Maya connections, Cacaxtla and Xochicalco, were abandoned by this time. It is probably no coincidence that the central Maya area itself was going through a complete collapse between AD 800 and 900, the sign of the times being their failure to erect dynastic monuments dated in the Long Count system, and by clearcut vandalism and defacement. As at the fall of Teotihuacan, there must have been much movement of peoples, shifting alliances, and a certain amount of social chaos at the end of the Epiclassic. Out of this was to emerge a new order, the Toltec, which was to link the Maya and ancient Mexico yet again, create a new capital, and initiate a new art style.

8 · The Post-Classic Period: The Toltec State

A time of troubles

Following in the wake of the disturbances and movements of peoples during the ninth century AD came a seemingly new mode of organized life. The Post-Classic continued and heightened the Epiclassic emphasis on militarism by parading seemingly endless lines of warriors throughout public art. There was now an entrenched class of tough professional warriors, grouped into military orders which took their names from the animals from which they may have claimed a kind of totemic descent: coyote, jaguar, and eagle. At the same time, new alliances and trade relationships were formed across ancient Mexico to the Maya area and even to Central America and the Southwest United States.

Throughout Mexico, this was a time which saw a great deal of confusion and movement of peoples, amalgamating to form small, aggressive, conquest states, and splitting up with as much speed as they had risen. The Epiclassic saw movement and conquest on a grand scale, but during certain spans of the Post-Classic the rhythm and intensity of these processes increased. Even groups of distinctly different speech sometimes came together to form a single state – as we know from their annals, for we have entered the realm of history. Naturally, such new conditions are mirrored in Post-Classic art styles, which are characterized by an interest in costume ornament over naturalistic human features and in a hard-edged carving style that is not overly concerned with the niceties of finish.

The introduction of metallurgy into Mexico took place over the Epiclassic 112 period and it continued to grow in popularity during the Post-Classic, but metal had only a slight effect upon the development of native civilization, in contrast to its history in South America and in the Old World. Mexican metalwork consists largely of ornaments, particularly small bells cast by the "lost-wax" method, while implements such as celts or axes are relatively rare and so had little significance in the native tool-kit, which remained on an essentially Neolithic level.

Related to the rise of metallurgy was the introduction of turquoise as a prestige stone on the order of jade. Both of these phenomena had their origins far to the north and west of central Mexico, but both materials were fervently embraced by much of Mexico, and indeed much of Mesoamerica, during this period. In the realm of both jewelry and turquoise work, the skill of the Mexican craftsman reached heights of great artistry, as we shall see below.

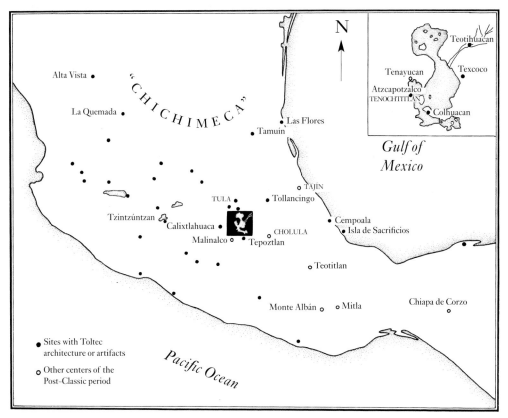

111 Distribution of Toltec sites and other important centers of the Post-Classic period. The inset map is the Valley of Mexico.

112 Copper tools and ornaments, Post-Classic period. The large "ax-money" is from Mitla, Oaxaca. The awls are from Lake Chapala in Michoacan, the bells and tweezers from unknown proveniences in Mexico.

The Chichimeca of northern Mexico

It was not only internal pressure brought by new conquest states that disturbed Mexico. Probably more far-reaching in their long-range effects were the great migrations into central Mexico of the northwestern frontier peoples and other marginal groups as the northern borders of Mesoamerica retracted near the beginning of this period. The two great northwestern centers, Alta Vista and La Quemada, both fell as the Post-Classic opens, and it is surely not coincidence that several traits seen in these centers, such as the skull rack and colonnaded hall, manifest themselves in central Mexico at this time. There is also evidence of an important influx of people and goods from the Bajío, a northern frontier zone centered on the modern states of Guanajuato and Querétaro. For those living in central Mexico, all these northern peoples were subsumed under the designation "Chichimeca," a name meaning something like "lineage of the dog." In later Aztec chronicles they are pictured as bow-and-arrow wielding nomadic barbarians, an image easily related to the hunting-and-gathering groups who inhabited the north Mexican desert from the Archaic period onward. At the same time, Chichimeca are described as obsidian and flint workers, turquoise artists, and feather workers – all things associated with Alta Vista and La Quemada, as well as other West Mexican peoples, all of whom were sedentary, urban-dwelling Mesoamericans. Further, several ruling dynasties in the Valley of Mexico were proud to claim Chichimec ancestry, and a group called the "Tolteca-Chichimeca" was instrumental in the conquest or founding of cities throughout the first half of Post-Classic Mexican history.

Given the conflicting images of the Chichimeca emerging from the chronicles, along with the rather complex history of northwest Mexico, who were these people? There is no simple answer to this important historical question, for it seems that many different sorts of groups were lumped into this category by those who wrote Mexican history. In the account recorded by Father Sahagún, the truly nomadic, "wild" people were called "Teochichimeca," the "real" Chichimeca, who lived in caves and clothed themselves in animal skins and yucca-fiber sandals, subsisting on wild fruits, roots, and seeds and on the meat of humble animals like the rabbit. Between them and the civilized peoples were the "Tamime," Chichimeca who had picked up a smattering of the customs and speech of their more advanced neighbors to the south; they wore the cast-off rags of civilization and did a little farming to supplement their wild diet. The portrait of the Teochichimeca is a fairly accurate description of the lifeways of desert-dwelling hunters and gatherers. The Tamime, if they may be identified with the frontier farmers and urban-dwellers of northwestern and West Mexico, could engage in much more complex forms of society than those described by Father Sahagún and other chroniclers. It is very likely that it is this latter group, those prosperous northwestern farmers and urban-dwellers, who on immigrating to central Mexico brought with them certain innovative cultural traits and whose presence disrupted the Epiclassic order, ushering in the Post-Classic.

Tula and the Toltecs

There have been four unifying forces in the pre-Spanish history of Mexico: the first of these was Olmec, the second Classic Teotihuacan, the third Toltec, and the last Aztec. In their own annals, written down in Spanish letters after the Conquest, the Mexican nobility and intelligentsia looked back in wonder to an almost semi-mythical time when the Toltecs ruled, a people whose very name means "the artificers." Of them it was said that "nothing was too difficult for them, no place with which they dealt was too distant." From their capital, Tollan (Tula), they had dominated much of northern and central Mexico in ancient times, as well as parts of the Guatemalan highlands and most of the Yucatan Peninsula. After their downfall, no Mexican or Maya dynasty worth its salt failed to claim descent from these wonderful people.

Like many other Post-Classic states, Toltec society seems to have been composed of disparate tribal elements that had come together for obscure reasons. One of these, which would appear to have been dominant, was called the Tolteca-Chichimeca. The other group went under the name Nonoalca, and according to some scholars was made up of sculptors and artisans from the old civilized regions of Puebla and the Gulf Coast, brought in to construct the monuments of Tula. The Tolteca-Chichimeca, for their part, were probably the original Nahua-speakers who founded the Toltec state. As their name implies, they were Chichimeca originating on the fringes of Mesoamerica among the urban Uto-Aztecans of western Mexico, for although it was said that "they came from the interior of the plains, among the rocks," their level of culture was substantially higher than that of the "real" Chichimeca.

The Toltec annals

Numerous accounts of the indigenous history of Tula were recorded soon after the Spanish Conquest. Most of these are especially concerned with the fall of Tula, for by tracing their lineage to the Toltec diaspora later kings could claim Toltec descent. Yet enough remains of earlier episodes to allow us to piece together a more complete story. Led by their probably entirely legendary ruler Mixcoatl ("Cloud Serpent," i.e. Milky Way), who was deified as patron of hunting after his death, the Tolteca-Chichimeca by the beginning of the ninth century had entered civilized Mexico at the southern extension of the Sierra Madre Occidental, passing through what now comprises northern Jalisco and southern Zacatecas. It is no easy matter to reconstruct their history from the contradictory accounts which we have been left, but according to the widely accepted scheme of Jiménez Moreno, Mixcoatl and his people first settled at a place in the Valley of Mexico called Colhuacan. His son and heir was the most famous figure in all Mexican history, a possibly real person named Topiltzin, born in the year 1 Reed (either AD 935 or 947), and later identified to the confusion of modern scholars with the Feathered Serpent, Quetzalcoatl. This king is described

113

113 Feathered Serpent from cornice of banquette, Tula, Hidalgo. Toltec culture, Early Post-Classic period.

in the post-Conquest literature as being of fair skin, with long hair and a black beard.

The first event in the rule of 1 Reed Topiltzin Quetzalcoatl was the transfer of the Toltec capital from Colhuacan via Tulancingo to Tula, the ancient Tollan, a name signifying "Place of the Rushes" but which to the ancients meant something like "the city." Some years after its founding, according to the annals, Tula was the scene of a terrible inner strife, for Topiltzin was supposedly a kind of priest-king dedicated to the peaceful cult of the Feathered Serpent, abhorring human sacrifice and performing all sorts of penances. His enemies were devotees of the fierce god Tezcatlipoca ("Smoking Mirror"), the giver and taker away of life, lord of sorcerers, and the patron of the warrior orders, the latter perhaps made discontented by the intellectual pacificism of their king.

As a result of this struggle for power, Topiltzin and his followers were forced to flee the city, perhaps in AD 987. Some of the most beautiful Nahuatl poetry records his unhappy downfall, a defeat laid at the door of Tezcatlipoca himself. Topiltzin and his Toltecs were said to have become slothful, the ruler having even transgressed the priestly rules of continence. Tezcatlipoca undermines the Toltecs by various evil stratagems: coming to Topiltzin in the guise of an old man and tricking him into drinking a magic and debilitating potion; then appearing without his loincloth in the marketplace disguised as a seller of green chile peppers, inflaming the ruler's daughter with such a desire for him that her father is forced to take him as son-in-law; next, as a warrior successfully leading a force of dwarfs and hunchbacks which had been given him in vain hope that he would be slain by the enemy; making a puppet dance for the Toltecs, causing them in their curiosity to rush forward and crush themselves to death. Even when they finally killed Tezcatlipoca by stoning, the Toltecs were unable to rid themselves of his now festering, rotted body.

At last, according to legend, Topiltzin Quetzalcoatl leaves his beloved city in exile after burning or burying all his treasures, preceded on his path by birds of precious feather. As Tula disappears from his sight:

Then he fixes his eyes on Tula and in that moment begins to weep:
as he weeps sobbing, it is like two torrents of hail trickling down:
His tears slip down his face;
his tears drop by drop perforate the stones.[4]

On his way trickster magicians cross his path again and again, trying to make him turn back. At last he reaches the stormy pass between the volcanoes

Iztaccihuatl and Popocatepetl, where his jugglers, buffoons, and the pages of his palace freeze to death. He continues on, his gaze directed at the shroud of the snows and eventually arrives at the shore of the Gulf of Mexico. One poem relates that there he set himself afire, decked in his quetzal plumage and turquoise mask; as his ashes rose to the sky, every kind of marvelously colored bird wheeled overhead, and the dead king was apotheosized as the Morning Star. Another version of the tale, the one claimed by the Spaniards to have been known to Motecuhzoma Xocoyotzin, tells us that he did not perform an act of self-immolation, but rather set off with followers on a raft formed of serpents on a journey to the east, from which he was supposed to return some day.

It may be evidence of the historical core within this legend that Maya accounts speak of the arrival from the west, perhaps in the year AD 987, of a Mexican conqueror named in their tongue Kukulcan ("Feathered Serpent"), who with his companions subjugated their country. There is also evidence in the archaeology of Yucatan for a seaborne Toltec invasion, successfully initiating in the late tenth century a Mexican period, with its capital at Chich'en Itza.

With the sanguinary rule of the Tezcatlipoca party now dominant at Tula, the Toltec empire may have reached its greatest expansion, holding sway over most of central Mexico from coast to coast. At the height of its power, Tula is pictured in the poems as a sort of marvelous never-never land, where ears of maize were as big as mano stones, and red, yellow, green, blue and many other colors of cotton grew naturally. There were palaces of jade, of gold, a turquoise palace, and one made of blue-green quetzal feathers. The Toltecs were so prosperous that they heated their sweat baths with the small ears of maize. There was nothing that they could not make; wonderful potters, they "taught the clay to lie." Truly, they "put their heart into their work."

The end of Tula approached with the last ruler, Huemac ("Big Hand"). Triggered by a disastrous series of droughts, factional conflicts broke out once more, apparently between the Tolteca-Chichimeca and the Nonoalca. In 1156 or 1168 Huemac transferred his capital to Chapultepec, the hill-crowned park in what is now the western part of Mexico City, where he committed suicide. Some Tolteca-Chichimeca hung on at Tula for another fifteen years, finally themselves deserting the city and moving south to the Valley of Mexico and as far as Cholula, subjugating all who lay in their way. Tula was left in ruins, with only memories of its glories. As the Nahuatl poet tells us:

> Everywhere there meet the eye,
> everywhere can be seen the remains of clay vessels,
> of their cups, their figures,
> of their dolls, of their figurines,
> of their bracelets,
> everywhere are their ruins,
> truly the Toltecs once lived there.[5]

The great Toltec diaspora had begun, bands of refugees wandering over highland and lowland Mexico, all claiming Tula as their homeland. They were said to give the right to rule even to groups in the Guatemala highlands, establishing new dynasties over the Maya and imposing Mexican customs. In death, as in life, Tula remained a potent force in Mesoamerican thought through its role in the definition of cultural and political ideals. But how do these stories compare with the actual physical remains of the city?

Archaeological Tula

It has been the misfortune of modern scholarship that there are not one, but many places named Tula in Mexico – a quite natural circumstance from the meaning of the original name *Tollan*, which can be translated not only as "Place of the Rushes," but also as "civilized urban space." Thus the term was applied indiscriminately to great ancient centers like Teotihuacan and Cholula. Given this premise, the glowing descriptions appearing in the native and Spanish accounts have led many an archaeologist, such as the late George Vaillant, to the erroneous conclusion that the Tula of the Toltecs must have been the admittedly magnificent Teotihuacan. In the late 1930s, however, documentary researches by the Mexican ethnohistorian Wigberto Jiménez Moreno proved that the city of Topiltzin and Huemac was the Tula lying some 50 miles (80 km) northwest of Mexico City, in the state of Hidalgo. Subsequent excavations have borne him out.

The first serious archaeological work at Tula took place as far back as the 1880s, when the pioneer French Mesoamericanist Desiré Charnay excavated a palace structure and noted close ties between the remains at Tula and those at distant Chich'en Itza. Intensive excavations were begun at the site in 1940 under the direction of the late Jorge Acosta of the National Institute of Anthropology and History, and continued for another twenty years. More recent projects undertaken by Eduardo Matos Moctezuma, Richard Diehl, Alba Guadalupe Mastache, and Robert Cobean have given us an even deeper knowledge of the Toltec capital.

The real Tula had not only been burned and sacked by its destroyers (whoever they might have been), but the later Aztecs had thoroughly looted sculptures, friezes, and offerings which were re-used in Tenochtitlan and elsewhere. Its reconstruction has been for that reason extremely difficult, and it is little wonder that it now seems unimpressive as one of the major sites of Mesoamerica, and unlikely that it was Tula that conquered Chich'en Itza, and not the other way around.

Placed in a defensible position on a limestone promontory, Tula is surrounded by steep banks on three sides. There were small villages here in Preclassic times, and a more substantial settlement during the apogee of Teotihuacan, when the extensive irrigation system in the broad valley to the northwest of Tula may have been begun. During the Epiclassic, when the area had been abandoned by the Teotihuacan group, a new people (perhaps the Tolteca-Chichimeca of the annals) moved in from the Bajío, bringing with them the Coyotlatelco pottery and new, rougher style of monument

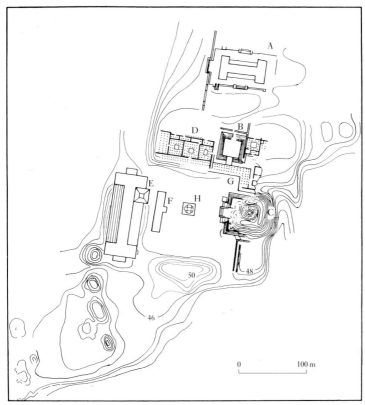

114 (*above*) View from the southeast of Pyramid B at Tula, Hidalgo. This step-pyramid rises in five tiers and has an overall height of 10 m.

115 Ground plan of Tula Grande, the central part of the site.

A   Ball Court I
B   Pyramid B
C   Pyramid C
D   Palacio Quemado ("Burnt Palace")
E   Ball Court II
F   *Tzompantli* (skullrack)
G   Vestibule
H   Adoratorio

Tula, the Toltec capital

116 (*right*) Colossal atlantean figure of stone, one of the four that surmount Pyramid B. Each figure is made of four sections of stone and represents a warrior carrying an atlatl (spearthrower) in one hand and a pouch for copal incense in the other. On the chest is worn the stylized butterfly emblem of the Toltec. Ht 4.6 m.

117 (*below*) Stone "chacmool" from Tula. Reclining figures of this sort are found wherever Toltec influence was felt. This "chacmool" wears the Toltec nose-plug and carries a sacrificial knife strapped to the upper arm.

118 East side of Pyramid B at Tula, bas-reliefs of prowling coyotes and felines alternate with rows of eagles eating hearts and composite monsters. Toltec culture, Early Post-Classic period.

carving that will eventually characterize Tula and the Toltecs. Their main source of obsidian at this time also came from the north and west, at Ucareo, Michoacán, as Dan Healan has shown. By AD 900, but perhaps a century earlier, there was a sizeable community of localized artisans specializing in the production of such items as pottery vessels, moldmade figurines, and obsidian blades, with a civic-religious center, dubbed Tula Chico, in the northeast part of the city.

The Tollan phase (traditionally AD 950–1150) marks the major occupation of the capital and the construction of a monumental civic/religious center called Tula Grande. The traditional dating is based on both archaeological evidence and interpretations of indigenous histories, but most of the absolute dates for this phase cluster in the AD 900–1000 range, as do new dates for comparable Basin of Mexico ceramics and Tohil Plumbate trade wares, suggesting that the apogee of Tula may be slightly earlier than we once thought. At this time the city – one of the largest, if not *the* largest in Early Post-Classic Mesoamerica – covered 5.4 sq. miles (16 sq. km), and contained an estimated population of 30,000–40,000. Tula's rulers had decreed a major reorganization of the city, for its streets and avenues, which had formerly been oriented to true north, were now changed to 15 degrees east of north (this was soon changed to 15 degrees west of north!). The old center of Tula Chico was abandoned, never to be reinhabited. Tula Grande, the sole major civic/religious center during the Tollan phase, consists of a wide central plaza bordered on

115

the east by the thoroughly despoiled Pyramid C, the largest structure at Tula and as yet unexcavated; on the west by an unexplored ball court; and on the north by Pyramid B and its annexes. On the north side of Pyramid B is a smaller plaza, beyond which is another I-shaped ball court about 120 ft (37 m) long, an exact copy of the prototype at Xochicalco.

Pyramid B is the most impressive building at Tula. Built in six successive stages, in its final form this stepped pyramid-platform was fronted by a colonnaded hall, along the back of which banquettes with polychromed bas-reliefs of marching warriors were ranged. An ancient visitor would have walked through the colonnade, climbed the stairway and passed through the entrance of the temple, flanked by two stone columns in the form of Feathered Serpents, with their rattles in the air and heads on the ground. The temple itself had two rooms; the roof of the outer one was supported by the heads of four colossal atlantean figures representing warriors carrying an atlatl in one hand and an incense bag in the other – perfect embodiments of Toltec artistic ideals. The rear room had four square pillars, carved on all sides with Toltec warriors adorned with the symbols of the knightly orders.

114

116

119 Bas-relief of an eagle eating a heart from the east side of Pyramid B at Tula. Toltec culture, Early Post-Classic period.

There, in the sanctuary, once stood a stone altar supported by little atlantean figures. Also in the temple and in other parts of the ceremonial precinct were
117   the peculiar sculptures called "chacmools," reclining personages bearing round dishes or receptacles for human hearts on their bellies.

118   Around the four sides of Pyramid B were bas-reliefs symbolizing the warrior orders on which the strength of the empire depended: prowling jaguars
119   and coyotes, and eagles eating hearts, interspersed with strange composite beasts that may descend from the great War Serpent of Teotihuacan.

Adjacent to this pyramid is the Palacio Quemado, or Burnt Palace, which consists of very spacious colonnaded halls with sunken courts in their centers. The columns were built up of rubble over wooden cores. Again, low banquettes extend along the walls, which were apparently frescoed. These halls served probably for meetings and ceremonies, rather than as palaces. In fact, two floor plans very closely resembling the palaces of Teotihuacan have been uncovered away from the center of Tula, and these were certainly residences for the rulers of the city.

On the north side of the pyramid and parallel to it is the 131-ft (40-m) long "Serpent Wall," embellished with painted friezes, the basic motif of which is a serpent eating a human; the head has been reduced to a skull, and the flesh has been partially stripped from the long bones.

The grim Toltec man-at-arms whose features are delineated in stone everywhere at Tula carried the feather-decorated atlatl in the right hand, and a cluster of darts in the left, the Chichimec bow never appearing in the art of civilized Mexico. Protection against enemy darts was provided by a heavy padding of quilted cotton on the left arm. Strapped to the small of the back was the *tezcacuitlapilli*, a round, pyrite mirror backed by a turquoise mosaic representing four encircling Fire Serpents. Headgear consisted of a pillbox-shaped hat topped by quetzal plumes and bearing on its front a bird flying downward. The customary nose ornament was something like a button through the alae, and a goatee often embellished the knight's chin. Over the chest was a breastplate worn under a highly abstract butterfly pectoral, both emblematic of warriors. Either the breechclout (*maxtli*) or the short kilt could be worn, while below leg and ankle bands the feet were shod with backed sandals.

A splendid shell breastplate and turquoise *tezcacuitlapilli* back mirror recently unearthed at Tula give some idea of how impressive this uniform must have been. The back mirror, which consisted of over 3,000 pieces of finely worked turquoise mixed with shell, was deposited 11.8 in (30 cm) above the breastplate in the center of a patio in the Palacio Quemado. Buried with the breastplate in a large earthen box were shells from both the Gulf of Mexico and the Pacific, which along with the turquoise from the Southwestern United States indicates the far-flung nature of the Toltec trading networks.

The most common foreign trade pottery at the site was the very distinctive Tohil Plumbate ware, one of the very few true glazed ceramics of the pre-Spanish Western Hemisphere, produced in kilns on the Pacific coastal plain near the Mexican-Guatemalan border.

XII Excavated near the El Corral Temple at the Toltec capital of Tula, this plumbate-ware jar is covered with mother-of-pearl and other shell mosaic. It depicts the face of a bearded man (possibly Quetzalcoatl) emerging from the jaws of a feathered coyote. Early Post-Classic period.

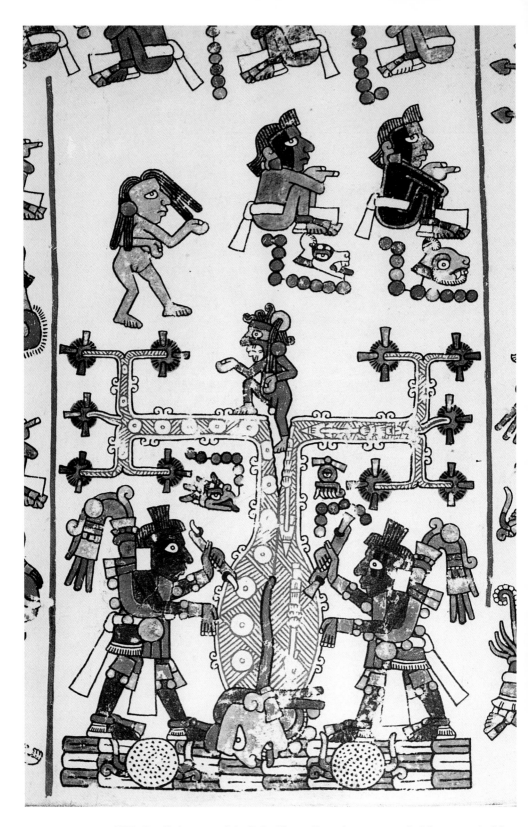

XIII Detail of page 37 of the Codex Vienna. Two priests cut open the Mixtec tree of origin at a place called Apoala, giving birth to gods, humans, and ancestors. Mixtec culture, Late Post-Classic period.

XIV Folio 2 of the Codex Mendoza illustrates the legendary founding of Tenochtitlan in
1325, with the eagle perched on the cactus at the center, surrounded by ten early Aztec chiefs.
Pictured below are the first two conquests of the young Aztec state. Early Colonial period.

XV Coatlicue, the Aztec mother goddess, was a terrifying figure; here she is shown with her characteristic skirt of intertwined snakes, and a skeletalized head.

XVI An Aztec shield of feathers and gold trim. On its face is a feathered coyote, emitting a device that combines water and fire, an Aztec metaphor for war.

XVII (*left*) This hollow, life-sized ceramic figure of an Aztec Eagle Warrior was recovered from the Eagle House, in the Great Temple excavations.

XVIII (*above*) Crude sculpture of a recumbent *chacmool* in the Sanctuary of Tlaloc, Stage II of the Great Temple. Such figures, common at Tula, indicate the importance that the Toltec cultural heritage had to the nascent Aztec state.

XIX Wooden Aztec mask encrusted with turquoise mosaic and shell, depicting an unknown god or ancestral figure. This object was certainly part of the Aztec treasure shipped by Hernán Cortés to Charles V.

a   b

120 Plumbate effigy jars from Teotihuacan and Tula. Toltec culture. *a*, bearded warrior in jaguar helmet; *b*, turkey effigy.

Plumbate was probably made to order for the Toltec taste, and one superb vessel was discovered at Tula showing the face of a bearded man (perhaps Quetzalcoatl) between the jaws of a coyote, all completely covered with small plaques of mother-of-pearl. A storage or cache pit in a room of one house produced five Tohil Plumbate goblets, along with three goblets and a bowl of Papagayo Polychrome, a kind of brightly painted pottery manufactured in quantity at this time in an area extending from eastern Honduras down to northwestern Costa Rica. 120
pl. XII

The Aztec testimony that the Toltecs were mastercraftsmen is validated by the breastplate and mirror above, but numerous other excavations have only come up with objects in *tecalli* (Mexican "onyx," a kind of travertine) as an elite product. Obsidian production, however, was on a large scale, similar to that at Teotihuacan, and like the Teotihuacanos, during the Tollan phase the Tula Toltec controlled the great mines of green obsidian at Pachuca, Hidalgo. In fact, Richard Diehl estimates that more than 40 percent of Tula's inhabitants were engaged in production of obsidian cores, blades, and projectile points for internal consumption and export.

In clay one also finds a small amount of Mazapan pottery, a red-on-buff ware featuring bowls whose interiors are decorated with parallel wavy or straight lines applied by a multiple brush, undistinguished moldmade figurines, and tobacco pipes with flaring bowls and long stems embellished with undulating snakes. To date, Tula has yielded no metal of any kind, neither copper nor gold, but this need scarcely surprise us, for as yet no fine tombs, where one would expect such treasures, have been located there. On the other hand, many of the ornaments portrayed in stone are painted yellow, a color reserved for gold in the Mexican canon. 121

There is a singularly secular cast to Tula, for representations of the gods are rare – a state of affairs usually interpreted as the result of the encroachment of the military over the spiritual power, but it could well be an artifact of

121 Mazapan ceramic artifacts, from Teotihuacan. Pottery of this sort underlies the Toltec culture at Tula. *a–b*, Mazapan red-on-buff bowls, 1/8; *c*, female figurine, 1/2.

Aztec collecting expeditions. Curiously, the supposedly victorious Tez-catlipoca himself is absent, and the Feathered Serpent ubiquitous. Quite recognizable are representations of several deities worshipped also by the Aztecs, such as Centeotl, the Maize Goddess; Xochiquetzal, the Goddess of Love; and Tlahuizcalpantecuhtli, an avatar of Quetzalcoatl as Morning Star. In line with the claim that human sacrifice was introduced in the last phase of Tula by the Tezcatlipoca faction, there are several depictions of the *cuauhxicalli*, the sacred "eagle vessel" designed to receive human hearts, as well as a *tzompantli*, the altar decorated with skulls and crossbones on which the heads of sacrificed captives were displayed. In fact, the base of an actual *tzompantli* has been found just to the east of Ball Court II, the largest at the site; fragments of human skulls littered its surface. In accordance with Mesoamerican custom, these were probably trophies from losers in a game that was "played for keeps"!

122   Richard Diehl's University of Missouri excavations brought to light some of the domestic architecture of the Toltecs. Individual houses were flat-roofed buildings of square or rectangular plan; these formed complexes of up to five houses, each group separated from others by exterior house walls and courtyard walls. Each such group had a small altar or shrine in the center of the courtyard. An important part of the rites celebrated there must have been the worship of the Rain God, represented by hour-glass-shaped pottery braziers with faces of Tlaloc indicated by clay fillets; there are also openwork ceramic censers with one long handle and two feet for supports. Less easy to explain are small wheeled figurines of animals – these could have been toys, but Diehl feels they also were part of the household cult. The dead were gen-erally buried in a pit beneath the house floor, and accompanied by pots; sacrificial victims formed an exception, these being tossed onto rubbish heaps in abandoned rooms after their bodies had been cannibalized. The general settlement pattern seems to be different from Teotihuacan's, but there is evidence that Tula also had an overall grid plan, organizing these household clusters into wards about 1,970 ft (600 m) on a side.

Tula is on the margins of Mesoamerica, and it was also marginal for farming, since summer rainfall is insufficient for effective cultivation, and there are winter frosts. Accordingly, food for Tula's population came from

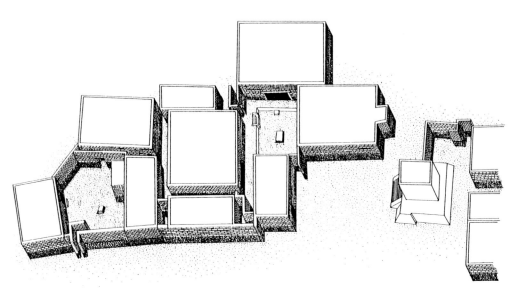

122 Reconstruction drawing of houses and associated small temple at Tula. Toltec culture, Early Post-Classic period.

the fields irrigated during the rainy season from small canals running from modest check dams.

All the evidence points to the death of the city through sudden and overwhelming cataclysm: the ceremonial halls were burned to the ground, and the Serpent Wall was toppled over. The fury of the destruction visited on Tula makes one wonder about the hand that performed the act. The mere fact that the subsequent reoccupation of the site was by a people who used so-called "Aztec" II pottery does not mean that the vanquishers of the capital were of the same affiliation. On the contrary the finger of accusation points most logically once more to the Chichimeca, for Tula was perilously close to their frontiers. It was just at this time that these peoples were again pushing south into cultivated lands. When Xolotl and his band of Chichimeca passed by Tula on their way to the Valley of Mexico, they found it already in ruins and spent some days exploring its shattered walls.

Tula and Chich'en Itza

As long ago as 1885, Desiré Charnay had concluded that Tula, Hidalgo, was the Toltec capital described in the histories; he recognized the close relationship between the architecture and sculpture of Tula and that of distant Chich'en Itza, in the middle of the Yucatan Peninsula; and he proposed that the Toltecs had invaded and conquered Yucatan. This last hypothesis has had its ups and downs over the subsequent century, in large part caused by the almost total lack of an archaeological culture history or even a chronology for Chich'en Itza, in spite of decades of research by the Carnegie Institution of Washington and the Mexican government.

The facts of the case are these. Chich'en Itza has two components which overlap to some extent. The first of these is native Maya, and consists of a number of buildings in an architectural style known as "Puuc," dated to the end of the Epiclassic and located in the southern part of the city. The other component is closely linked to Tula of the Toltecs, so closely, in fact, that Richard Diehl has said that "despite the 1,100 km that separate them, these two communities were more alike than any other two archaeological sites in Pre-Columbian America." C. Kristan-Graham has listed some of the more significant of the many traits shared by the two as "feathered serpent columns, atlantids, chacmools, *cipactli* [crocodile day-sign] glyphs, banquettes decorated with processional reliefs, colonnaded halls, similarly attired profile figures, and low relief images of feathered serpents, composite man-bird-serpent creatures posed frontally, profile raptors, canines and felines." One might add that both have a major *tzompantli* of the same shape placed just east of the principal ball court. Even further, personal names at both Tula and Chich'en Itza are expressed in a glyphic system that is yet unstudied, but which is not Maya.

The greatest novelty for the Maya area is the Feathered Serpent imagery so ubiquitous in Toltec-related Chich'en Itza. This is specifically a rattlesnake covered with quetzal feathers, a concept totally unknown among the Classic Maya, but ancient in central Mexico (and even among the Preclassic Olmec). It really breaks the rule of Occam's razor to see this as anything other than the direct appropriation of a major cult coming directly from Tula of the Toltecs, along with several other specific, non-Maya traits, such as the *tzompantli* and the colonnaded hall. It may be recalled that these latter two traits began far north and west of Tula, and would certainly have come through the Toltec on their way to the Maya area. Given the geography and the close ties between Tula and northwest Mexico, it is difficult to believe that these traits originated at Chich'en Itza and then were passed back to Tula, as some scholars have asserted. There may never have been such a personage as Topiltzin Quetzalcoatl – archaeologist and ethnohistorian Susan Gillespie has marshaled impressive evidence that much of his "history" was fabricated in the early Colonial period – but this has no bearing on the material evidence for Toltec traits at Chich'en Itza.

Given this situation, may it still be argued that Toltec warriors invaded Chich'en Itza and imposed these Toltec traits? While the paucity of specific Tula ceramic types and the cohabitation of Puuc and Toltec traits at Chich'en Itza do not completely rule out an invasion, they do not support such a scenario. The late Sir Eric Thompson suggested another possibility: that all these non-Maya elements were brought to Chich'en not from Tula, but by the highly Mexicanized Putún Maya of the Gulf Coast, who presumably had been subjected to Toltec influence at some unknown point in time. This hypothesis cannot be tested, for like the Olmeca-Xicallanca with whom the Putún are sometimes conflated, we have little knowledge of their homeland and thus little definition of the archaeological traces needed to map their movements. It seems likely, however, that if there had ever existed a Tula-like center with stone monuments in that area, it would have been discovered by now.

Recently Alfredo López Austin and Leonardo López Luján have suggested that Toltec traits at the two cities are evidence not of conquest, but of a shared political and economic system that was cemented through the knowledge of an esoteric language: that of "Zuyuá," which was still known and recited in the Yucatan during the Colonial period. Through the shared identity offered by this language and the related architectural and art forms, Chich'en and Tula were able to overlay their now Mesoamerican-wide power on trade routes controlled earlier by local elites. William Ringle and George Bey define with great precision the archaeological basis of a shared cult, based on Quetzalcoatl, that united the two cities. According to their exegesis, both cities brought a certain amount of material to the cult, but neither Tula nor Chich'en were the originators of cult materials or practices. Both the Quetzalcoatl and the Zuyuá models locate the genesis of Toltec symbolism and Toltec economic strategy in the network of Epiclassic cities that Tula and Chich'en largely supplanted.

The striking similarities between Tula and Chich'en cannot be ignored, but recently the explanatory mechanisms have generally shifted from influence and invasion to appropriation and trade. Until we know more of the beginnings of Tula and Chich'en Itza, and have a firmer chronological grip on their interaction, all these scenarios will remain hypothetical. What all this means is that there is much yet to be learned about the Toltec phenomenon in Mesoamerica, and that there continues to be a pressing need for large-scale excavation and mapping at Chich'en Itza, as well as for all areas of early Tula occupation.

9 · The Post-Classic Period: Rival States

Late Zapotec culture at Mitla

Of all peoples of Mexico, the Zapotecs were among the most fortunate, for they had long been undisturbed in their beautiful valley by troublemakers from outside. This state of affairs was ended, however, when Monte Albán was abandoned at the end of the eighth century and a new force was spearheaded by a people infiltrating the Valley of Oaxaca from the mountainous country lying to the northwest. But more of this later.

In the early Post-Classic, a new center of Zapotec civilization sprang up at Mitla, about 25 miles (40 km) southwest of Oaxaca City. The name is derived from the Nahuatl *Mictlan*, or "Land of the Dead," but to the Zapotecs it was known as *Lyobaá*, "Place of Rest." Not very much is known of the archaeology of Mitla, but it is thought to have been constructed in the Monte Albán V period, corresponding to the Toltec and Aztec eras; it was still in use when the Spaniards arrived.

Mitla is one of the architectural wonders of ancient Mexico – not grandiose, not a mighty city it is true, but of unparalleled beauty. Five architectural groups are scattered over the site, three of which are Post-Classic 123 palaces, while the remaining two are Classic-period temple precincts, re-used in the Post-Classic. During this latter period the ensemble was guarded by a fortified stronghold on a nearby hill. A Colonial church is built into one of the palaces and during fiestas native Zapotec ceremonies are still carried out within its precincts, side by side with Christian rites. Most remarkable among these complexes is the Group of the Columns, comprising very long masonry halls arranged on platforms around the four sides of a plaza. Here and elsewhere at Mitla long panels and entire walls are covered with geometric stonework mosaics, the intricate arabesques of which are almost entirely 124 based on the step-and-fret motif, each piece of veneer being set into a red stucco background. From the descriptions handed down from the Colonial period, it is known that the spacious rooms of the palaces had flat roofs supported by huge horizontal beams of wood.

If we can believe the somewhat sensational but highly detailed account of pre-Spanish Mitla given us by Father Burgoa, who visited the district in the

123 (*left, above*) North facade of the Building of the Columns, Mitla, Oaxaca. Late Post-Classic period. Overall height about 8 m.

124 (*left, below*) Portion of inner chamber in Palace II, Mitla, Oaxaca. Late Post-Classic period.

seventeenth century, this was once the residence of the High Priest (*Vuijatao*, or "Great Seer") of the Zapotec nation, a man so powerful that even the king bowed to his commands. Mitla's groups of buildings were apparently precincts, one for the holy man himself; one for secondary priests; one for the Zapotec king and his court when on a visit; and one for the officials and military officers of the king. Priests carried out the ceremonies garbed in white robes and figured chasubles, amid clouds of perfumed copal incense. Hidden from vulgar eyes in an inner chamber of his palace, the High Priest ruled from a throne covered by a jaguar skin; even the king, when in his presence, took a lesser seat. Kept scrupulously clean and covered by mats, the floors were the place of repose for all occupants at night.

Burgoa asserts that gruesome sacrifices took place there continuously: numberless captives had their hearts torn out and offered to the High Priest and the Zapotec gods. Somewhere underneath Mitla was supposed to be a great secret chamber where the Zapotec kings and nobles, as well as heroes killed on the battlefront, were interred, accounting for the name of the site. The exact location of this catacomb is not known, but according to Burgoa the passage leading to it was found in his day and entered by some enterprising Spanish priests, who were soon forced by the horror of the place to scurry out again and seal it up as an abomination against God.

The Mixtecs

"A succession of very small, rather prosperous valleys surrounded by large areas of nearby desert" is how the late Ignacio Bernal once characterized the homeland of the Mixtec people. This is the rugged, mountainous land in western and northern Oaxaca called the Mixteca. Archaeological survey carried out by Ronald Spores of Vanderbilt University has shown that initially, during the Classic, Mixtec settlements were located on hilltops; but by the outset of the Post-Classic, they had moved down into the valleys, where (as John Pohl and Bruce Byland have demonstrated) they were organized into multiple kingdoms or polities, with no large-scale political integration and no large cities. Each kingdom was under the domination of one independent lord. Since arable land was scarce in this precipitous landscape, there was fierce competition for it along the borders between kingdoms, and warfare was endemic.

Miraculously, there have survived four pre-Conquest codices which, through the researches of Alfonso Caso, have carried Mixtec history back to a time beyond the range of any of the annals of other Mexican, non-Maya peoples. Analysis of this material by Emily Rabin has established that it covers a 600-year time span beginning about AD 940. These codices are folding, deerskin books in which the pages are coated with gesso and painted; they were produced late in the Post-Classic for the Mixtec nobility. As Jill Furst notes, "they are concerned with historical events and genealogies, and present records of births, marriages, offspring, and sometimes the deaths of native rulers, and their conflicts to retain their lands and wars to extend their pl. XIII domains." The one exception is the front, or obverse, of the Vienna Codex, which she has found to be a land document that begins in the mythical "first time" (when the ancestral Mixtecs sprang from a tree at a place called Apoala), and establishes the rights of certain lineages to rule specific sites through the approval and sanction of the gods and sacred ancestors.

The reader is taken through these largely pictorial texts by means of red guidelines (generally horizontal), but there is no standard layout for the entire codex: some proceed from right to left, and some from left to right. Dates are given only in the 52-year Calendar Round; the year itself is given with a sign that looks like an interlaced A and O, accompanied by the Year Bearer (i.e. 12 Reed, 7 House, and the like), followed by the day in the 260-day count. There is no attempt at portraiture, and there was no need for it, for each personage in the histories is indicated by his or her birthdate in the 260-day count, plus an iconic "nickname," so there is little ambiguity. Each individual received further specificity through detailed renderings of costume, which for the Mixtecs often identified precise offices or ceremonies.

Compared with the Maya script and the Zapotec writing system from which it may have sprung, Mixtec writing was fairly rudimentary. As art historians Nancy Troike and Mary Elizabeth Smith have pointed out, Mixtec is a tonal language, and there were many opportunities for the artist scribes to indulge in phonetic substitutions and word play in the writing of place-names. This generally took the form of rebus or "puzzle-writing," in which a concept difficult to picture is substituted by another sign of different meaning but identical, or near-identical, sound. An example of this is provided by the town called Teozacoalco in Nahuatl; its Mixtec name means "Great Foundation." The place sign in the codices is a base being bent or broken by a small figure. Since, except for a difference in tone, the words for "breaking" and for "great" are homonyms in Mixtec, the reader would have no difficulty in identifying this place.

That the Mixtecs managed to bring under their sway not only all of the Mixteca proper but also most of Zapotec territory by Post-Classic times is a tribute to their statecraft. This was of a simple sort, quite familiar in European history, namely for an aggressive prince to marry into the royal line of a coveted town if he was unable to take it by force; polygamy made this strategy fairly common. Often, if he actually subdued the enemy by force of arms, he would further consolidate his rule by a judicious marriage with a native princess. Extensive intermarriage eventually resulted in the Mixtec aristocracy being one family, under a single dynastic house. As with royalty of Egypt, Hawaii, and Peru, policy considerations led even to brother-sister marriage.

By the beginning of the Post-Classic period, the leading power in the Mixteca was a town called Hill of the Wasp, a Classic-period hilltop settlement in the southern Nochixtlan Valley, where it is still referred to today by its codical name in Mixtec, *Yucu Yoco*. When it was overthrown in the late tenth century, its rulers were sacrificed, and an epic cycle of conflict referred to as the "War Of Heaven" commenced. According to the codices, three Mixtec factions fought for sixteen years, eventually founding the Mixtec political landscape of the Post-Classic period. Scenes of these battles in the codices are highly schematized, with capture indicated by grasping the hair, and defeat by the burning of mummy bundles. The bundles were very important to the Mixtec, for it was through access to the divine ancestors in the form of bundles that family tradition and prestige were upheld. Supernaturals like the Mixtec culture hero 9 Wind also played an important role in the indigenous account, giving the results a divine sanction. The War of Heaven ends with the establishment of the first dynasty of Tilantongo (its Mixtec name means "Black Town"); this jointly ruled several valleys with a place called Xipe Bundle, until it too fell.

In the second dynasty of Tilantongo, the codices have much to tell about a great warlord named 8 Deer "Jaguar Claw," who lived during the Calendar Round which began in AD 1063 and ended in 1115. When he rose to power, he attacked a town known as Red and White Bundle, located to the east of Tilantongo, sacrificing both the lord of that place and (somewhat unchivalrously) his wife Lady 6 Monkey, who had been a princess of Mountain of the Place of Sand. In 1097, 8 Deer "Jaguar Claw" seems to have made a journey to Tollan (a place of the rushes, or place of legitimacy), where he was invested with the Toltec nose button under the auspices of the Toltec king himself, a man called 4 Jaguar; this probably marks his accession to the throne of Tilantongo, the ruler of the Toltec capital fulfilling the same function as the pope who crowned the Holy Roman Emperor.

125   We follow in the books the machinations of 8 Deer "Jaguar Claw," as he tries to bring rival statelets under his sway: marrying no fewer than five times, all his wives were princesses of other towns, some of whose families he had subjected to the sacrificial knife (or had shot with darts while strapped to a scaffold, another Mixtec way of dispatching captives). "Who lives by the sword dies by the sword" goes the European saying, and this formidable warrior was ultimately killed by Lady 6 Monkey's son. This latter personage became ruler of a town called Place of Flints, and married the daughter of 8 Deer "Jaguar Claw" himself! 8 Deer's exploits were so fundamental to Mixtec history that they still served as legitimating claim for several Mixtec royal houses when the Spanish arrived, 400 years later.

By approximately AD 1350 the Mixtecs began to infiltrate even the Valley of Oaxaca by the usual method of state marriage, Mixtec royal brides insisting on bringing their own retinues to the Zapotec court. By the time the Spaniards arrived, practically all Zapotec sites were occupied by the Mixtecs. Of their great wealth and high artistry – for they were the finest goldsmiths and workers in turquoise mosaic in Mexico – the fantastic treasure from Tomb 7 at Monte Albán is eloquent testimony. Here, in a Classic period 126, 127 tomb, the Mixtecs laid the remains of one of their nobles, accompanied by slaughtered servants, some time in the mid-fourteenth century. Accompanying the central figure were magnificent objects of gold, cast in the lost-wax process, and silver; turquoise mosaics; necklaces of rock crystal, amber, jet, and coral; thousands of pearls, one as big as a pigeon's egg; and sections of jaguar bone carved with historical and mythological scenes. While Alfonso Caso and his team had identified the central skeleton as male, other evidence, especially the presence of a weaving kit with battens, picks, spindle whorls, and spindle bowls, suggests strong female associations. Certainly the Mixtecs had a tradition of politically powerful females, and several of these are featured in the codices, but there is as yet little firm evidence to suggest that the skeleton was female. It is likely, however, that the central figure was a

125 (*left*) Scenes from the life of the Mixtec king, 8 Deer, from the Codex Nuttall. Right, 8 Deer has his nose pierced for a special ornament in the year AD 1045. Center, 8 Deer goes to war. Left, town "Curassow Hill" conquered by 8 Deer.

126 (*right*) Gold pendant from Tomb 7, Monte Albán, Oaxaca. The pendant was cast in one piece by the lost-wax process. The uppermost elements represent, from top to bottom, a ball game played between two gods, the solar disk, a stylized butterfly, and the Earth Monster. Mixtec culture, Late Post-Classic period. Length 22 cm.

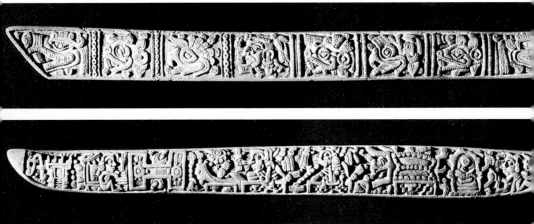

127 Two carved bones from Tomb 7, Monte Albán, Oaxaca. The representations are calendrical and astronomical in meaning. Mixtec culture, Late Post-Classic period. Length about 18 cm.

female deity impersonator. Both the Mixtecs and the Aztecs had important political and ritual posts based on female deities, the costumes of which often contained spinning and weaving implements.

Zaachila, a Valley town still bitterly divided between the descendants of the Zapotecs and the Mixtecs, was a Zapotec capital after the demise of Monte Albán, and had a Zapotec king, but its culture was Mixtec. One of its structures has produced two tombs with a treasure trove of Mixtec-style objects almost equal to those in Tomb 7, including some of the

128 Small polychrome pedestal bowl from Zaachila, Oaxaca. A bright blue hummingbird perches on the rim. Mixtec culture, Late Post-Classic period. Ht of bowl rim 5.4 cm.

most remarkable polychrome pottery ever discovered in the New World: the ceramic gem in this case is a beautifully painted cup with the three-dimensional figure of a blue hummingbird perched on its rim.

128

Not only to the south, but as far north as Cholula, Mixtec artistic influence was felt, resulting in the hybrid Mixteca-Puebla style which produced some of the finest manuscripts, sculpture, pottery, and turquoise mosaics of latter-day Mexico. Although, like several other rival states in Mexico, the Mixtecs were marked down for conquest in its aggressive plans, they were never completely vanquished by the Aztec empire. They united successfully with the Zapotecs against the intruder and thus avoided the fate of so many other once independent nations of Post-Classic Mexico.

The Tarascan kingdom

The Aztecs called the territory of the Tarascans, whom they were never able to conquer, *Michoacan*, meaning "the place of the masters of fish." This is a fitting name, for much of Tarascan history centers on Lake Pátzcuaro in western Mexico, which abounds in fish. The Tarascans' own name for themselves and for their unique language is *Purépecha*. While very little field archaeology has yet been carried out in Michoacan, we fortunately have a long and rich ethnohistoric source, the *Relación de Michoacan*, apparently an early Spanish translation of one or more original documents in Tarascan, which gives important details of their past and of their life as it was on the eve of the Spanish Conquest.

In the Late Post-Classic, the Tarascan state was bounded on the south and west by areas under Aztec control, and on the north by the Chichimecs. The people were ethnically mixed, but dominated by the "pure" Tarascans, who made up about 10 percent of the population; many of the groups within their territory were in fact Nahuatl-speakers. The *Relación* tells us of migrations of various tribes into Michoacan, among whom the most important ethnic group was "Chichimec" – probably semi-barbaric speakers of Tarascan, who established themselves on islands in the midst of Lake Pátzcuaro, and who called themselves *Wakúsecha*. Their first capital was the town of Pátzcuaro, which was "founded" about AD 1325 under their hero-chief Taríakuri; from there they imposed their language and rule on the native peoples and on the other tribes.

Eventually, the Tarascans conquered all of present-day Michoacan and established a series of fortified outposts on their frontiers. Ihuátzio, located on the southeastern arm of the lake, became the capital, to be succeeded by Tzintzúntzan, the royal seat of power when the Spaniards arrived on the scene in 1522.

At the top of the Tarascan hierarchy was the Kasonsí, the king; he acted as war chief and supreme judge of the nation, and was the ruler of Tzintzúntzan. Under him were the rulers of the two other administrative centers, Ihuátzio and Pátzcuaro, and four boundary princes. The Kasonsí's court was large and attended by a wide variety of officials whose functions give a good idea of the division of labor within the royal household. For

129   Funeral ceremonies for the Tarascan Kasonsí or king, from the *Relación de Michoacan*.

instance, there were the heads of various occupational groups, such as the masons, drum-makers, doctors, makers of obsidian knives, anglers, silver-smiths, and decorators of cups, along with many other functionaries including the king's zookeeper and the head of his war-spies.

129   The chronicler of the *Relación* spends many pages on the funeral of the Kasonsí, which was indeed spectacular, but probably not very different from that of any other Mesoamerican ruler of the time. He was borne to his final resting place attended by Tarascan and foreign lords, with elaborate rites and music. Accompanying him in death were seven important women from his palace, such as his "keeper of the gold and turquoise lip-ornaments," his cook, his wine-bearer, and the "keeper of his urinal." Also sacrificed were forty male attendants, including the doctor who had failed to cure him in his last illness! Quite clearly the Kasonsí's palace was to be replicated for him in the land of the dead.

Unlike the Aztec (but like the late pre-Conquest Maya), the Tarascan priesthood was not celibate; the badge of the priests was the gourd container for tobacco which was strapped to their backs. At the top of the religious organization was the Supreme High Priest, heading a complex hierarchy with many ranks of priests divided as to function.

The Tarascan state religion, which was probably codified within the last 150 years of the pre-Conquest era, seems remarkably un-Mesoamerican. There was no rain god analogous to Tlaloc, and no Feathered Serpent. Even more remarkable was the absence of both the 260-day count and the use of the calendar for divinatory ends. They did, however, have the approximate solar year of 18 months of 20 days each, plus the five "extra" days. Ball courts were apparently rare, and none are known for Tzintzúntzan itself.

According to data gathered by anthropologist Helen Perlstein Pollard, the universe was made up of three parts: 1) the sky, associated with eagles, hawks, falcons, and the *Wakúsecha* elite; 2) the earth, viewed as a goddess with four world-directions; and 3) the Underworld, the place of death and caves, inhabited by burrowing animals like mice, gophers, moles, and snakes. The sky was the domain of Kurikaweri, the sun god, the most important deity in the state cult; his worship demanded huge offerings of firewood which, along with agricultural clearances, must have resulted in extensive deforestation of the Michoacan landscape. Kurikaweri was also the tribal god of the *Wakúsecha* and a war god, in whose honor there was performed not only human sacrifice but also auto-sacrifice (the shedding of blood from one's own body), and his earthly form was the Kasonsí himself.

Like the gods on the Greek Mount Olympus, the Tarascan deities were considered to belong to one large family. Kurikaweri's consort was Kwerawáperi, the earth-mother, a creator divinity from whom all the other gods were born; she controlled life, death, and the rains and drought. The most important fruit of the union between the sky and earth deities was Xarátenga, the goddess of the moon and the sea; her domain was in the west (towards the Pacific Coast), and she could take the form of an old woman, a coyote, or an owl. Naturally, there were many local cults, and each of the ethnic groups subdued by the Tarascan war machine had its own tutelary supernaturals, but these were all subsumed in the cosmological kinship system of the official state religion.

There was no formal education for Tarascan boys, who were trained by their fathers for a particular profession or calling, but young women of the *Wakúsecha* aristocracy were educated in a special communal house; these were considered "wives" of the tribal god Kurikaweri, and usually married off to army officers.

The ruins of the final Tarascan capital, Tzintzúntzan, rest on a terraced slope above the northeast arm of Lake Pátzcuaro. An enormous rectangular

130 View of one of five *yákatas* or rectangular platforms at Tzintzúntzan, Michoacan, looking north. Tarascan culture, Late Post-Classic period.

130 platform 1,440 ft (440 m) long supports five of the superstructures known as *yákatas*; each *yákata* is a rectangular stepped pyramid joined by a stepped passageway to a round stepped "pyramid." The *yákatas* were once entirely faced with finely fitted slabs of volcanic stone that recall the perfection of Inca masonry in South America. Those that have been investigated contained richly stocked burials, and it is probable that their primary function was to contain the tombs of deceased Kasonsís and their retainers.

What little archaeological evidence we have suggests that the Tarascans were extraordinary craftsmen; many luxury objects in collections that are ascribed to the Mixtecs may well come from Michoacan instead, and it has been suggested that the Tarascans may have taken over some of the northern Toltec trade routes, in particular the commerce in Southwestern turquoise, after the downfall of Tula. The most astonishing of their productions were paper-thin obsidian earspools and labrets, faced with sheet gold and turquoise inlay, but they were master workers in gold and silver, and in bimetallic objects using both of these precious substances.

Casas Grandes and the northern trade route

Central to any interaction with the Southwest during this period would have been Casas Grandes, Chihuahua, not far south of the border with New Mexico. The site, also referred to as Paquimé, may now be dated to *c.* 1200–1475. While the population lived in Southwestern-style apartment houses, the Mesoamerican component can be seen in the presence of platform temple mounds, I-shaped ball courts, and the cult of the Feathered Serpent. Warehouses filled with rare Southwestern minerals, such as turquoise, were found by Charles DiPeso, the excavator of Casas Grandes. While it is now clear that the regional elite consumed large quantities of these precious materials, a substantial amount must also have found its way south, where turquoise especially continued to grow in importance for the Tarascans and other Mesoamericans. What was traveling north? The Pueblo Indians have a deep ritual need for feathers from tropical birds like parrots and macaws, since these symbolize fertility and the heat of the summer sun. Special pens were discovered at the site in which scarlet macaws were raised; certainly some of these must have found their way north to pay for the precious turquoise. Initially, these birds must have come from Mesoamerica, the original habitat of the scarlet macaw.

The rise of the Aztec state

The beginnings of the Aztec nation, as we know them from their own accounts, were so humble and obscure that their rise to supremacy over most of Mexico in the space of a few hundred years seems almost miraculous. It is somehow inconceivable that the magnificent civilization witnessed and destroyed by the Spaniards could have been created by a people who were not many generations removed from the most abject barbarism, yet this is what their histories tell us.

But these histories, all of which were written down in Nahuatl (the Aztec language) or in Spanish early in the Colonial period, must be considered in their context, and rigorously evaluated. First, given the nature of central Mexican chronology during the Post-Classic, which was based on the 52-year Calendar Round, it is clear that at least some of the supposedly historical data we are given in the chronicles is cyclical rather than linear: that is, an event which occurs at one point in a given cycle could also have taken place, and will take place, at similar points in other such cycles. Secondly, given the above, there were ample opportunities for the Aztec royal dynasty to rewrite its own history and the history of the nation as changing times demanded; we are told that this was done in the reign of the ruler Itzcoatl, but it apparently was done on a far larger scale during the course of the sixteenth century to cope with the cataclysm of the Spanish invasion and Conquest. The fully developed Aztec state had a cosmic vision of itself and its place in the universe which demanded a certain kind of history, and we now realize that even royal genealogies could be tailored to fit this vision.

It is thus no easy task to reconcile the often-conflicting native chronicles into a coherent story of Aztec origins and rise to power; yet there is consider-able agreement on the broad outlines. The story begins with events which followed Tula's destruction in the twelfth century. Refugees from this center of Toltec civilization managed to establish themselves in the southern half of the Valley, particularly at the towns of Colhuacan and Xico, both of which became important citadels transmitting the higher culture of their predeces-sors to the savage groups who were then streaming into the northern half. Among the latter were the band of Chichimeca under their chief Xolotl, arriving in the Valley by 1244 and settling at Tenayuca; the Acolhua, who founded Coatlinchan around the year 1160; the Otomi at Xaltocan by about 1250; and the powerful Tepanecs, who in 1230 took over the town of Atzcapotzalco, which much earlier had been a significant Teotihuacan settlement. There is no question that all of these with the exception of the Otomi were speakers of Nahuatl, now the dominant tongue of central Mexico. Thus, by the thirteenth century, all over the Valley there had sprung up a group of modestly sized city-states, those in the north founded by Chichimec upstarts eager to learn from the Toltecs in the south.

According to Edward Calnek, this was a time of relative peace in the Valley. The Toltec refugees, occupying the rich lands in the south and west, intro-duced the organization and ideology of rule by the elite (called *pipiltin* in Nahuatl); its guiding principle was that only someone descended from the ancient royal Toltec dynasty could be a ruler or *tlatoani* ("speaker," a term that will be explained in the next chapter). Those who lacked such descent could demand – if they were powerful enough – women of royal rank as wives. As time passed, the *pipiltin* came to hold a nearly complete monopoly of the highest offices in each city-state. As for the non-Toltec groups, some adopted the system sooner than others; the Aztecs were to prove the last hold-outs.

Into this political milieu stepped the Aztecs themselves, the last barbaric tribe to arrive in the Valley of Mexico, the "people whose face nobody knows." The official Aztec histories claimed that they had come from a place called "Aztlan" (meaning "Land of White Herons"), supposedly an island in a lake in the west or northwest of Mexico, and thus called themselves the "Azteca." One tradition says that they began their migration toward central Mexico in AD 1111, led by their tribal deity Huitzilopochtli ("Hummingbird on the Left"), whose idol was borne on the shoulders of four priests called *teomamaque*. Apparently they knew the art of cultivation and wore agave fiber clothing, but had no political leaders higher than clan and tribal chieftains. It is fitting that Huitzilopochtli was a war god and representative of the sun, for the Aztecs were extremely adept at military matters, and among the best and fiercest warriors ever seen in Mexico.

Along the route of march, Huitzilopochtli gave them a new name, the Mexica, which they were to bear until the Conquest. Many versions of the migration legend have them stop at Chicomoztoc, "Seven Caves," from which emerge all of the various ethnic groups which were to make up the nascent Aztec nation. There is a further halt at the mythical Coatepec ("Snake Mountain") where, somewhat confusingly, Huitzilopochtli is miraculously born as the sun god – a supernatural tale of supreme importance that we shall examine in Chapter 10.

It needs no saying that none of the above is to be taken literally: like many other Mesoamerican peoples, such as the highland Maya, the Aztecs had myths and legends describing a migration from an often vague land of origin to a historically known place where they settled, inspired by the prophecy of a god. Similar legends can be found in the Book of Genesis and among a number of tribal states in Africa and Polynesia. Their function seems clear: to tell the world that the rule by a particular elite was given by history and supported by divine sanction.

Exactly when these Aztecs arrived in the Valley of Mexico is far from clear, but it must have already taken place by the beginning of the fourteenth century. Now, all the land in the Valley was already occupied by civilized peoples; they looked with suspicion upon these Aztecs, who were little more than squatters, continually occupying territory that did not belong to them and continually being kicked out. It is a wonder that they were ever tolerated since, women being scarce as among all immigrant groups, they took to raiding other peoples for their wives. The cultivated citizens of Colhuacan finally allowed them to live a degraded existence, working the lands of their masters as serfs, and supplementing their diet with snakes and other vermin. In 1323, however, the Aztecs repaid the kindness of their overlords, who had given their chief a Colhuacan princess as bride, by sacrificing the young lady with the hope that she would become a war goddess. Colhuacan retaliated by expelling these repulsive savages from their territory.

We next see the Aztecs following a hand-to-mouth existence in the marshes of the great lake, or "Lake of the Moon." On they wandered, loved by none, until they reached some swampy, unoccupied islands, covered by pl. XIV rushes, near the western shore; it was claimed that there the tribal prophecy, to build a city where an eagle was seen sitting on a cactus, holding a snake in its mouth, was fulfilled. By 1344 or 1345, the tribe was split in two, one group under their chief, Tenoch, founding the southern capital, Tenochtitlan, and the other settling Tlatelolco in the north. Eventually, as the swamps were drained and brought under cultivation, the islands became one, with two cities and two governments, a state of affairs not to last very long.

The year 1367 marks the turning point of the fortunes of the Aztecs: it was then that they began to serve as mercenaries for the mightiest power on the mainland, the expanding Tepanec kingdom of Atzcapotzalco, ruled by the unusually able Tezozomoc. One after another the city-states of the Valley of Mexico fell to the joint forces of Tezozomoc and his allies; sharing in the resulting loot, the Aztecs were also taken under Tepanec protection.

Up until this time, the Aztec system of government had essentially been egalitarian, and there were no social classes: the *teomamaque* and the other traditional leaders had remained in control. But in 1375, Tezozomoc gave them their first ruler or *tlatoani*, Acamapichtli ("Bundle of Reeds"), although during his reign there was still a degree of tribal democracy, in that he was not allowed to make or execute important decisions without the consent of the tribal leaders and the assembly. During these years, and in fact probably beginning as far back as their serfdom under Colhuacan, the Aztecs were taking on much of the culture that was the heritage of all the nations of the Valley from their Toltec predecessors. Much of this was learned from the mighty Tepanecs themselves, particularly the techniques of statecraft and empire-building so successfully indulged in by Tezozomoc. Already the small island kingdom of the Aztecs was prepared to exercise its strength on the mainland.

The consolidation of Aztec power

The chance came in 1426, when the aged Tezozomoc was succeeded as Tepanec king by his son Maxtlatzin, known to the Aztecs as "Tyrant Maxtla" and an implacable enemy of the growing power of Tenochtitlan. By crude threats and other pressures, Maxtlatzin attempted to rid himself of the "Aztec problem"; and in the middle of the crisis, the third Aztec king died. Itzcoatl, "Obsidian Snake," who assumed the Aztec rulership in 1427, was a man of strong mettle. More important, his chief adviser, Tlacaelel, was one of the most remarkable men ever produced by the Mexicans. The two of them decided to fight, with the result that by the next year the Tepanecs had been totally crushed and Atzcapotzalco was in ruins. This great battle, forever glorious to the Aztecs, left them the greatest state in Mexico.

In their triumph, and with the demotion of the traditional leaders, the Aztec administration turned to questions of internal polity, especially under Tlacaelel, who remained a kind of grand vizier to the Aztec throne through three reigns, dying in 1475 or 1480. Tlacaelel introduced a series of reforms that completely altered Mexican life. The basic reform related to the Aztec conception of themselves and their destiny; for this, it was necessary to rewrite history, and so Tlacaelel did, by having all the books of conquered peoples burned since these would have failed to mention Aztec glories. Under his aegis, the Aztecs acquired a mystic-visionary view of themselves as the chosen people, the true heirs of the Toltec tradition, who would fight wars and gain captives so as to keep the fiery sun moving across the sky.

This sun, represented by the fierce god Huitzilopochtli, needed the hearts of enemy warriors; during the reign of Motecuhzoma Ilhuicamina, "the Heaven Shooter" (reigned 1440–1469), Tlacaelel had the so-called "Flowery War" instituted. Under this, Tenochtitlan entered into a Triple Alliance with the old Acolhua state of Texcoco (on the other side of the lake) and the dummy state of Tlacopan in a permanent struggle against the Nahuatl-speaking states of Tlaxcala and Huexotzingo. The object on both sides was purely to gain captives for sacrifice.

Besides inventing the idea of Aztec grandeur, the glorification of the Aztec past, other reforms relating to the political-juridical and economic administrations were also carried out under Tlacaelel. The new system was successfully tested during a disastrous two-year famine which occurred under Motecuhzoma Ilhuicamina, and from which this extraordinary people emerged more confident than ever in their divine mission.

Given these conditions, it is little surprise that the Aztecs soon embarked with their allies on an ambitious program of conquest. The elder Motecuhzoma began the expansion, taking over the Huaxteca, much of the land around Mount Orizaba, and rampaging down even into the Mixteca. Axayacatl (1469–1481) subdued neighboring Tlatelolco on trumped-up charges and substituted a military government for what had once been an independent administration; he was less successful with the Tarascan kingdom of Michoacan, for these powerful people turned the invaders back. Greatest of all the empire-builders was Ahuitzotl (1486–1502), who succeeded the weak and vacillating Tizoc as sixth king. This mighty warrior conquered lands all the way to the Guatemalan border and brought under Aztec rule most of central Mexico. Probably for the first time since the downfall of Tula, there was in Mexico a single empire as great as, or greater than, that of the Toltecs. Ahuitzotl was a man of great energy; among the projects completed in his reign was a major rebuilding of the Great Temple of Tenochtitlan, completed in 1487, and the construction of an aqueduct to bring water from Coyoacan to the island capital.

Ahuitzotl's successor, Motecuhzoma Xocoyotzin ("The Younger") (1502–1520) is surely one of history's most tragic figures, for it was his misfortune to be the Aztec ruler when Mexican civilization was destroyed. He is described in many accounts, some of them eye-witness, as a very complex person; he was surely not the single-minded militarist that is so well typified by Ahuitzotl. Instead of delighting in war, he was given to meditation in his place of retreat, the "Black House" – in fact, one might be led to believe that he was more of a philosopher-king, along the lines of Hadrian. Like that Roman emperor, he also maintained a shrine in the capital where all the gods of captured nations were kept, for he was interested in foreign religions. In post-Conquest times, this was considered by Spaniards and Indians alike to have been the cause of his downfall: according to these *ex post facto* sources, when Cortés arrived in 1519, the Aztec emperor was paralyzed by the realization that this strange, bearded foreigner was

Quetzalcoatl himself, returned from the east as the ancient books had allegedly said he would, to destroy the Mexican peoples. All of his disastrous inaction in the face of the Spanish threat, his willingness to put himself in the hands of Cortés, was claimed to be the result of his dedication to the old Toltec philosophy. The triumphant Spaniards were only too glad to spread the word among their new subjects that this was Motecuhzoma's destiny, and that it had been foretold by a series of magical portents that had led to an inevitable outcome. We shall examine the life and death of the Aztec civilization in subsequent chapters.

10 · The Aztecs in 1519

The island city

Let the soldier Bernal Díaz, who was with Hernán Cortés when the Spaniards first approached the island capital of Tenochtitlan on 8 November 1511, tell us his impressions of his first glimpse of the Aztec citadel:

> During the morning, we arrived at a broad causeway and continued our march towards Iztapalapa, and when we saw so many cities and villages built in the water and other great towns on dry land and that straight and level Causeway going towards Mexico, we were amazed and said that it was like the enchantments they tell of in the legend of Amadis, on account of the great towers and temples and buildings rising from the water, and all built of masonry. And some of our soldiers asked whether the things that we saw were not a dream.[6]

132 The island was connected to the mainland by three principal causeways, "each as broad as a horseman's lance," says Cortés, running north to Tepeyac, west to Tlacopan, and south to Coyoacan. These were broken at intervals by openings through which canoes could pass, and were spanned by removable bridges, thus also serving a defensive purpose; moreover, access to the city by the enemy was barred by manned gatehouses. Across the western causeway ran a great masonry aqueduct carrying water to Tenochtitlan from the spring at Chapultepec, the flow being "as thick as a man's body."

The Spanish conquerors called the Aztec capital another Venice, and they should have known, for many of them had actually been to that place. With a total area of about 5 sq. miles (14 sq. km), the city (meaning by this Tenochtitlan and its satellite Tlatelolco) was laid out on a grid, according to a fragmentary sixteenth-century map of one section. Running north and south were long canals thronged with canoe traffic and each bordered by a lane; larger canals cut these at angles. Between these watery "streets" were arranged in regular fashion rectangular plots of land with their houses. In effect, this was a *chinampa* city.

A brief description of *chinampa* cultivation, mentioned in Chapter 1, will not be out of place here. The technique is well known, for it is still used in the Xochimilco zone to the south of Mexico City, and may have originated with the Teotihuacanos in the Classic. It belongs to the general category of "raised field cultivation," which is widespread in the New World tropics, and was in use among the lowland Classic Maya.

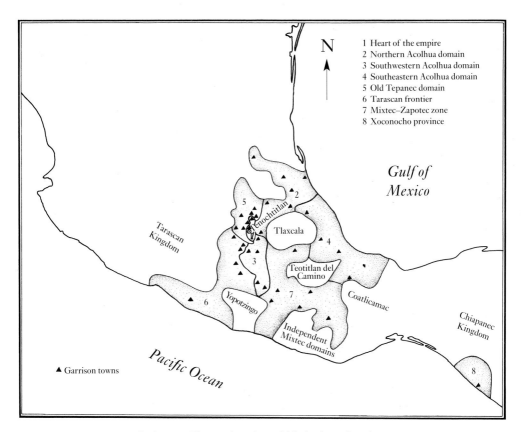

1 Heart of the empire
2 Northern Acolhua domain
3 Southwestern Acolhua domain
4 Southeastern Acolhua domain
5 Old Tepanec domain
6 Tarascan frontier
7 Mixtec–Zapotec zone
8 Xoconocho province

131 Extent of the Aztec empire in 1519. The provinces into which the Aztec domains were organized are indicated.

The first Aztec settlers on the island constructed canals in their marshy habitat by cutting layers of thick water vegetation from the surface and piling them up like mats to make their plots; from the bottom of the canals they spread mud over these green "rafts," which were thoroughly anchored by planting willows all around. On this highly fertile plot all sorts of crops were raised by the most careful and loving hand cultivation. This is why Cortés states that half the houses in the capital were built up "on the lake," and how swampy islands became united. Those houses on newly made *chinampas* were necessarily of light cane and thatch; on drier parts of the island, more sub-stantial dwellings of stone and mortar were possible, some of two stories with flower-filled inner patios and gardens. Communication across the "streets" was by planks laid over the canals.

The greatest problem faced by the inhabitants of the island was the saltiness of the lake, at least in its eastern part. With no outlet, during floods those nitrous waters inundated and ruined the *chinampas*. To prevent this, the Texcocan poet-king Nezahualcoyotl bountifully constructed a 10-mile (16-km) long dyke to seal off a spring-fed, freshwater lagoon for Tenochtitlan.

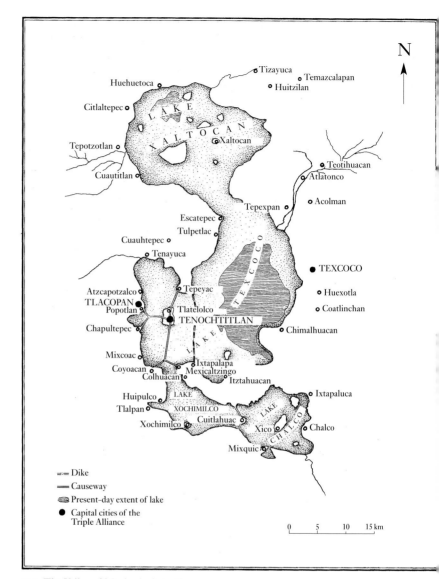

132 The Valley of Mexico in Aztec times.

With its willows, green gardens, numerous flowers, and canals bustling with canoes, Tenochtitlan must have been of impressive beauty, as the Nahuatl poem suggests:

> The city is spread out in circles of jade,
> radiating flashes of light like quetzal plumes,
> Beside it the lords are borne in boats:
> over them extends a flowery mist.[7]

It is extraordinarily difficult to estimate the population of the capital in 1519. Many early sources say that there were about 60,000 houses, but none say how many persons there were. Basing himself on the Aztec tribute lists, Rudolf van Zantwijk estimates that there were enough foodstuffs in the warehouses of Tenochtitlan to support a population of 350,000, even without taking into account local *chinampa* production. The data which we have, however flimsy, suggest that Tenochtitlan (with Tlatelolco) had at least 200,000 to 300,000 inhabitants when Cortés marched in, five times the size of the contemporary London of Henry VIII. Quite a number of other cities of central Mexico, such as Texcoco, also had very large populations; all of Mexico between the Isthmus of Tehuantepec and the Chichimec frontier had about 11,000,000 inhabitants, most of whom were under Aztec domination.

The houses of the ordinary class of people, especially those who lived on the *chinampa* plots, were generally of reeds plastered with mud, and roofed with thatch; better-off people had dwellings of adobe bricks with flat roofs; while those of the wealthy were of stone masonry, also with flat roofs, and probably made up house complexes arranged around an inner court, like

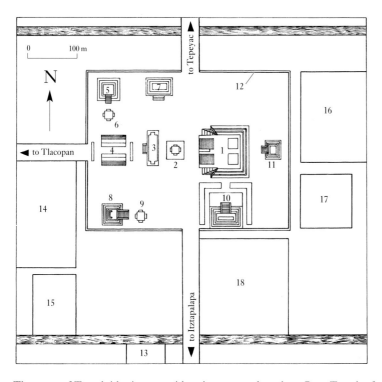

133 The center of Tenochtitlan in 1519, with main streets and canals. *1*, Great Temple of Tlaloc and Huitzilopochtli; *2*, Platform for Stone of Tizoc; *3*, *Tzompantli* (skullrack); *4*, Ball court; *5*, "Eagle House" of the Sun Temple; *6*, Platform of the "Eagle House," base for Calendar Stone; *7*, Snake Temple; *8*, Temple of Xipe Totec, God of Spring; *9*, Platform for gladiatorial stone; *10*, Temple of Tezcatlipoca; *11*, Temple of Colhuacan, the former temple of Huitzilopochtli; *12*, Snake Wall, enclosing the sacred precinct; *13*, "Black House" of the Temple of Coatlicue; *14*, Palace of Motecuhzoma Ilhuicamina (1440–69); *15*, "House of the Songs"; *16*, Palace of Axayacatl (1469–81); *17*, Royal Aviary; *18*, Palace of Motecuhzoma Xocoyotzin (1502–20).

those of Tula. The highest officials dwelt in great palace complexes, the greatest of which were reserved for the ruler or *Huei Tlatoani* ("Great Speaker") and for the descendants of his predecessors.

133   On the higher ground at the center of Tenochtitlan, the focal point of all the main highways which led in from the mainland, was the administrative and spiritual heart of the empire, and the conceptual center of the universe. This was the Sacred Precinct, a paved area surrounded by the Coatepantli ("Snake Wall"), and containing, according to Fray Bernardino de Sahagún – our great authority on all aspects of Aztec life – seventy-eight buildings; however, the late Jacques Soustelle was of the opinion that some of these were religious buildings in other parts of the city. The Sacred Precinct was dominated by the double Temple of Huizilopochtli and Tlaloc (the Great Temple), its twin stairways reddened with the blood of sacrificed captives. Other temples were dedicated to the cults of Tezcatlipoca, his adversary Quetzalcoatl, and Xipe Totec, the god of springtime. A reminder of the purpose of the never-ending "Flowery War" was the *tzompantli*, or skull rack, on which were skewered for public exhibition thousands of human heads. Near it was a very large ball court, in which Motecuhzoma Xocoyotzin was said to have played a game with and lost to the king of Texcoco on the truth of the latter's prediction that the former's kingdom would fall. The magnificent palaces of the Aztec royal line surrounded the Sacred Precinct.

Both in Tenochtitlan and in Tlatelolco proper were great marketplaces, very close to the main temples. The latter market was described by Bernal Díaz in superlative terms; Cortés says that it was twice as large as the main square of Salamanca, in Spain, and some of the soldiers who had been in Rome and Constantinople claimed that it was larger than any there. Every day over 60,000 souls were engaged in buying and selling in the Tlatelolco market, so many that there were market inspectors appointed by the ruler to check the honesty of transactions and to regulate prices. Thieves convicted in the market court were immediately punished by being beaten to death (Aztec law was draconian). As for "money," cacao beans (which sometimes were counterfeited), cotton cloaks, and transparent quills filled with gold dust served that purpose. Befitting its role as the commercial center of an empire, in the Great Market of Tlatelolco one could buy luxury products of gold, silver, jade, turquoise, or feathers; clothing of all sorts; foods both cooked and unprepared; pottery, the most esteemed being lovely polychrome dishes and cups from Cholula; chocolate and vanilla; carpenter's tools of copper; cane cigarettes, tobacco pipes, and aromatic cigars; and slaves, brought in by dealers from the slave center of Atzcapotzalco and exhibited in wooden cages. The market people had the obligation to furnish war provisions to the state, mainly maize in forms that would not spoil on long marches.

Aztec society

The basic unit of Aztec social organization in the heart of the empire was the *calpolli* (pl. *calpoltin*), a word meaning "big house." Often mistakenly called a "clan" – which would imply real or fictive descent from a common ancestor –

the *calpolli* has been defined by Rudolf van Zantwijk as a group of families related by kinship or proximity over a long period of time. Elite members of the group provided its commoner members with arable land and/or nonagricultural occupations, in return for which the commoners would perform various services for their chiefs and render them tribute. The *calpolli* was thus a localized, land-holding corporation, but it also had ritual functions in that it had its own temple and gods, and even an association with a day in the 260-day count. Its principal chief, the *calpollec*, was elected for life by the inhabitants, and confirmed in office by the ruler. There were approximately twenty *calpoltin* in Tenochtitlan, some of which have actually persisted as traditional barrios near the center of modern Mexico City. The *calpoltin* were arranged into the four great quarters into which the Aztec city was divided, separated by imaginary north–south and east–west lines which met at the Sacred Precinct.

The vast bulk of the population in the cities, towns, and villages of the empire consisted of commoners or *macehualtin* (sing. *macehualli*). These worked lands belonging to the *calpoltin*; each family with its plot maintained rights over it as long as it did not lie unused for over two years at a time. Many of these farmers also had a *calmil*, or house garden, which was managed at the household level. The rural *macehualtin* formed the majority of commoners. These people lived in dispersed settlements, constructing small check dams and terrace systems to increase agricultural yield. The modest scale of rural dam and terrace systems suggests that they were organized by the *macehualtin* themselves, unlike the large-scale irrigation systems found throughout the empire that required state-level organization. Whether they had access to state-supported projects or not, all *macelhualtin* were required to pay tribute to their overlords, the Aztec nobility.

Near the top of the social ladder were the noblemen or *pipiltin* (sing. *pilli*), who were all the sons of lords: "precious feathers from the wings of past kings," as one source puts it. It was from their rank that the imperial administrators were drawn; these had the use of lands belonging to their office and also owned private lands. Yet the social stratification so apparent in Aztec life was not entirely rigid, for there were also *cuauhpipiltin*, "eagle nobles" – commoners who had distinguished themselves on the field of battle and who were rewarded for their gallantry with noble titles and with private lands.

Above the *pipiltin*, at the apex of the social pyramid, were the *teteuhctin* (sing. *tecuhtli*), the rulers of towns and cities; the emperor himself was a *tecuhtli*. These received the honorific suffix *-tzin* at the ends of their names, and were entitled to wear clothes of the utmost richness. From their palaces they exercised legal powers, and ensured that tribute payments were made to all appropriate levels of the imperial administration. As far as conquered territories were concerned, the Aztecs wisely followed a system of indirect rule, by leaving the indigenous *tecuhtli* and nobles in place, but demoting them to the status of middle- and lower-rank officials.

At the bottom of the social scale were the *mayeque*, bondsmen or serfs who tilled the estates of the noblemen. These, according to van Zantwijk, comprised about 30 percent of the empire's population, and were often former *macehualtin* who had lost their rights either through conquest or through suppression of rebellion. A study by Edward Hicks shows that the produce from about one third of the land worked by a serf went to his lord, while the rest could be retained by himself and his family (although he was expected to pay tribute from this). Some *mayeque* occasionally became richer and more powerful than the *macehualtin* through the inheritance of tangible property and other rights.

Slaves or *tlacohtin* ("bought ones") were persons who had not been able to meet their obligations, particularly gambling debts. Such individuals could pawn themselves for given lengths of time (including in perpetuity), or they might even be pawned by needy spouses or parents. The institution of slavery was closely defined under Aztec law: for instance, slaves could not be resold without their consent, unless they violated the rules frequently, in which case they might end up in the slave market. They were generally well treated; and often – as among the ancient Romans – they became domestic servants, farm laborers, and even estate managers. Some achieved considerable prosperity. Comely young female slaves could be taken by rulers as concubines, and were considered as suitable diplomatic gifts (witness the women presented to Cortés).

The long-distance merchants

Although relatively small in number, the long-distance merchants or *pochteca* constituted a powerful group in Aztec society. These were of far higher status than the ordinary market-vendors, for the emperor treated them like nobility, and if one of them died on an expedition, he went to the paradise of the Sun God like a fallen warrior. The *pochteca* were directly responsible to the royal palace and the *tlatoani*, for whom they traveled into foreign territories many hundreds of miles from the capital, to obtain luxury goods such as precious quetzal feathers, amber, and the like for the use of the crown. Allied with the *pochteca* was a more specialized group, the *oztomeca*, who went disguised in the local garb and who spoke the local language; their task was to gather military intelligence as well as exotic goods. Like the businessmen-spies of modern days, the *oztomeca* were often the vanguard for the Aztec takeover of another nation, acting sometimes as *agents-provocateurs*.

Membership in the *pochteca* was hereditary. There were twelve merchants' organizations or guilds, all located in the heart of the empire, and all under the control of the head merchants in Tenochtitlan-Tlatelolco. The most important commerce of this kind linked the capital with the tropical coasts of southeast Mesoamerica, particularly the Putún Maya port-of-trade at Xicallanco on the Gulf of Mexico; a key nodal point was the Aztec garrison town of Tochtepec, in northern Oaxaca, from which human caravans were sent out to the hot country, and to which they returned. It is apparent from detailed descriptions given by Father Sahagún that the goods exported largely consisted of cotton mantles and other textiles from the royal warehouses which had been received as tribute, along with cast-gold jewelry fashioned by Tenochtitlan's master craftsmen.

Because the *pochteca* could themselves pay taxes to the palace in luxury goods rather than the produce of their lands, and grew rich and powerful as a consequence, some have seen them as an entrepreneurial middle-class in formation. But there were powerful sanctions against them flaunting their wealth: as an example, they had to creep into the city at night after a successful trading expedition, lest they arouse the jealousy of the ruler. There was an additional leveling mechanism operating here, as Rudolf van Zantwijk has stressed. As a merchant rose up the social ladder of the guild, the special ceremony that he was obligated to give on his return from abroad became more and more costly. One of these was a Song Feast, a lavish banquet for a large number of guests; as he achieved even higher office within the *pochteca* organization, the ritual would include not only another and even more grand banquet (at which presents would have to be given out), but the human sacrifice of slaves bought in the market.

While this was a highly honorable enterprise, it was also a highly dangerous one, and many died of disease or injury on the road, or were slain. Because of this, the activities of the *pochteca* were surrounded by ritual dictated by the solar calendar. They even had their own gods, in particular Xiuhtecuhtli, the Fire God, and Yacatecuhtli ("Nose Lord"), a deity with a Pinocchio-like nose, a traveler's staff in one hand and a woven fan in the other.

Becoming an Aztec

The enculturation experience – turning an unformed human being into an Aztec – began at birth. After she had cut the umbilical cord, the midwife recited set speeches to the newborn. To an infant girl she would say:

> Oh my dear child, oh my jewel, oh my quetzal feather, you have come to life, you have been born, you have come out upon the earth. Our lord created you, fashioned you, caused you to be born upon the earth, he by whom all live, God. We have awaited you, we who are your mothers, your fathers; and your aunts, your uncles, your relatives have awaited you; they wept, they were sad before you when you came to life, when you were born upon the earth.[8]

A boy was told that the house in which he was born was not a true home, but just a resting place, for he was a warrior: "your mission is to give the sun the blood of enemies to drink, and to feed Tlaltecuhtli, the earth, with their bodies," in contrast to girls, who were admonished to be homebodies.

Baptism took place not long after birth, on an auspicious day in the 260-day calendar, with the midwife doing the washing and naming of the child. The sex roles were again emphasized, boys being given a miniature breech clout, a cape, a shield, and four arrows; and girls a little skirt (*cueitl*) and blouse (*huipilli*), along with weaving implements. The early Colonial Codex Mendoza shows that a child's subsequent upbringing was Spartan and strict. Until the age of fifteen, education took place in the family, a boy at first going out with his father to gather firewood, and later learning how to fish, a girl learning how to spin and later advancing to weaving and grinding of the *nix-tamal* for tortillas. Punishments for infractions were drastic: a disobedient boy might be left out naked to the night cold, pricked with maguey spines, or held over burning chile peppers.

In 1519, the Aztecs may have been the only people in the world with universal schooling for both sexes. This began at fifteen for all boys and girls, and lasted until they were of marriageable age (about twenty). There were two kinds of schools, the *calmecac* and the *telpochcalli*. The *calmecac* was a seminary, generally attached to a specific temple, attended by the sons and daughters of the *pipiltin*, but also by some *pochteca* children; in it, the priest-teachers instructed the students in all aspects of Aztec religion, including the calendar, the rituals, the songs which were to be chanted over the sacred books, and certainly much of the glorious past of the Aztec nation. Like the English public school, having attended a *calmecac* was a prerequisite to holding any kind of high office in the Aztec administration. Those who really wanted to enter the priesthood then passed to a kind of theological graduate school termed the *tlamacazcalli* ("priest's house") for further training.

The *telpochcalli* or House of Youths was basically a military academy, attended by the offspring of *macehualtin* (the commoners) and presided over by Tezcatlipoca, the god of warriors. As in the *calmecac*, the sexes were strictly segregated, and females were here assigned to a *cuicalco*, House of Song. Male students were trained in the martial arts, and could even take leave to accompany seasoned warriors as their squires on the field of battle, while girls seem to have concentrated on less bellicose subjects such as song and dance. Conditions in the male part of the academy seem to have been far less austere than in the *calmecac*, and some of our sources tell us that the cadets were often visited by ladies of pleasure in their communal quarters.

Marriage

For commoners, marriage took place at around the age of twenty; one was expected to marry someone within one's own *calpolli*. This union was considered to be a contract between families, not individuals, and was arranged by an old woman acting as go-between. This was a complicated matter, for consent had to be obtained not only from the prospective bride's family, but also from the young man's masters in the school he had attended. After an auspicious day in the 260-day calendar had been selected for the ceremony, there was an elaborate banquet in the bride's house, when she was arrayed and painted for the event. The actual marriage took place at night. First she was placed on the back of an old woman and borne in a procession to the groom's house by the light of torches. The young couple were placed on a mat spread before the hearth, they were given presents, and the union was finalized by the tying together of her blouse and his cloak, followed by feasting at which the old people were allowed to get drunk.

There may have been equality of the sexes in the sphere of education, but it was otherwise with matrimony. This being a male-oriented society, the new couple always made their home with the bridegroom's family. Moreover, a man could take as many secondary wives or concubines as he could afford: great princes and lords had dozens of such wives, sometimes even hundreds, and Nezahualpilli, the *tlatoani* of Texcoco, was said to have had 2,000 (and 144 children)! On the other hand, women seem to have had equal rights in divorce, which was never easy in any circumstance.

The Triple Alliance and the empire

A glance at a map showing the Aztec dominions as they were in 1519 would disclose that while the empire spanned the area between the Gulf of Mexico and the Pacific, it by no means included all of Mesoamerica. Left in place within it were enemy states like Tlaxcallan (which was to provide tens of thousands of quisling troops for Cortés), Huexotzingo, and Chollolan (Cholula). Under Axayacatl (1469–1481), the Aztec armies had tried to conquer the Tarascans, and been repelled once and for all, while much of southeastern Veracruz remained free of Aztec control, as did the entire Maya area. Nevertheless, this was an empire equivalent to those of the Old World, with an enormous population held in a mighty system whose main purpose was to provide tribute to the Valley of Mexico.

Nations which had fallen to Aztec arms and those of their allies in the Triple Alliance of Tenochtitlan, Texcoco, and Tlacopan were speedily organized as tribute-rendering provinces of the empire. Military governors in Aztec garrisons ensured that such tribute, which was very heavy indeed, was paid promptly and on fixed dates. Most of our sources state that on arrival in the Valley, this was distributed in a 2:2:1 ratio (Tenochtitlan and Texcoco got two-fifths each, and Tlacopan one-fifth). It is fortunate that the tribute list in Motecuhzoma's state archives has survived in the form of copies, for the Spaniards were also interested in what they could extract from the old Aztec provinces. Incredible as it may seem, each year Tenochtitlan received from all parts of the empire 7,000 tons of maize and 4,000 tons each of beans, chia seed, and grain amaranth, and no fewer than 2,000,000 cotton cloaks, as well as war costumes, shields, feather headdresses, and luxury products, such as amber, unobtainable in the central highlands. Certainly some of this loot, especially the cloaks, was farmed out by the royal treasury to the *pochteca* as barter goods to carry to distant ports of trade. But a good deal of the tribute acted as the main financial support of the state edifice, since in an essentially moneyless economy state servants had to be paid in goods and land, and artisans had to receive something for the fine products which they supplied to the palace. Each page of the tribute list covers one province, the various subject towns within it being listed vertically along the edge of the page. The names of these places are written by means of the rebus principle (the only form of script in use among the Aztecs, and employed exclusively for toponyms and personal names). Thus, the town called Mapachtepec ("Raccoon Hill") would be expressed by a hand (*ma-itl*) grasping a bunch of Spanish moss (*pach-tli*), over a picture of a hill (*tepe-tl*). Aztec numbers on the list were given in a

134

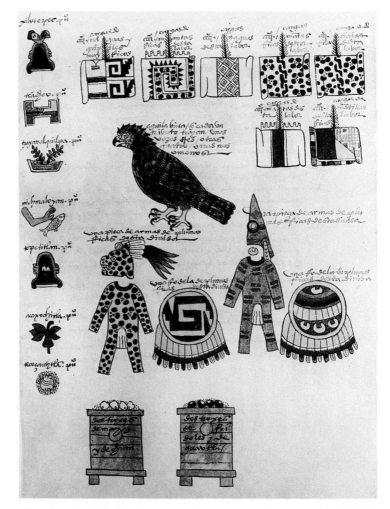

134 Page from the Codex Mendoza, a post-Conquest copy of an Aztec original. This is the tribute list of Motecuhzoma Xocoyotzin. Pictured on this sheet is the biannual tribute due from the six towns of Xilotepec, an Otomí-speaking province northwest of the Valley of Mexico. Enumerated are women's skirts and blouses, men's mantles of various sorts, two warrior's costumes with shields, four wooden cribs filled with maize, beans, and other foodstuffs, and an eagle.

vigesimal (base 20) system: 1–19 by dots or occasionally by fingers, 20 by a flag, 400 by a sign which resembles a feather or fir tree, and 8,000 by a bag or pouch.

Exempt from the payment of tribute were certain specialists like painters and singers, along with *pipiltin* who enjoyed the revenues from private lands, and outstanding warriors. Commoners, no matter where they were, had to pay both with maize ears and with labor, and each was expected to furnish one cotton mantle a year; merchants and ordinary artisans paid in the goods that they produced or that passed through their hands.

As the late scholar Fernando Horcasitas once said, the Aztec empire was not so much an empire in the Roman or British sense as an economic empire based on the provision of tribute, paid in full and on a regular basis. Obviously, some of the peoples participating under this arrangement were unwilling partners in the system, and chafed under the Aztec yoke. There was thus an inherent weakness in the empire that Cortés was quick to perceive and to exploit.

The emperor and the palace

The Aztec emperor was in every sense an absolute ruler, although only in certain domains. His Nahuatl title was *Huei Tlatoani* or "Great Speaker"; as the researches of Rudolf van Zantwijk have made clear, his function, like that of the "talking chiefs" among North American tribes, was principally to deal with the external side of the Aztec polity – warfare, tribute, and diplomacy. His counterpart handling the internal affairs of Mexico-Tenochtitlan was the man who held the office of *Cihuacoatl* or "Female Snake." Based on an Aztec female deity, the very title celebrates the opposition of male and female principles in the philosophy of dualism so dear to the Aztecs. This man acted as a kind of grand vizier, and was always a close relative of the *Huei Tlatoani*; the most famous *Cihuacoatl* of all was the great Tlacaelel, who transformed the Aztec realm from a kingdom into an empire.

The *Huei Tlatoani* was elected from the royal lineage by a council composed of the nobles, chief priests, and top war officers; at the same time, the four principal lords who were to act as his executive arm were also chosen. All sources agree on the openness of the process but, while many names were advanced during the convocation, only one was put forth by the council. The exact rules of Aztec dynastic succession are still being debated by scholars, but during the last hundred years of the empire brothers seem to have inherited the office more often than sons.

On his installation, the new king was taken by the chief priests to pay homage at the temple of the national god, Huitzilopochtli; while he censed the sacred image, the masses of citizens waited expectantly below, in a din caused by the blowing of shell trumpets. Four days were spent by the king in meditation and fasting in the temple, which included prayers and speeches in honor of Tezcatlipoca, the patron deity of the royal house. Before the image of this all-powerful god the new king stood naked, emphasizing his utter unworthiness in speeches like this:

> O master, O our lord, O lord of the near, of the nigh, O night, O wind...
> Poor am I. In what manner shall I act for thy city? In what manner shall I
> act for the governed, for the vassals [*macehualtin*]? For I am blind, I am
> deaf, I am an imbecile, and in excrement, in filth hath my lifetime been...
> Perhaps thou mistaketh me for another; perhaps thou seekest another in
> my stead.[9]

Then the *Huei Tlatoani* was escorted to his palace, which stood adjacent to the Sacred Precinct. To his coronation banquet came even the kings of distant lands, such as the rulers of the Tarascan kingdom, the king of the Totonacs (a puppet prince), and great personages from as far away as Tehuantepec.

The descriptions of the Spaniards make it clear that the *Huei Tlatoani* was semi-divine. Even great lords who entered into his presence approached in plain garments, heads bowed, without looking on his face. Everywhere he went, he was borne on the shoulders of noblemen in a litter covered with precious feathers. If he walked, nobles swept the way and covered the ground with cloths so that his feet would not touch the ground. When Motecuhzoma ate, he was shielded from onlookers by a gilt screen. No fewer than several hundred dishes were offered at each meal for his choosing by young maidens; during his repast he was entertained by buffoons, dwarfs, jugglers, and tumblers.

Motecuhzoma's gardens and pleasure palaces amazed the Spaniards. The royal aviary had ten large rooms with pools of salt and fresh water, housing birds of both lake and sea, above which were galleries bordered by hanging gardens for the imperial promenade. Another building was the royal zoo, staffed by trained veterinarians, in which were exhibited in cages animals from all parts of his realm – jaguars from the lowlands, pumas from the mountains, foxes, and so forth, making an unearthly clamor with their roars and howls. Carefully tended by servants, many kinds of deformed persons and monstrosities inhabited his private sideshow, each with his own room.

Less frivolous activities of the royal household included separate courts of justice for noblemen (and warriors) and for commoners; the overseeing by stewards of the palace storehouse; the maintenance of the state arsenal, officers' quarters, and the military academy; and the management of the empire-wide tribute system.

Food and agriculture

All of these state functions, the Aztec war machine, and the Aztec economy itself, ultimately rested on the agricultural basis of the Mexican peoples – the farming of maize, beans, squash, chile peppers, tomatoes, amaranth, chia, and a host of other cultigens. Thousands of canoes daily crowded the great lake, bearing these products to the capital either as direct tribute or as merchandise to be traded for craft items and other necessities in the marketplaces. A tremendous surplus for the use of the city was extracted from the rich *chinampas* fringing the shallow lake and from fields nearby, while the upper slopes of the surrounding hills were probably largely given over to the cultivation of maguey, the source of the mildly alcoholic beverage so important to Aztec culture.

Most of the Aztec people, from nobles to serfs, were very well fed, although Lucullan repasts and other excesses were proscribed by the puritanical Aztec ethic. Much of the diet of ordinary citizens consisted of tortillas dipped in a *molli* or sauce made of chiles ground with water; maize could also be taken in the form of steamed tamales, to which could be added ground or whole beans, but unlike their modern counterparts, these contained no fat or grease. Sahagún's informants gave him a long list of dishes with their ingredients, and these show that the Aztec cuisine was extremely sophisticated: for example, there were dozens of ways to prepare tamales, not just one. Meat and fish dishes were for the elite, or were reserved for feast days, while poorer people ate large quantities of greens instead. Although some of these are not to modern taste, many animal and plant species entered the Aztec cuisine, such as the *axolotl*, a large larval salamander found in *chinampa* canals which could be stewed in a sauce of yellow chiles, or tadpoles prepared in a variety of styles. Insects, in the form of eggs, larvae, and adults, were widely consumed, as was *tecuilatl*, a scum-like algae (*Spirulina* sp.) gathered from lake margins; this latter was pressed into cakes. A wide variety of fruits, from both the highlands and the tropical lowlands, were available in the markets, and highly appreciated.

Amaranth occupied a special place in the Aztec diet. This eminently nutritious grain crop was imported into the capital in large quantities, but it was destined not so much for the kitchens of ordinary folk as for ceremonial use: it was mixed with ground maize, along with honey or maguey sap, formed into idols of the great god Huitzilopochtli, and consumed in this manner on his feast days – to the horror of the Spanish priests, who saw this as a travesty of Holy Communion!

Maize could be consumed not only as tortillas and tamales, but also in liquid form, as a maize gruel called *atolli*; another kind of maize drink called *pozolli* was made from slightly fermented maize dough; both could be taken to the fields in gourd containers for the repast of farmers. Chocolate drinks were generally reserved for the elite and the wealthy, for the bean was expensive. Chocolate could be prepared in a variety of ways, with an array of flavors (such as chile pepper, vanilla, and other spices); it could even be mixed with *atolli*. As might be expected, given their ethic of moderation and austerity, the Aztecs were ambivalent about *octli* (called by the Spaniards *pulque*), the fermented sap of the maguey plant. One was not supposed to drink more than four cups during a feast, and drunkenness was punished with severity and even death; although old people were released from this prohibition and allowed to get thoroughly inebriated whenever they pleased. Nonetheless, *octli* played a major role in Aztec ritual, and there was a whole group of *octli* gods, as well as a major goddess of the maguey plant, about whom a mythic cycle was created.

War and human sacrifice

The Aztec army, like armies everywhere, traveled on its stomach, and the Aztec military successes which resulted in their empire were in part the outcome of their ability to supply their forces with food – principally dried tortillas – wherever they went. The main goal of the Aztec state was war. Every able-bodied man was expected to bear arms, even the priests and the long-distance merchants, the latter fighting in their own units while ostensibly on trading expeditions. To the Aztecs, there was no activity more glorious than to furnish captives or to die oneself for Huitzilopochtli:

> The battlefield is the place:
> where one toasts the divine liquor in war,
> where are stained red the divine eagles,
> where the jaguars howl,
> where all kinds of precious stones rain from ornaments,
> where wave headdresses rich with fine plumes,
> where princes are smashed to bits.[10]

In the rich imagery of Nahuatl song, the blood-stained battlefield was described as an immense plain covered by flowers, and lucky was he who perished on it:

> There is nothing like death in war,
> nothing like the flowery death
> so precious to Him who gives life:
> far off I see it: my heart yearns for it![11]

Aztec weapons were the terrible sword-club (*macuahuitl*), with side grooves set with razor-sharp obsidian blades; spears, the heads of which were also set with blades; and barbed and fletched darts hurled from the atlatl. Seasoned Aztec warriors were gorgeously arrayed in costumes of jaguar skins or suits covered with eagle feathers, symbolizing the knightly orders; for defense, Aztec troops were sometimes clad in a quilted cotton tunic and always carried a round shield of wood or reeds covered with hide, often magnificently deco-

pl. XVI   rated with colored designs in feathers. While the battle raged, high-ranking officers could be identified by ensigns worn on the shoulders – towering constructions of reeds, feathers, and the like, which made it all too easy for the soldiers of Cortés to identify and destroy them. Acting as mercenaries, fierce Otomí tribesmen accompanied the army as bowmen.

War strategy included the gathering of intelligence and compilation of maps. On the field of battle, the ranks of the army were arranged by generals. Attacks were spearheaded by an elite corps of veteran warriors, followed by the bulk of the army, to the sound of shell trumpets blown by priests. The idea was not only to destroy the enemy town but also to isolate and capture as many of the enemy as possible for transport to the rear and eventual sacrifice in the capital.

Although the Aztec authority Henry Nicholson has said that among the Aztecs "human sacrifice…was practiced on a scale not even approached by any other ritual system in the history of the world," many scholars are now convinced that this scale was immensely exaggerated by the Spaniards to justify their own violence and aggression against the New World natives. One of our Spanish sources, for example, reports that over 80,000 victims, all of them war captives, were dispatched to celebrate the dedication of the Great Temple in 1487, probably a physical impossibility. Yet it is true, as Nicholson has maintained, that "some type of death sacrifice normally accompanied all important rituals," a custom that surely goes back to the Olmecs; it was practiced in Teotihuacan, as the warrior sacrifices of the Temple of Quetzalcoatl so abundantly prove. In all likelihood, several hundreds, perhaps even a few thousand, young men so lost their lives in the Aztec capital each year, but there is no way to test this.

The victims were ideally enemy warriors; when an Aztec took a captive in action, he said to him, "Here is my well-beloved son," and the captive responded "Here is my revered father," establishing the kind of fictive kinship that characterized the warrior-captive relationship in the New World from the Tupinambá of Brazil to the Iroquois of New York State. All warriors believed that they were destined to die this way, being transformed on death into hummingbirds which went to join the Sun God in his celestial paradise.

After the victim had been ritually bathed, there were five possible modes of sacrifice. The usual one was by stretching the prone body over a sacrificial stone, opening the chest with a knife of flint or obsidian, and ripping out the heart, which was then offered to the gods in a *cuauhxicalli*, or "eagle vessel" of carved stone. A second was decapitation, but this was customarily reserved for female victims impersonating goddesses. A third method was gladiatorial sacrifice, in which the war captive was tethered to a round stone, and forced to defend himself against a seasoned warrior with a sword-club which lacked the usual obsidian blades; as Father Durán laconically says, "Whether one defended himself well or whether one fought badly, death was inevitable." Sacrifice of warriors strapped to scaffolds and shot with darts or arrows was another. And finally, there was heart sacrifice after the captive had been thrown repeatedly into a fire, probably the most unpleasant end of all.

It is incontrovertible that some of these victims ended up by being eaten ritually. That said, the sensational theory put forth by Michael Harner, that the Aztec elite practiced cannibalism on an allegedly massive scale so as to monopolize protein in a protein-poor environment, fails on two grounds: 1) there were abundant sources of protein available to the residents of the Valley of Mexico, not the least of which was *Spirulina* lake scum; and 2) a close reading of the historical records demonstrates that human flesh was eaten very sparingly and only during tightly controlled rituals – in fact, the practice was more like a form of communion than a cannibal feast.

Aztec religion

Aztec mythology and religious organization are so incredibly complex that little justice can be given them in the space of this chapter. The data that we have from the early sources, particularly from the pictorial books and from Fray Bernardino de Sahagún, are more complete in this respect than for any other Mesoamerican people.

The Aztec concept of the supernatural world was a result of the reconciliation by mystic intellectuals of the tribal gods of their own people to the far richer cosmogony of the older civilizations of Mexico, welding both into a single great system. The bewildering multiplicity of Mexican gods was to these thinkers but an embodiment of one cosmic principle of duality: the unity of opposites, as personified in the great bisexual creator deity, Ometeotl or "Dual Divinity." In Aztec philosophy, this was the only reality, all else being illusion. Ometeotl presided over a layered universe, dwelling in the thirteenth and uppermost heaven, while various celestial phenomena such as the sun, moon, stars, comets, and winds existed in lower heavens. Beneath the surface of the earth were nine stratified underworlds, through which the souls of the dead had to pass in a perilous journey until reaching extinction in the deepest level, Mictlan Opochcalocan, "The Land of the Dead, Where the Streets Are on the Left." This was presided over by another dual divinity, the dread "Lord and Lady of the Land of the Dead," the infernal counterpart of Ometeotl.

Out of the sexual opposition embodied in Ometeotl were born the four Tezcatlipocas. Like all the Mesoamericans and many other American Indian groups as well, the Aztecs thought of the surface of our world in terms of the four cardinal directions, each of which was assigned a specific color and a specific tree on the upper branches of which perched a distinctive bird. Where the central axis passed through the earth was the Old Fire God, an avatar of Ometeotl since his epithet was "Mother of the Gods, Father of the Gods." Of these four offspring, the greatest was the Black Tezcatlipoca ("Smoking Mirror") of the north, the god of war and sorcery, and the patron deity of the royal house, to whom the new emperor prayed on his succession to office. He was everywhere, in all things, and could see into one's heart by means of his magic mirror. This, the "real" Tezcatlipoca, was the giver and taker away of life and riches, and was much feared. The White Tezcatlipoca of the west was the familiar Quetzalcoatl, the lord of life and the patron of the priestly order.

135   Visually expressed on the famous Calendar Stone and other Aztec monuments was the belief that the world had gone through four cosmic ages or Suns (like the Hindu *kalpas*), each destroyed by a cataclysm; this process of repeated creations and destructions was the result of the titanic struggle between the Black Tezcatlipoca and Quetzalcoatl, in each of which one or the other would be triumphant and would dominate the next age. The previous age perished in floods, when the sky fell on the earth and all became dark. We ourselves live in the Fifth Sun, which was created at Teotihuacan when the gods gathered there to consider what to do. After each had declined in turn the honor of sacrificing himself to begin the world anew, the least and most miserable of them, "The Poxy (or Purulent) One," hurled himself in a great fire and rose up to the sky as the new Sun. Another god then repeated this altruistic act, rising as the Moon; but this luminary was casting rays as bright as the Sun, so to dim it the gods hurled a rabbit across the Moon's face, where it may still be seen.

Human beings had existed in the previous world, but they had perished. To recreate them, Quetzalcoatl made a perilous journey into the Underworld, stealing their bones from Mictlantecuhtli, "Lord of the Land of the Dead." When he reached the earth's surface, these were ground up in a bowl, and the gods shed blood over them from their perforated members. From this deed, people were born, but they lacked the sustenance that the gods had decreed for them: maize, which had been hidden by the gods inside a magic mountain. Here again Quetzalcoatl came to the rescue: by turning himself

135 Aztec Calendar Stone, part of the sculptural programme around the Great Temple.
The interior contains glyphs referring to the five cosmic ages, surrounded by the 20 day signs
of the sacred calendar. A central devouring deity represents the need for sacrifice.

into an ant, he entered the mountain and stole the grains which were to
nurture the Aztec people.

Central to the concepts of the Aztec destiny codified by Tlacaelel was the
official cult of Huitzilopochtli, the Blue Tezcatlipoca of the south. The
result of a miraculous birth from Coatlicue (an aspect of the female side of   pl. XV
Ometeotl), he was the tutelary divinity of the Aztec people; the terrible
warrior god of the Sun, he needed the hearts and blood of sacrificed
human warriors so that he would rise from the east each morning after a
nightly trip through the Underworld.

On the east was the Red Tezcatlipoca, Xipe Totec "Our Lord the Flayed   136
One." He was the god of spring and the renewal of the vegetation, imperson-
ated by priests and those doing penance, wearing the skin of a flayed captive –
the new skin symbolizing the "skin" of new vegetation which the earth puts
on when the rains come. At the end of twenty days the god impersonator

136 Stone head from the Great Temple excavations of Xipe Totec, god of spring and fertility, wearing the flayed skin of a sacrificial victim. Ht 11.9 cm.

could take the skin off, but by this time he "stank like a dead dog," as one source tells us.

Tlaloc was another nature god, the source of rain and lightning and thus central to Aztec agricultural rites; he could also be quadruple, so that there were black, white, blue, and red Tlalocs, but he was generally depicted as blue-colored, with serpent-like fangs and goggles over the eyes. One of the more horrifying of Aztec practices was the sacrifice of small children on mountain tops to bring rain at the end of the dry season, in propitiation of Tlaloc. It was said that the more they cried, the more the Rain God was pleased. His cult yet survives among central Mexican peasants, although humans have probably not been sacrificed to him since early Colonial days.

The cults were presided over by a celibate clergy. Every priest had been to a seminary at which he was instructed in the complicated ritual that he was expected to carry out daily. Their long, unkempt hair clotted with blood, their ears and members shredded from self-mutilations effected with agave thorns and sting-ray spines, smelling of death and putrefaction, they must have been awesome spokesmen for the Aztec gods.

137   The daily life of all Aztecs was bound up with the ceremonies dictated by the machine-like workings of their calendar. The Almanac Year (*tonalpo-hualli*) of 260 days was the result of the intermeshing of 20 days (given names like Crocodile, Wind, House, Lizard, etc.) with the numbers 1 to 13, expressed in their books by dots only. To all individuals, each day in the *tonalpohualli* brought good or evil tidings in accordance with the prognostications of the priests; but the bad effects could be mitigated, so that if a child was born on an unfavorable day, his naming ceremony could be postponed to a better one. For each of the twenty 13-day "weeks" there were special rites

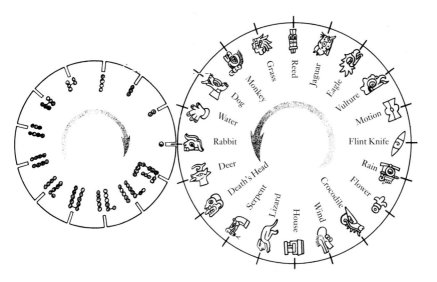

137 Schematic representation of the *tonalpohualli* or 260-day period of the Aztecs. The 20 named days intermesh with the numbers 1 to 13.

and presiding gods; there were also supernatural birds ruling over each of the 13 days of the "week," and a constantly repeating series of 9 gods who reigned during the night.

The Solar Year was made up of 18 named months of 20 days each, with an unlucky and highly dangerous period of 5 extra days before the commencement of the next year. Again, every month had its own special ceremonies in which all the citizens of the capital participated; given this kind of cycle, it is hardly surprising that the months were closely correlated with the agricultural year, but there must have been a constant slippage in this respect since neither the Aztecs nor any other Mesoamericans used Leap Years or any other kind of intercalation to adjust for the fact that the true length of the year is a quarter-day longer than 365 days. The Solar Years were named after one of the four possible names of the Almanac Year that could fall on the last day of the eighteenth month, along with its accompanying numerical coefficient.

Observations of the Sun, Moon, planets, and stars were carried out by the Aztec priests, and apparently even by the rulers, but they were not so advanced in this respect as the Maya. After the Sun, the most important heavenly body to the Aztecs was Venus, particularly in its first appearance, or heliacal rising, as Morning Star in the east, which they calculated took place every 584 days (the true figure is 583.92 days). While the Morning Star was thought to be the apotheosis of Topiltzin Quetzalcoatl, ruler of Tula, its heliacal rising was viewed as fraught with danger and they feared its rays at that time. It is a remarkable fact that every 104 Solar Years, all parts of their calendar coincided: the Almanac Year of 260 days, the Solar Year of 365 days, and the 584-day synodic period of Venus.

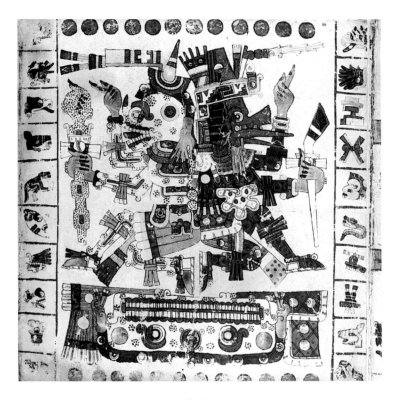

138 Page from the Codex Borgia, now in the Vatican Library. This, the finest of all Mexican manuscripts, might have been painted in Cholula, Puebla. The codex is of deerskin and is folded in screen fashion; it is 10.3 m long and 27 cm wide. The scene illustrates the dual aspect of existence, the Death God back-to-back with Quetzalcoatl, the Lord of Life. Around the edge of the page are various days from the 260-day count, one half assigned to the rule of one god and one half to the other. Mixteca-Puebla culture, Late Post-Classic period.

It was impressed on the Aztec mind that the close of every 52-year Calendar Round was a point at which the Fifth Sun could be destroyed. On this day, all fires in every temple, palace, and household were extinguished. On the Hill of the Star, just east of Colhuacan in the Valley of Mexico, the Fire Priests anxiously watched to see if the Pleiades would cross the meridian at midnight on this date; if they did, then the universe would continue. A fire was kindled on fire-sticks in the newly opened breast of a captive, and the glowing embers were carried by runners to every part of the Aztec realm.

138, 139   All this complex information was recorded in pictorial codices, folding-screen books of deerskin or bark paper, kept in the temples and seminaries by the priests. The state archives also included economic accounts, maps, and, possibly, historical works. Given the somewhat rudimentary nature of the Aztec script, such books must have been mainly mnemonic aids, to assist the priests in bringing to mind the details of immensely long oral recitations. It is a sad fact that, as a result of the massive book-burnings carried out by the Franciscan friars following the Conquest, no truly Aztec codices from the Valley of Mexico have survived. The Codex Borbonicus, preserved in the

139 Page from the Codex Borgia. Depicted is the host of the night sky. Represented here, reading from left to right and from top to bottom, are Mixcoatl, the Milky Way; the Traveler of the Southern Sky; Xolotl, the planet Venus; the Traveler of the Northern Sky; the Moon Goddess, before the moon; Tonatiuh, the Sun. Mixteca-Puebla culture, Late Post-Classic period.

library of the French Assembly, while dating from the very early Colonial period, probably comes close to what these may have looked like. Scholars are still debating the exact place of manufacture of demonstrably pre-Conquest ritual books like the magnificent Codex Borgia in the Vatican Library, or the Codex Cospi in Bologna, but it was probably within the confines of the empire.

The ritual round must have provided year-long excitement and meaning to the life of the ordinary citizen of Tenochtitlan, with feasts, decoration of the idols, and dances and songs to the accompaniment of two-toned slit drums, upright drums, conch-shell trumpets, rattles, and flutes. Homage to the gods prescribed individual penances and burning of blood-spattered paper, burning of perfumed copal incense, and immolation of hundreds or thousands of human captives yearly.

As has been said, the souls of warriors who had died under the sacrificial 140 knife or on the field of battle went not to the Land of the Dead in the Underworld, but directly to the Paradise of the Sun God. Curiously, so did the dread spirits of women who died in childbirth (for they also had fought their

140 Sacrificial knife of flint with mosaic-incrusted handle in the form of an Eagle Knight. Aztec culture, Late Post-Classic period. Length 30 cm.

"warrior" and lost); they rose dutifully from the west each day to greet the Sun at noon, conducting it into the nether regions. Others who too avoided extinction in Mictlan were those who had died in some manner connected with the Rain God: by lightning, drowning, or sufferers from dropsy and gout. They ascended to the Paradise of Tlaloc, where they spent an idyllic afterlife among flowers, butterflies, and other heavenly delights.

Most famous among the Aztec sacrifices was that of the handsome young captive annually chosen to impersonate the god Tezcatlipoca. For one year he lived a life of honor, worshipped literally as the embodiment of the deity; towards the end, he was given four beautiful maidens as his mistresses. Finally, he left them sadly, mounted the steps of the temple, smashing one by one the clay flutes on which he had played in his brief moment of glory, then was flung on his back so that the flint dagger might be plunged into his breast.

Aztec art and architecture

The Aztecs were the greatest sculptors seen in Mexico since the demise of the Olmec civilization, capable of turning out masterpieces from tiny works in semi-precious stones like rock crystal and amethyst, to truly monumental carvings. To some eyes, Aztec sculpture may be repulsive, and there is no doubt that the colossal figures of gods like Coatlicue may be terrifying, but there is no denying their awesome power. Power is also reflected in the more "realistic" works such as the seated stone figure of Xochipilli ("Prince of Flowers"), the god of love and summertime, which continue traditions of workmanship perfected by the Toltecs. Or, in the same vein, the lovely sculptured drum from Malinalco, which recalls the Nahuatl war song:

141

142

143

> The earth shakes: the Mexica begins his song:
> He makes the Eagles and Jaguars dance with him!
> Come to see the Huexotzinca:
> On the dais of the Eagle he shouts out,
> Loudly cries the Mexica.[12]

141 Colossal statue of Coatlicue, the old goddess of the earth and mother of gods and men. The head has been severed from the body, and two serpents rise from the neck, meeting to form a face. Her necklace is fashioned from human hearts and hands, with a pendant skull. The skirt is a web of writhing snakes. Since the goddess feeds on human corpses, her hands and feet are tipped with monstrous claws. Aztec, Late Post-Classic period. Ht 2.5 m.

143 (*above*) Carved wooden drum (*huehuetl*) from Malinalco, State of Mexico. The drum is carved in relief with scenes representing the "Flowery," or Sacred, War of the Aztecs, symbolized by dancing eagles and jaguars, the sign 4 Motion (the present age of the world), and, as seen here in the upper register, the figure of the Sun as an eagle. Aztec, Late Post-Classic period. Ht 1.15 m.

142 (*above*) Statue of Xochipilli, the Aztec "Prince of Flowers," patron god of dances, games, and love, and symbol of summertime. The god sits crosslegged on a temple platform which is adorned with a flower, butterflies, and clusters of four dots signifying the heat of the sun. He wears a mask and is decorated with hallucinogenic mushrooms and flowers from psychotropic plants, as well as with animal skins. Aztec, Late Post-Classic period. Ht of figure with base 1.2 m.

Aztec artisans in Tenochtitlan were arranged in an approximation of guilds and were famous for their fine work in feather mosaics; but they were hardly rivals to the great craftsmen of the Cholula area, who under influence from the Mixtecs in the south, Aztecs in the north, and possibly Tarascans in the west produced the magnificent Mixteca-Puebla style. Motecuhzoma himself would eat only from cups and plates of Cholula ware, and it is sure that much of the goldwork as well as practically all the fine masks and other

144

144 Polychrome pottery cup, from Cholula, Puebla. Three jaguars prance around the exterior of the bowl. Mixteca-Puebla culture, Late Post-Classic period. Ht 12 cm.

ceremonial paraphernalia of wood encrusted with turquoise mosaic were also manufactured there. The stupendous collection of mosaic pieces once in the hands of Charles V and now in the British Museum, in Florence, and in Rome bears eloquent testimony to late Mexican workmanship in this medium, although most examples are said to have been consumed in the *pietre dure* "laboratories" of Florence in the early nineteenth century.

pl. XIX

Aztec architecture was primarily ecclesiastical, rather than secular in nature. The leveling of the Sacred Precincts of Tenochtitlan and Tlatelolco by the Spaniards for their own administrative buildings, cathedral, and churches destroyed all but the foundations of the major Aztec temples, but some idea can be gained of their magnificence by those that remain elsewhere

145 Facade of Temple I, Malinalco, State of Mexico, a circular temple cut from the living rock. The work was carried out under orders from the Aztec emperors Ahuitzotl and Motecuhzoma Xocoyotzin, between AD 1501 and 1515 (in the Late Post-Classic period). The outer wall is now about 3 m high. Entrance to the interior was gained through a giant serpent face. Within can be seen an outspread eagle in the center of the floor and above it a feline and other eagles stretched out on a circular banquette.

146 Temple I at Malinalco as it is today, with its reconstructed thatched roof.

145, 146   in the Valley of Mexico, such as the huge double temple at Tenayuca, or the wonderful rock-carved sanctuary at Malinalco, circular and therefore certainly sacred to Quetzalcoatl.

147–52   It has long been known that the ruins of the Great Temple of Tenochtitlan were located a short distance to the northeast of the Cathedral, underneath the buildings of Colonial and modern-day Mexico City. The chance discovery in 1978 of a huge oval monument by workers digging a pit for the installation of power transformers led to one of the most important Aztec archaeological discoveries of all time. This stone lies directly at the base of the Huitzilopochtli side of the temple, directly in front of one of seven successive rebuildings which the temple had undergone since its foundation. It bears on its upper surface a deep relief of the dismembered body of the goddess Coyolxauhqui, the malevolent sister of Huitzilopochtli, and is one of the masterpieces of Aztec sculptural art.

To understand the significance of this monument, we must recount the legend which lies behind it. Huitzilopochtli, the terrible warrior god of the Sun, was the miraculous result of the impregnation of his widowed mother, Coatlicue ("She of the Serpent Skirt"), by a ball of feathers as she was sweeping one day on Coatepec ("Serpent Mountain"), near Tula. Angered by what they perceived as her dishonor, her 400 sons (the stars of the southern sky), egged on by their sister Coyolxauhqui (almost certainly an avatar of the Moon), decided to kill her; they eventually managed to behead Coatlicue, an event commemorated in a magnificent statue of the goddess, a pair of snakes representing the gushing blood issuing from her severed neck. Nevertheless, Huitzilopochtli emerged fully armed from her womb, and slew his sister Coyolxauhqui, hurling her body down from the summit of Coatepec, then pursued and defeated his 400 brothers – surely an astral myth of the defeat by the Sun of the Moon and the stars.

141

The importance of the legend, and of its confirmation by the find of the oval monument, is that the Huitzilopochtli side of the Great Temple was

147   Plan of the excavated foundations of the Great Temple, showing remains of the successive construction stages; the oldest is Stage II. The Coyolxauhqui Stone (ills. 150, 151) is associated with Stage IV. The conquistadores would have seen Stage VI.

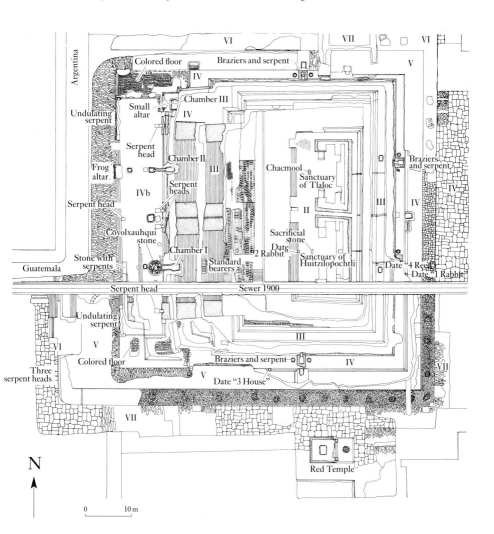

The Great Temple of Tenochtitlan

148 Polychrome jars, stone masks, and other offerings found in Chamber III beneath Stage IVb of the Great Temple.

149 Gruesome depictions in stone of skulls on a *tzompantli* or skullrack, excavated in the Great Temple precinct.

150 Colossal stone relief of the dismembered goddess Coyolxauhqui, discovered at the foot of an early building of the Great Temple of Tenochtitlan. Aztec culture, Late Post-Classic period. Longest dimension 3.4 m.

151 Detail of the Coyolxauhqui Stone, showing the severed head of the goddess; her cheek is marked with a golden bell.

152 Excavations in progress at the Great Temple site, looking northeast. The oldest remaining pyramid-platform (Stage II Temple) lies under the protective roof at right. The Coyolxauhqui Stone can be seen beneath the scaffolding near the center of the picture.

known to the Aztecs as "Coatepec." This would suggest that there was a representation of Coyolxauhqui in front of each successive Huitzilopochtli pyramid, and such seems to have been the case, since two earlier versions of the goddess were found in the right position in older renovations. The spectacular Coyolxauhqui find has led to a massive archaeological project for the Great Temple, with the clearing of the burden of post-Conquest structures.

The Mexican archaeological team under Eduardo Matos Moctezuma has found that the earliest stages of the Great Temple were remarkably crude, as was the associated statuary, in line with the traditional Aztec notion that their ancestors had truly been barbarians when they settled on their island. For example, the murals of the oldest structure were painted not upon plaster, but on mud-daubed walls. All stages of rebuilding were associated with offertory caches, the later ones often containing great deposits of objects from all over the empire, especially Mezcala figurines which the Aztecs had clearly looted from Late Preclassic burials in the newly conquered Guerrero; one remarkably fine Olmec mask even turned up in one offering.

From its earliest stages until the latest, the Great Temple was split between a right or south half, dedicated to the sun cult of Huitzilopochtli, and to a left or north half devoted to the worship of the Rain God, Tlaloc. In the offering caches in the latter were found marvelous, blue-painted Tlaloc vases in both pottery and stone, along with shells, coral, and the like imported from the sea, while a dread sacrificial stone is still in place in the floor of an early stage of the Huitzilopochtli temple. The Great Temple was the conceptual center of the Aztec universe, so it is no surprise that this immense construction expressed the ancient duality implicit in all Aztec life: the contrast between rain and crop fertility, on the one hand, and war and the continued survival of the Fifth Sun, on the other.

pl. XVIII

Aztec thought and literature

The amount of surviving literature in the Nahuatl language is truly remarkable; written down in the letters of the European alphabet after the fall of the Aztec nation, these texts have given us a view into native philosophy that has no parallel elsewhere in the New World. The language used by Aztec poets and thinkers is richly metaphorical, making abundant use of double epithets, in which paired nouns have a third, inner meaning, thusly:

Nahuatl	Translation	Meaning
Atl, tepetl	Water, mountain	City
Cuitlapilli, atlapilli	Tail, wing	The commoners
Petlatl, icpalli	Mat, seat	Rulership
Teoatl, tlachinolli	Divine water, blaze	War
Yollotli, eztli	Heart, blood	Cacao
Topco, petlacalco	In a box, in a coffer	Secretly
Teuhtli, tlazolli	Dust, filth	Evil, vice
Mixtitloan, ayautitlan	Out of the clouds, out of the mist	A wonder

References to supernaturals in the prayers and hymns are often shrouded in epithets, the divinity seldom being addressed by his or her true name. This was especially true of the awesome Tezcatlipoca, for whom were reserved such terms as "Lord of the Near, of the Nigh" (an epithet mistakenly applied by the early friars to the Christian God), "Night, Wind," "The Enemy on Both Sides," or "The Mocker." To be able to narrate such discourse, and to understand it, was the mark of an educated person.

The most stylized of these texts were the *Huehuetlatolli*, the "Orations of the Elders"; these were didactic discourses directed to children in the *calmecac* and *telpochcalli*, as well as to adults, and were highly embellished with these literary devices. Book 6 of Sahagún's encyclopedia of Aztec life presents these stock speeches in abundance, including the orations of parents to children, and orations delivered during *pochteca* banquets. From them, one may learn something of the mentality that enabled the Aztec people not only to survive misfortunes, disasters, and privations that would have broken others, but also to create one of the most advanced political states ever seen in Mexico. Raised in the most stern fashion in their homes and schools, trained to withstand cold and hunger, Aztec individuals embodied ideals which would have done credit to an "old Roman." Self-restraint and humility were expected even of those whose fortunes soared, including the emperors themselves.

> The mature man:
> a heart as firm as stone,
> a wise countenance,
> the owner of a face, a heart,
> capable of understanding.[13]

Not for them the megalomaniac self-esteem and lust for riches exhibited to the Aztec disgust by the Spaniards!

The image of the Aztec people as bloodthirsty savages bent only on rapine and murder – an image carefully fostered by the conquistadores – is belied by the great compendium of Nahuatl poetry preserved to us in the *Cantares Mexicanos*. Poetry was known as *in xochitl, in cuicatl*, "flowers, songs," and was recited in the royal courts to the accompaniment of the *teponaztli*, a log

153 The Old World meets the New, AD 1519. Cortés and friendly nobles of the Tlaxcalan state. From the *Lienzo de Tlaxcala*.

slit-drum played with rubber-tipped drumsticks; the tones and beats of the drum are given in nonsense syllables for some poems, such as *totocoto tototo cototo tiquititi titiqui tiquito*. Although some of the compositions celebrate war and death on the "flowery field" (the battleground), through many of them there runs a singular streak of melancholy and pessimism, a philosophical theme particularly developed by the closely allied Texcocan royal house, known for its learning and cultivation. The transitoriness of life on this earth and the uncertainty of the hereafter appear in a song ascribed to the *tlatoani* Nezahualcoyotl, the poet-king of Texcoco:

> I, Nezahualcoyotl, ask this:
> Is it true one really lives on the earth?
> Not forever on earth,
> only a little while here.
> Though it be jade it falls apart,
> though it be gold it wears away
> Not forever on earth,
> only a little while here.[14]

To another poet, Tochihuitzin Coyolchiuhqui, life itself is an illusion:

> Thus spoke Tochihuitzin,
> thus spoke Coyolchiuhqui:
> We only rise from sleep,
> we only come to dream,
> it is not true, it is not true,
> that we come on earth to live.
> As an herb in springtime,
> so is our nature.
> Our hearts give birth, make sprout,
> the flowers of our flesh.
> Some open their corollas,
> then they become dry.
> Thus spoke Tochihuitzin,
> thus spoke Coyolchiuhqui.[15]

Yet finally Nezahualcoyotl came to the realization that "flowers, songs" never perish, and it is only through them that the truly wise man will approach the ultimate reality, the dual creator divinity in whom all things are contained, the Giver of Life. As an artist paints a book, so he has painted us with flowers and songs:

> With flowers You paint,
> O Giver of life!
> With songs You give color,
> with songs You shade
> those who will live on the earth.

Later You will destroy eagles and jaguars:
we live only in Your painting
here, on the earth.

With black ink You will blot out
all that was friendship,
brotherhood, nobility.

You give shading
to those who will live on the earth.
We live only in Your book of paintings,
here on the earth.[16]

Epilogue

The Spanish Conquest

To the victor go not only the spoils, as the old saw would have it, but also the opportunity to tell the story of a victory without fear of contradiction. The Spaniards and generations of historians, including even the renowned William Prescott, have presented the Conquest of Mexico by a handful of brave and resourceful soldiers as the inevitable consequence of the cultural superiority of European over native cultures. As the Aztec scholar Inga Clendinnen has forcefully put it, "Historians are the camp-followers of the imperialists." Thanks to a closer and more critical reading of the sources, we can now see that there was considerable rewriting and often blatant distortion of the course of events, even with such otherwise impeccable figures as Father Sahagún. Particularly untrustworthy are the self-serving letters of Hernán Cortés to his sovereign Charles V, since that wily commander was acting illegally and without royal permission throughout his campaigns on Mexican soil.

In the history partially fabricated by the Spaniards, the Aztecs' terrible destiny had been preordained in the weak and vacillating figure of Motecuhzoma Xocoyotzin, held spellbound by a series of sinister omens, and by the myth of the "returning god-ruler": that Topiltzin Quetzalcoatl had come back in the person of Cortés himself. According to these accounts, now held in suspicion by specialists in Aztec culture, strange portents had appeared to the terrified monarch in the final ten years of his reign. The first of these was a great comet "like a tongue of fire, like a flame, as if showering the light of the dawn." Then, in succession, a tower of the Great Temple burned mysteriously; the water of the lake foamed and boiled and flooded the capital; and a woman was heard crying in the night through the streets of Tenochtitlan. Two-headed men were discovered and brought to the ruler, but they vanished as soon as he looked at them. Worst of all, fisherfolk snared a bird like a crane, which had a mirror on its forehead; they showed it to Motecuhzoma in broad daylight, and when he gazed into the mirror, he saw the shining stars. Looking a second time, he saw armed men borne on the backs of deer. Consulting his soothsayers, they could tell him nothing, but Nezahualpilli, King of Texcoco, forecast the destruction of Mexico.

Inflicting great cruelties on his magicians for their inability to forestall the doom that he saw impending, the Aztec monarch was said to be dumbfounded when an uncouth man arrived one day from the Gulf Coast and demanded to be taken into his presence. "I come," he announced, "to advise you that a great mountain has been seen on the waters, moving from one part

154 Nezahualpilli, *tlatoani* of Texcoco, attired for a dance. From the Codex Ixtlilxochitl, folio 108r

to the other, without touching the rocks." Quickly clapping the wretch in jail, he despatched two trusted messengers to the coast to determine if this was so. When they returned they confirmed the story previously told, adding that strange men with white faces and hands and long beards had set off in a boat from "a house on the water." Secretly convinced that these were Quetzalcoatl and his companions, he had the sacred livery of the god and food of the land offered to them, which they immediately took back with them to their watery home, thus confirming his surmises. The gods had left some of their own foods in the form of sweet-tasting biscuits on the beach; the monarch ordered the holy wafers to be placed in a gilded gourd, covered with rich cloths, and carried by a procession of chanting priests to Tula of the Toltecs, where they were reverently interred in the ruins of Quetzalcoatl's temple.

The "mountain that moved" was in reality the Spanish ship commanded by Juan de Grijalva, which after skirting the coast of Yucatan made the first Spanish landing on Mexican soil in the year 1518, near modern Veracruz. This reconnaissance was followed up in 1519 by the great armada that embarked from Cuba under the leadership of Hernán Cortés. The peoples of the Gulf Coast, some of whom were vassals of the Aztec *Huei Tlatoani*, put up little resistance to these strange beings, and Cortés soon learned of their disaffection with the Aztec state and with the heavy tribute that they had been forced to pay. On their way to the Valley of Mexico and the heart of the empire, the conquistadores met with opposition from the Tlaxcallans; after crushing these fierce enemies of the Triple Alliance, Cortés gained them as willing allies; the Tlaxcallans would come to play a key role in the overthrow of Mexican civilization.

A figure crucial to Cortés' plans was his native interpreter and mistress, known to history as La Malinche. This beautiful and intelligent woman was of noble birth, and had been presented to Cortés by a merchant prince of coastal Tabasco. Much of his success in dealing with the Aztecs must be attributed to the astuteness and understanding of this remarkable personage. But misunderstandings nevertheless seem to have been the rule in the con-frontation and clash of these two cultures. For instance, far from being held in thrall by a view of Cortés as the returned Quetzalcoatl, Motecuhzoma appears to have dealt with him as what he said he was, namely, an ambassador from a distant and unknown ruler. As such, Cortés had to be treated with respect and hospitality. Welcomed into the great capital and even into the royal palace, Cortés chose to take his host captive, to the chagrin and disgust of the *Huei Tlatoani*'s subjects.

The dénouement of this tragic story is well known. Learning that a rival military expedition under Panfilo Narváez had been sent to Veracruz by his enemy the governor of Cuba, with orders for his arrest, Cortés moved down to the coast and defeated the interlopers. On his return to Tenochtitlan, he found the capital in full revolt. During the uprising, Motecuhzoma was killed – the Spaniards being the likely perpetrators – and the booty-laden conquis-tadores were forced to flee the city by night, with great loss of life.

Thus ended the first phase of the Conquest. Withdrawing to the friendly sanctuary of Tlaxcallan, the invaders recovered their strength while Cortés made new plans. Eventually, both armies met in a pitched battle on the plains near Otumba, a confrontation in which Spanish arms triumphed. Then, joined by his ferocious allies from Tlaxcallan, Cortés once again marched against Tenochtitlan, building an invasion fleet along the shores of the Great Lake. The siege of Tenochtitlan began in May 1521, and ended after a heroic defense led by Cuauhtemoc, the last and bravest of the Aztec emperors, on 13 August of that year. There then ensued a blood bath at the hands of the revengeful Tlaxcallans that sickened even the most battle-hardened conquistadores. Although Cortés received Cuauhtemoc with honor, he had him hanged, drawn, and quartered three years later. The Fifth Sun had indeed perished.

How was it that a tiny force of about 400 men had been able to overthrow a powerful empire of at least 11 million people? First of all, there is little ques-tion that the weaponry of these men of the Renaissance was superior to the essentially Stone Age armament of the Aztecs. Thundering cannon, steel swords wielded by mounted horsemen, steel armor, crossbows, and mastiff-like war dogs previously trained in the Antilles to savor the flesh of Indians – all contributed to the Aztec downfall.

A second factor was that of Spanish tactics. The Spaniards fought by rules other than those that had prevailed for millennia in Mesoamerica. To the Aztecs, as Inga Clendinnen has noted, "battle was ideally a sacred duel between matched warriors"; in fact, before the Aztecs waged war on a town or province, they would often send them arms to make sure that the contenders were so matched. The "level playing field" meant nothing to the Spaniards, whom the Aztecs perceived as cowards – they shot their weapons at a distance, avoided hand-to-hand combat with native warriors, and took refuge behind their cannons; the Spaniards' horses were held in far higher estimation! Equally incomprehensible and thus devastating to the Aztecs' defense was the Spanish policy of wholesale terror, so well exemplified by the act of Cortés in cutting off the hands of over 50 Tlaxcallan emissaries admitted in peace into the Spanish camp, or the massacre of vast numbers of unarmed warriors at the order of the terrible Pedro de Alvarado, while they were dancing in a feast.

Thirdly, the role played by thousands upon thousands of seasoned Tlaxcallan warriors – the deadliest enemies of the Triple Alliance – can hardly be overlooked. Not only were they vital to the defeat of the Aztec empire, but they continued to serve as an auxiliary army in the conquest of the rest of Mesoamerica, even participating in the takeover of the highland Maya states.

But most significant of all was that invisible and deadly ally brought by the invaders from the Old World: infectious disease, to which the New World natives had absolutely no resistance. Smallpox was apparently introduced by a black who arrived with the Narváez expedition of 1520, and ravaged Mexico; it had decimated central Mexico even before Cortés began his siege. Along with measles, whooping cough, and malaria (and perhaps yellow fever as well), it led to a terrible mortality that must have enormously reduced the size and effectiveness of Aztec field forces and led to a general feeling of despair and hopelessness among the population. Given these four factors, it is a wonder that Aztec resistance lasted as long as it did. The completeness of the Aztec defeat is beautifully defined in an Aztec lament:

> Broken spears lie in the roads;
> we have torn our hair in our grief.
> The houses are roofless now, and their walls
> are red with blood.
>
> Worms are swarming in the streets and plazas,
> and the walls are splattered with gore.
> The water has turned red, as if it were dyed,
> and when we drink it,
> it has the taste of brine.
>
> We have pounded our hands in despair
> against the adobe walls,
> for our inheritance, our city, is lost and dead.
> The shields of our warriors were its defense,
> but they could not save it.[17]

New Spain and the Colonial world

Within the space of about three years following the fall of Tenochtitlan, most of Mexico between the Isthmus of Tehuantepec and the Chichimec frontier had fallen to the Spaniards and their grim Tlaxcallan allies. During this period, there were a number of native revolts (such as occurred among the Tarascans), but these were quickly suppressed. This vast territory became organized as New Spain, with a viceroy responsible to the Spanish king through the Council of the Indies.

The conquistadores had not been ordinary soldiers, but adventurers expecting riches. To placate them, the Crown granted them *encomiendas*, in which each *encomendero* would receive tribute payments from vast numbers of Indians; in return, the *encomendero* would ensure that their souls would be saved through conversion to Christianity. In time, this led to incredible abuses against the natives, and in 1549 a new system, *repartimiento*, was substituted, in which the natives were theoretically supposed to get fair wages for their labor. However, through the cupidity of their Spanish overlords and bureaucratic abuse, *repartimiento* swiftly turned into a system of forced labor.

Almost immediately following the Conquest, Mexico's social, economic, and religious life were transformed; even the landscape suffered immense changes. The fate of the elite class that had ruled the old pre-Spanish cities was two-fold: many of them disappeared altogether, and with them the elite culture that they had created, while others – perhaps more pliant – were given titles by the new regime and used as tribute and labor gatherers; it was these latter who were significant agents of acculturation, as they were converted to the new religion and learned the Castilian language.

The great native cities and towns of Mexico were leveled, along with thousands of pagan temples, to be replaced by urban settlements laid out on the grid pattern favored by the authorities in urban America. The old *calpoltin* became barrios, and the *calpolli* temples parish churches.

The economic transformation of Mexico began with the introduction of chickens, pigs, and the herd animals so important to life in the old country, cattle, horses, sheep and goats (the two latter contributing to the destruction of the landscape through overgrazing); iron tools and the plow; European fruit trees, and crops like wheat and chickpeas (the Spaniards initially spurned native foods such as maize and beans). The *repartimiento* system led to the growth of vast *haciendas*, at first dependent upon forced labor; after abolition in later centuries, this was transformed into debt bondage, a state of affairs that was to last until the Mexican Revolution. New Spain proved to be the Spanish empire's richest source of silver, and hundreds of thousands of natives were put to work in the silver mines under the most terrible conditions.

In line with the doctrine promulgated by the papacy – that the New World natives had souls and thus must not be enslaved but converted to the True Faith – the conquistadores were truly serious about conversion. This task was placed in the hands of the mendicant orders, and twelve Franciscan friars duly arrived in the newly founded Mexico City (built on the ruins of Tenochtitlan); as they walked unshod and in patched robes through the city's streets, the native population was truly awestruck by their poverty and sincerity. The Franciscans viewed the Indians with paternalistic kindliness, and saw them as raw material on which to fashion a new, Utopian world, free from the sins that were so apparent in the Spanish settlers. They quickly learned Nahuatl, and began early to instruct the sons of the native nobility in Christian values and learning. Naturally, they came into frequent conflict with the *encomenderos*. Other orders soon followed – Augustinians, Dominicans, and eventually the Jesuits.

Conversion, though, was often only skin deep and, later on in the sixteenth century, the secular and religious clergy came to recognize this. The basic similarity between many aspects of the Aztec religion and Spanish Catholicism has led to a syncretism between the two that persists today in the more indigenous parts of Mexico: there truly were (and often are) "idols behind altars." The Church's attempts to stamp out paganism, however, were hampered by the exemption that Indians had from the investigations of the Inquisition, and many old beliefs and practices flourished, particularly in the field of medicine.

Away from the mines and the great *haciendas*, many Indian communities preserved their self-sufficiency, and had their own lands. These were known as "*Repúblicas de Indios*," and were organized on the Spanish *cabildo* system of town administration. On top was an elected governor, in early years often a native noble. Below him were *alcaldes* (judges for minor crimes or civil suits) and *regidores* (councillors who legislated laws for local matters). At first, all electors were from the nobility, but as this dwindled, the commoners or *macehualtin* took over. Under the friars' tutelage, native communities had adopted the religious cofraternities so important to Spanish life, and these became intertwined with the *cabildo* system: one advanced in this civil religious hierarchy through a series of *cargos*, or burdensome offices, that became more and more costly as one achieved ever higher rank and honor. One can see such a hierarchy in many indigenous communities today.

The "ladinoization" of Mexico

As historian Woodrow Borah has demonstrated, after 1600 New Spain entered a profound "Century of Depression," when supplies of both food and labor suffered an enormous drop. That this was a direct result of a crash in the Indian population is shown by the following figures: in 1519, on the eve of the Conquest, there were an estimated 11 million souls in central Mexico; by the close of the sixteenth century, there were only about 2½ million Indians left, and by 1650 no more than 1½ million, just 13.6 percent of the pre-Conquest total. While the Spanish clergy was prone to ascribe this demographic disaster to the allegedly drunken habits of their charges, it is clear that the major cause was a series of great epidemics, beginning in 1520 but especially drastic in 1545–46 and 1576–79. Intolerable working conditions in the silver mines and on the great estates certainly added to the toll.

At the same time that the Indian demographic collapse was taking place, the white and *mestizo* (mixed) population was steadily increasing. When the great sugarcane *haciendas* were established in the Gulf Coast lowlands, landowners like Cortés had imported African slaves, and these certainly contributed to the racial mixture in those areas. But it was the people of mixed Indian-white race, or *ladinos* as they are known, who came to represent the majority of the Mexican people, at least toward the end of the Colonial era. Peninsular Spanish notions of purity of race and superiority of the Catholic religion were transformed during the centuries to a system of values in which hispanicized people of light skin, wearing European clothing and living in or near the center of a community, having Spanish surnames and able to read and write, were considered inherently far better than the darker skinned, "superstitious," frequently illiterate Indians. Accordingly, the *ladinos* came to occupy the middle rank of the political and economic hierarchy, while the Indians occupied the lowest. This is the situation that yet prevails in many parts of Mexico. If there had been no demographic catastrophe among the natives, the political and cultural status of the native population would have been very different indeed.

Aftermath

The independence from Spain that Mexico had achieved by 1821 did little to ameliorate the unhappy lot of its indigenous people; in fact, the Crown and the Church had been the principal protectors of native rights throughout Colonial history, against the abuses of the settlers. For much of the nineteenth century, Mexico was in the throes of continuous wars, a situation only brought to an end with the dictatorial regime of Porfirio Díaz, himself a largely Zapotec *ladino* from Oaxaca. The Mexican Revolution which began in 1910 brought sweeping changes to the Mexican countryside, and thus to the native peoples who were mainly poor, rural peasants. The old *haciendas* were broken up and the land distributed to farming communities in the form of *ejidos*, communal land-holding groups supposedly based (according to Revolutionary ideology) on Aztec institutions. Debt slavery was abolished.

Especially under the radical presidency (1934–40) of Lázaro Cárdenas, the rights of Indians to economic well-being were at last recognized by the Mexican government. With the establishment of a National Indigenous Institute, rural schools and economic assistance centers were set up in native communities. But the goal of these government programs remains incorporation of these communities into "national life," in other words "ladinoization" in modern dress. Every effort is made to wean people away from their language and from their traditional culture, a process that has been accelerated in some areas where massive hydroelectric projects have uprooted many thousands of native peoples from their traditional lands.

Like "Fourth World" populations elsewhere in the "Third World," where rapid economic development is the national goal, the right of Mexico's original inhabitants to their own cultures and their own languages is under constant pressure. Whether they will be able to maintain their cultural integrity as change becomes inevitable remains to be seen.

Visiting Mexico

General information

Mexico is one of the richest archaeological zones in the world. While interesting and breathtaking sites may be found in the northern half of the country, the huge majority of the larger and more important sites are located south of the Tropic of Cancer. There are literally thousands of sites in this area: some of these are grand capitals, but many more are villages and small towns. Most of the latter are found on private property, have not been excavated, and are not open to visitors. Even so, it would take many years to visit the hundreds of sites that have been excavated to some extent and are open to tourists. Those with only a few weeks at their disposal should concentrate on the most accessible and well-known sites; often these have engaging museums attached and good accommodations nearby. For those willing to leave the beaten track and put up with less-than-luxurious lodging, there are ruins across the country that are no less spectacular and a good deal less crowded.

Mexico is a land of extreme physical contrasts: the experience of lush tropical regions abutting snow-covered peaks is one that shapes the travel experience, as it has shaped much of the country's history. All but the simplest itinerary will bring the traveler from the cool nights of Mexico City and environs to the hot, humid tropical lowlands of Veracruz and Tabasco. You will need a sweater for the higher elevations and loose-fitting, comfortable clothing for the lowlands. Sturdy, comfortable shoes are a must in both areas.

When deciding on a season for your trip, remember that Mexico has two: a winter dry season and a summer rainy season. Traditional wisdom often holds that the best time to visit the area is during the dry season, when visits are not interrupted by tropical downpours. That said, these rains are often predictable, occurring in the afternoon or early evening, just as the heat reaches a maximum. In many areas the rains revivify a landscape that has become brown and rather drab over the course of the dry season. In either season the sun can be strong, even dangerous, during the middle of the day. Keep a hat and other sun protection handy at all times, as well as a canteen of purified water.

Medical advice can be found in any good travel guide to Mexico and Central America. The most common complaint afflicting not only tyros but also seasoned archaeologists, is the ubiquitous *turista* – travelers' diarrhea – which can make an otherwise enjoyable trip a misery. Prevention is imperative here. Under *no* circumstances should one drink any water other than that from sealed bottles or which has been boiled for at least 20 minutes; ice is equally treacherous. And one should avoid salads, uncooked vegetables and garnishes, and the skins of unpeeled fruits. The good news is that most cases of *turista* clear themselves up in a few days.

Mexico offers a tremendous range of transportation, from the adequate airline systems to remarkable first-class bus services. Reaching truly out of the way ruins may prove more challenging, however, and for those visitors with ample funds, car rental gives a great deal of freedom and the ability to cover many more sites than would be possible by public transportation. A few sites, such as Cantona, Puebla, can only be reached by private car, but the great majority can be accessed by public transportation of some sort.

Should one hire a guide? One of the advantages of an organized tour is that one's group is almost always accompanied by a professional archaeologist or art historian, well versed in ancient Mexican culture history. Locally hired guides may or may not have been adequately trained, and it is best that they come recommended by a specialist. The true aficionado of ancient Mexico would do well to read as much as possible beforehand, beginning with some of the key works cited in the bibliography of this book.

Good site maps for the major ancient Mexican sites are available in various publications. It is always a good idea to have photocopies of these in hand, as well as a pocket compass to aid in orientation, when exploring a particular ruin.

The "must-see" sites

These are the cities that stand above the rest in historical importance and spectacular architecture and art. While specialists and travel buffs differ on their favorite lesser-known sites, several appear on everyone's list: Teotihuacan, Tula, Tenochtitlan (Templo Mayor), Xochicalco, Monte Albán; Mitla in the highlands, and El Tajín and the La Venta monument park in the lowlands. These sites encompass the great majority of ancient Mexican history, from the earliest cities to the Aztec capital. No one who has failed to see these can really be said to know ancient Mexico. Most of the above sites require more than one day to know well, and the giant Teotihuacan warrants a good deal more time. Add to this the spectacular National Museum of Anthropology in Mexico City, with objects from around ancient Mexico and a portion of the Maya area, which also requires at least two days to acquaint oneself with adequately.

There are, of course, many dozen "lesser" sites, some of which rival or surpass most of the above in size, but these are so little excavated or so hard to get to that only the more dedicated enthusiasts would find it worth the difficulties which must be overcome to visit them. Other secondary centers reward the visitor without being too difficult of access: among the most notable of these are Xochitecatl and Cacaxtla, Cuicuilco, Malinalco, Yagul, La Quemada and Zempoala. Casas Grandes (Paquimé) in the far north, about three hours from El Paso, Texas, is the closest important ruin to the United States and well worth a visit.

Around Mexico City are Teotihuacan, Tula, Templo Mayor, and the National Museum of Anthropology. Teotihuacan is a one-hour drive or bus ride from Mexico City, making it an easy day trip from the capital. The site is an overwhelming experience if attempted in a day, however, and accommodations nearby are often a good idea if you are exploring over two days or more. There are several layers to any visit to Teotihuacan: the sheer scale of the Avenue of the Dead and its twin pyramids, the smaller but profusely decorated Temple of the Feathered Serpent and its stadium-sized court, and the intimate murals decorating the apartment compounds that cluster around the monumental center. Add to this two recently created museums of very high quality at the site, and it is easy to understand how one could spend at least three days at this site alone.

Also just north of Mexico City is the Toltec capital of Tula. While lauded in Aztec accounts as the fount of all artistry, the city was stripped by these same Aztecs of much of its finery, with some of the booty taken back to Tenochtitlan and used in the decoration of Aztec structures. While Tula is now a shadow of its former self, the reliefs of Pyramid B still enthrall, as does a trip to the top of that temple where the monumental warrior figures survey the Tula valley.

The remains of the most sacred Aztec pyramid may now be visited in the center of Mexico City, only steps from the Cathedral. Here one is struck by the complex layering of Latin American civilization, as each pyramid is covered by the next, grander pyramid only to be buried in turn by Spanish princely houses and the great Cathedral. The dramatic presentations in the accompanying museum, most culled from the deposits placed in the pyramid itself, are also well worth a visit.

No trip to Mexico is complete without time spent at the National Museum of Anthropology, located in Chapultepec Park near the center of Mexico City. While exhibits on the Maya area are artificially cropped at the nation's boundaries, the entire extent of ancient Mexican culture is on display here, from Casas Grandes (Paquimé) in the north to Oaxaca and Veracruz in the south. The large culture areas are each given their own rooms, with an introductory hall and an early cultures room just to the right of the entrance. Don't try to do the entire museum in one day: like other great world museums, this one rewards multiple visits and long stays near captivating displays. The Aztec room is particularly noteworthy, for unlike other sites or cultures that have major museums elsewhere, the National Museum itself is the central repository for the most important Aztec sculpture.

Xochicalco and environs

The state of Morelos is home to some of the most beautifully sited ruins in all of ancient Mexico. The easiest way to reach Xochicalco is via Cuernavaca, the starting point for many of the buses that pass by the ruins. The hilltop siting is magnificent, and the recently constructed museum houses many of the major finds of the last 40 years of archaeology at the site. The heart of any trip to Xochicalco is a visit to the Pyramid of the Plumed Serpent, with its monumental, deeply cut reliefs. The Aztec site of Malinalco, with its temple cut into the living rock overlooking the colonial town of the same name, is further along the same road. Chalcatzingo, a major Preclassic ruin also beautifully situated, is reachable from Cuernavaca.

Monte Albán and Mitla

The Valley of Oaxaca is a destination all its own, with a fascinating and important melange of Colonial and indigenous, surrounded by arid but stunning mountains. On the outskirts of Oaxaca City and easily reached from there is Monte Albán, the Classic capital of the Zapotec people and home to early writing and imagery as well as important Classic-period buildings and sculpture. The hilltop siting with its view down the arms of the valley is breathtaking, as it must have been for the lords of the place at its apogee. A much more intimate courtly society may be seen at the later Mitla, at the eastern end of the Valley of Oaxaca and easily reachable from Oaxaca City. The valley sites of Yagul and Dainzú are also well worth a visit if time permits, although this would require at least two days and preferably a rental car.

The Veracruz Coast:
El Tajín and the La Venta Monument Park

El Tajín may be accessed from Poza Rica or Papantla in northern Veracruz; the latter has a strong indigenous (Totonac) presence and a much more pleasant town center. Unlike the highland sites, the heat here is intense and it is best to start your tour as early as possible. But the beautifully proportioned architecture and the wealth of striking relief sculpture and mural painting here make any hardships bearable. Don't miss Structure I, in the area called Tajín Chico that overlooks the rest of the site. Inside this building are striking, well-preserved murals. Much farther down the coast is Villahermosa, the capital of Tabasco state. Many of the sculptures of the great Olmec site, La Venta, were moved here and given a park setting after the site itself became an oil field. Although the city itself lacks charm, the presence of such important early sculptures within easy reach of the traveler makes this a must-see, especially if one is then heading into Maya country. If Villahermosa is not a convenient destination, then the regional museum at Xalapa, Veracruz, between El Tajín and Villahermosa, is more than adequate as a substitute, with many of the great Olmec pieces housed in a superb building. In addition to the Olmec, here one finds the major collections of Classic Veracruz culture, including a recent reconstruction of important murals, as well as the life-size ceramic sculptures found to the south. All of this lies in an extremely pleasant colonial town center with a lively cafe and night life, due largely to the University of Veracruz. Xalapa is a major bus hub which may be reached easily from the coast or from Mexico City.

Recommended reading

Coe, Andrew. *Archaeological Mexico: A Traveler's Guide to Ancient Cities and Sacred Sites*. Chico, California, 2nd edn. 2001.
Kelly, Joyce. *An Archaeological Guide to Central and Southern Mexico*. Norman, Oklahoma 2001.

Reigning Monarchs of the Aztec State

Acamapichtli (1375–1395)

Huitzilihuitl (1396–1417)

Chimalpopoca (1417–1426)

Itzcoatl (1427–1440)

Motecuhzoma Ilhuicamina (1440–1469)

Axayacatl (1469–1481)

Tizoc (1481–1486)

Ahuitzotl (1486–1502)

Motecuhzoma Xocoyotzin (1502–1520)

Cuitlahuac (1520)

Cuauhtemoc (1520–1525)

Text References

References 1–5, 7, and 10–13 were translated by Michael Coe from Spanish versions of the original Nahuatl texts. Other translations are as follows: 6, A.P. Maudslay; 8, Louise Burkhart; 9, Charles E. Dibble and Arthur J.O. Anderson; 14–17, Miguel León-Portilla.

1 M. León-Portilla, *Los Antiguos Mexicanos a través de sus Crónicas y Cantares*, pp. 1–2. Mexico City 1961.
2 Op. cit., p. 23.
3 Op. cit., p. 26–7.
4 A.M. Garibay, *Historia de Literatura Nahuatl*, p. 316. Mexico City.
5 León-Portilla, op. cit., p. 33.
6 B. Díaz del Castillo, *The Discovery and Conquest of Mexico*. Routledge and Kegan Paul, London 1938. By permission.
7 León-Portilla, op. cit., p. 63.
8 Unpublished translation by Louise Burkhart, from Book 6, Sahagún. By permission.
9 B. de Sahagún, *General History of the Things of New Spain*, Book 6, p. 42. Santa Fe 1969. By permission.
10 Garibay, op. cit., p. 76.
11 Garibay, op. cit., p. 215.
12 A.M. Garibay, *Poesia Nahuatl*, vol. 3, p. 20. Mexico City 1968.
13 León-Portilla, op. cit., p. 147.
14 M. León-Portilla, *Fifteen Poets of the Aztec World*, p. 80. © 1992 University of Oklahoma Press, Norman.
15 León-Portilla, op. cit. p. 153. © 1992 University Oklahoma Press.
16 León-Portilla, op. cit. p. 83. © 1992 University Oklahoma Press.
17 M. Leon-Portilla, *The Broken Spears: Aztec Accounts of the Conquest of Mexico*, pp. 137-8. © 1966, Beacon Press, Boston.

Further Reading

There has been no attempt to present here anything like an exhaustive coverage of Mexican archaeology, the titles of which run into the many thousands. Rather, we have tried to guide the interested reader to those works used to prepare this and previous editions, and which might be profitably consulted for further information. Many of these publications themselves contain quite extensive bibliographies. Several ongoing journals contain up-to-date articles on Mexican archaeology and ethnohistory; especially recommended are *Ancient Mesoamerica*, *Estudios de Cultura Nahuatl*, and *Arqueología Mexicana*. The various volumes resulting from the Dumbarton Oaks Conferences also present significant advances in the field.

AVELEYRA ARROYO DE ANDA, LUIS. "The primitive hunters," in *Handbook of Middle American Indians*, vol. 1, ed. Robert Wauchope and Robert C. West, 384–412. Austin, Texas 1964. (Excellent treatment of the Early Hunters in Mesoamerica.)

AVENI, ANTHONY. *Skywatchers of Ancient Mexico*. Austin, Texas 1980. (Clearly written presentation of Mesoamerican astronomy.)

BARLOW, R.H. "The extent of the empire of the Culhua Mexica," *Ibero-Americana*, 28. Berkeley and Los Angeles 1949. (Classic study defining the Aztec empire on the basis of tribute lists.)

BENSON, ELIZABETH P. (ed.). *Dumbarton Oaks Conference on the Olmec*. Washington 1968. (First conference on Olmec problems since the California project at La Venta, and the Yale excavations at San Lorenzo.)

—— and MICHAEL D. COE (eds.). *The Olmec and Their Neighbors: Essays in Memory of Matthew W. Stirling*. Washington 1981. (Still the most comprehensive treatment of Olmec archaeology and civilization.)

—— and BEATRIZ DE LA FUENTE. *Olmec Art of Ancient Mexico*. Washington 1996. (Catalogue of an important show with descriptions of recent work at all major Olmec sites.)

BERDAN, FRANCES F. et al. *Aztec Imperial Strategies*. Washington 1996. (Detailed look at the empire through documents and artifacts.)

BERLO, JANET CATHERINE (ed.). *Art, Ideology and the City of Teotihuacan*. Washington 1992. (Essays on Classic Teotihuacan civilization.)

—— and RICHARD A. DIEHL (eds.). *Mesoamerica after the Decline of Teotihuacan*. Washington 1989. (Results of a Dumbarton Oaks Conference on Epi- and Post-Classic Mesoamerica.)

BERRIN, KATHLEEN and ESTHER PASZTORY (eds.). *Teotihuacan: Art from the City of the Gods*. San Francisco, New York, and London 1993.

BLANTON, RICHARD E. *Monte Albán: Settlement Patterns at the Ancient Zapotec Capital*. New York 1978. (Deals with the nature of urbanism and political control.)

BLANTON, RICHARD E. et al. *Ancient Oaxaca: the Monte Albán State*. Cambridge 1999. (Summary of settlement pattern, urban, and political studies.)

BOONE, ELIZABETH HILL (ed.). *The Aztec Templo Mayor*. Washington 1987. (Essays from a Dumbarton Oaks Conference dealing with the discoveries in the Great Temple.)

—— *Stories in Red and Black: Pictorial Histories of the Aztec and Mixtec*. Austin, Texas 2000. (The richest introduction to the codices.)

BORAH, WOODROW. "New Spain's century of depression," *Ibero-Americana*, 35. Berkeley and Los Angeles 1951. (Analysis of the great economic and demographic collapse in 17th-century Mexico.)

BRICKER, VICTORIA R. and JEREMY A. SABLOFF (eds.). *Supplement to the Handbook of Middle American Indians, vol. 1: Archaeology*. Austin, Texas 1981. (An important updating of Wauchope 1964–76.)

BURGOA, FR. FRANCISCO DE. *Geográfica Descripción*. 2 vols. Mexico City 1934. (Contains an early account of Mitla.)

BURKHART, LOUISE M. *The Slippery Earth: Nahua-Christian Moral Dialogue in Sixteenth-century Mexico*. Tucson 1989. (Perceptive study of early understandings and misunderstandings between two cultures and religions.)

BYERS, DOUGLAS S. and RICHARD S. MACNEISH (gen. eds.). *The Prehistory of the Tehuacan Valley*. 5 vols. Austin, Texas 1967–77. (Comprehensive final report on MacNeish's Tehuacan project, especially important for its information on agricultural origins.)

CABRERA CASTRO, RUBEN, SABURO SUGIYAMA, and GEORGE L. COWGILL. "The Templo de Quetzalcoatl Project at Teotihuacan," *Ancient Mesoamerica*, 2, 77–92. Cambridge 1991. (Spectacular discovery of warrior sacrifices in a major Teotihuacan structure.)

CARLSON, JOHN B. *Star Wars and Maya Merchants at Cacaxtla*. College Park, Md. 1990. (The most recent mural finds at Cacaxtla.)

CARRASCO, DAVID (ed.). *To Change Place: Aztec Ceremonial Landscapes*. Boulder 1991. (Examines how the Aztec calendar and ceremonialism are related to sacred landscapes in the Valley of Mexico.)

——, LINDSAY JONES, and SCOTT SESSIONS (eds.). *Mesoamerica's Classic Heritage: from Teotihuacan to the Aztecs*. Boulder 2000. (Important essays on Teotihuacan's place in Mexican and Maya history.)

CASO, ALFONSO. "Calendario y escritura de las antiguas culturas de Monte Albán," in *Obras Completas, Miguel Othón de Mendizabal*, 6 vols., i, 113–45. Mexico City 1946–7. (Pioneering study of the Zapotec script of Monte Albán I and II.)

—— *The Aztecs, People of the Sun*. Norman, Oklahoma 1958. (Clearly written general treatment of Aztec religion.)

—— "Mixtec writing and calendar," in *Handbook of Middle American Indians*, vol. 3, pt. 2, ed. Robert Wauchope, 948–61. Austin, Texas 1965.

—— *Calendarios prehispánicos*. Mexico City 1967. (Indispensable collection of essays on non-Maya calendars of Mesoamerica.)

—— *El Tesoro de Monte Albán*. Memorias del Instituto Nacional de Antropología e Historia 3. Mexico City 1969. (Final report on the great Mixtec tomb of Monte Albán.)

—— and IGNACIO BERNAL. *Urnas de Oaxaca*. Mexico City 1952. (Study of the iconography of Zapotec funerary urns.)

CLARK, JOHN E. (ed.). *Los Olmecas en Mesoamerica*. Mexico 1994. (Treatments of early pottery, Teopantecuanitlan, and the objects found in El Manatí, among other contributions.)

—— and MICHAEL BLAKE. "The power of prestige: competitive generosity and the emergence of rank societies in Lowland Mesoamerica," in *Factional Competition in the New World*, eds. Elizabeth M. Brumfiel and John W. Fox, 17–30. Cambridge 1994. (Provocative analysis of the earliest Mesoamerica pottery.)

CLENDINNEN, INGA. *Aztecs: An Interpretation*. Cambridge and New York 1991. (Eloquent, authoritative account, generally from the Aztecs' point of view.)

COE, MICHAEL D. *America's First Civilization: Discovering the Olmec*. New York 1968. (Popular description of the Olmec, and Olmec research.)

—— and RICHARD A. DIEHL. *In the Land of the Olmec*. 2 vols. Austin, Texas 1980. (The final report on archaeological and ecological investigations at San Lorenzo Tenochtitlan.)

—— et al. *The Olmec World: Ritual and Rulership*. Princeton 1995. (Key iconographic studies with a beautifully illustrated catalogue.)

CORTÉS, HERNÁN. *Letters from Mexico*, trans. and ed. Anthony Pagden. New Haven and London 1986. (Fascinating but devious and unreliable reports, written by Cortés to justify his actions to the Hapsburg court.)

COWGILL, GEORGE. "Discussion," *Ancient Mesoamerica* 7:325–31. Cambridge 1996. (Discussion of some recent changes in Teotihuacan and Aztec chronologies.)

—— "State and society at Teotihuacan," *Annual Review of Anthropology* 26, 129–61. Palo Alto 1997. (Thoughtful, fundamental synthesis of Teotihuacan history.)

DAVIES, NIGEL. *The Aztecs, A History*. New York 1973. (General synthesis, based on ethnohistoric sources.)

—— *The Toltecs until the Fall of Tula*. Norman, Oklahoma 1977. (Compilation of ethnohistoric data on the Toltecs, using native and Spanish sources.)

DÍAZ DEL CASTILLO, BERNAL. *The True History of the Conquest of New Spain*, trans. A.P. Maudslay. London 1908–16. (American edition, New York 1958.) (Gripping, eyewitness account, written by a conquistador in his old age.)

DIEHL, RICHARD A. *Tula, the Toltec Capital of Ancient Mexico*. London and New York 1983. (Semi-popular account of Tula and the University of Missouri archaeological project.)

—— "Olmec archaeology: what we know and what we wish we knew," in *Regional Perspectives on the Olmec*, ed. R.J. Sharer and D. C. Grove. Albuquerque 1989. (Well-reasoned summary of problems in Olmec archaeology.)

DRUCKER, PHILIP. "The Cerro de las Mesas offering of jade and other materials," *Bureau of American Ethnology, Bulletin* 157, 25–68. Washington 1955. (An Early Classic cache with heirloom materials.)

—— ROBERT F. HEIZER and ROBERT J. SQUIER. "Excavations at La Venta, Tabasco, 1955," *Bureau of American Ethnology, Bulletin* 170. Washington 1959. (Final report on the University of California excavations at a key Olmec site.)

DURÁN, FR. DIEGO. *The History of the Indies of New Spain*, trans. and annotated Doris Heyden. Norman, Oklahoma 1993. (After Sahagún, the most important early source on Aztec life and history.)

EUBANKS, MARY W. "The origin of maize: evidence for Tripsacum ancestry," *Plant Breeding Reviews* 20, 15–66. New York 2001. (Considers recent advances in both the molecular biology and the archaeology of domestication.)

FLANNERY, KENT V. (ed.). *The Early Mesoamerican Village*. New York 1976. (Highly influential volume on the Mesoamerican Preclassic, with important data on early Oaxaca.)

—— and JOYCE MARCUS (eds.). *The Cloud People: Divergent Evolution of the Zapotec and Mixtec Civilizations*. New York 1983. (A major collection of essays on all aspects of pre-Conquest Oaxaca.)

—— ,—— and STEPHEN A. KOWALEWSKI. "The Preceramic and Formative of the Valley of Oaxaca," in *Supplement to the Handbook of Middle American Indians*, vol. 1: *Archaeology*, 48–93. Austin, Texas 1981.

FONCERRADA DE MOLINA, MARTA. *Cacaxtla: La Iconografía de los Olmeca-Xicalanca*. Mexico 1993. (Detailed analysis of the murals.)

FUENTE, BEATRIZ DE LA (ed.). *La Pintura Mural Prehispánica en México I: Teotihuacan*. 2 vols. Mexico City 1995. (Complete catalogue of the murals along with substantial essays.)

FURST, PETER T. "House of Darkness and House of Light," in *Death and the Afterlife in Pre-Columbian America*, ed. Elizabeth P. Benson, 33–68. Washington 1975. (Application of ethnological data to the understanding of West Mexican tomb sculpture.)

GARIBAY, ANGEL MARÍA. *Historia de la literatura nahuatl*. 3 vols. Mexico City 1953–54. (Classic study of Aztec poetry and prose.)

GERHARD, PETER. *A Guide to the Historical Geography of New Spain*. Cambridge 1972. (Basic work on the civil and ecclesiastical organization of Colonial Mexico, and to the documentary sources.)

GILLESPIE, SUSAN. *The Aztec Kings*. Tucson 1989. (Iconoclastic study of Aztec dynastic succession and Toltec "history," based on a structural analysis of the data.)

GROVE, DAVID C. "The Olmec paintings of Oxtotitlan, Guerrero, Mexico," *Dumbarton Oaks Studies in Pre-Columbian Art and Archaeology*, no. 6. Washington 1970.

—— *Chalcatzingo: Excavations on the Olmec Frontier*. London and New York 1984. (General account of the most important highland Olmec site, famed for its relief carvings.)

—— (ed.). *Ancient Chalcatzingo*. Austin, Texas 1987. (Final report on the University of Illinois project.)

HARBOTTLE, GARMAN and PHIL C. WEIGAND. "Turquoise in Pre-Columbian America," *Scientific*

American 78–85. 1992. (Archaeological data and neutron-activation analysis of the turquoise trade between the American Southwest and Mesoamerica.)

HASSIG, ROSS. *Aztec Warfare*. Norman, Oklahoma 1988. (The definitive study of the subject.)

HEALAN, DAN M. (ed.). *Tula of the Toltecs*. Iowa City 1989. (Final report on the University of Missouri project.)

HEYDEN, DORIS. "Caves, gods and myths: world-view and planning in Teotihuacan," in *Mesoamerican Sites and World Views*, ed. Elizabeth P. Benson, 1–39. Washington 1981. (Implications of the discovery of a cave beneath the Pyramid of the Sun.)

IRWIN-WILLIAMS, CYNTHIA. "Summary of archaeological evidence from the Valsequillo region, Puebla, Mexico," in *Cultural Continuity in Mesoamerica*, ed. David Broman, 7–22. The Hague 1978. (Report on a key site of the Early Hunters stage in Mexico.)

JIMÉNEZ MORENO, WIGBERTO. "Tula y los Toltecas segun las fuentes históricas," *Revista Mexicana de Estudios Antropológicos* 5, 79–83. Mexico City 1941. (The article that established Tula, Hidalgo, as the Toltec capital.)

JORALEMON, PETER DAVID. "A study of Olmec iconography," *Dumbarton Oaks Studies in Pre-Columbian Art and Iconography*, no. 7. Washington 1971. (This and the following are the key works on Olmec religion and iconography.)

—— "The Olmec Dragon: a study in Pre-Columbian iconography," in *Origins of Religious Art and Iconography in Preclassic Mesoamerica*, ed. H.B. Nicholson, 27–71. Los Angeles 1976.

JUSTESON, JOHN S. and TERENCE KAUFMAN. "A decipherment of epi-Olmec hieroglyphic writing," *Science* 259, 1703–11. Washington 1993. (Identification of the Isthmian script as proto-Zoquean, and partial reading of the text on Stela 1, La Mojarra.)

KAMPEN, MICHAEL E. *The Sculptures of El Tajín, Veracruz, Mexico*. Gainesville, Florida 1972. (Excellent drawings of the El Tajín reliefs.)

KAN, MICHAEL, CLEMENT MEIGHAN, and H.B. NICHOLSON. *Sculpture of Ancient West Mexico*. Los Angeles 1970. (Important for style spheres in this area.)

KIRCHHOFF, PAUL. "Meso-America," in *Heritage of Conquest*, ed. Sol Tax, 17–30. Glencoe, Illinois 1952. (The first definition of "Mesoamerica.")

KRISTAN-GRAHAM, CYNTHIA. *Art, Rulership and the Mesoamerican Body Politic at Tula and Chichén Itzá*. Ph.D. dissertation, University of California at Los Angeles, 1989. (Analysis of traits shared by Tula and Chich'en Itza.)

KUBLER, GEORGE. "Chichén Itzá y Tula," *Estudios de Cultura Maya* 1, 47–79. Mexico City 1961. (Argues that it was Chich'en Itza that influenced Tula, and not the reverse.)

LEÓN-PORTILLA, MIGUEL. *Aztec Thought and Culture*. Norman, Oklahoma 1963. (A profound study of Aztec philosophy and religion.)

—— *The Broken Spears: Aztec Accounts of the Conquest of Mexico*. Boston 1966. (A deeply affecting antidote to the self-glorifying accounts of the victors in the great struggle for Mexico.)

—— *Fifteen Poets of the Aztec World*. Norman, Oklahoma 1992.

—— (ed. and trans.). *Coloquios y doctrina cristiana*. Mexico City 1986. (An extraordinary dialogue conducted in Nahuatl during a 1524 meeting between the Franciscan friars and native Aztec intellectuals.)

LÓPEZ AUSTIN, ALFREDO. *The Human Body and Ideology: Concepts of the Ancient Nahuas*. Salt Lake City 1988. (Innovative, detailed account of indigenous concepts of the body.)

LÓPEZ DE M., DIANA and DANIEL MOLINA F. *Cacaxtla, Guia Oficial*. Mexico City 1980. (Brief pamphlet describing this central Mexican site and its Maya murals.)

LÓPEZ LUJÁN, LEONARDO, R.H. COBEAN T., and A. GUADALUPE MASTACHE F. *Xochicalco y Tula*. Milan, 1995. (Summary of what is known along with recent excavations, all gloriously illustrated.)

MacNEISH, RICHARD S. "Preliminary archaeological investigations in the Sierra de Tamaulipas, Mexico," *Transactions of the American Philosophical Society*, 48, pt. 6. 1958. (Early Hunters and Archaic occupation in northeasternmost Mexico.)

—— *The Origins of Agriculture and Settled Life*. Norman, Oklahoma, and London 1991. (Chapter 3 covers Mesoamerica, in a theoretical work by the leading authority on the Archaic period.)

MADSEN, WILLIAM. *Christo-Paganism: A Study of Mexican Religious Syncretism*. New Orleans 1957. (The blending of Christian beliefs and worship with Aztec supernaturalism in a modern village in the Valley of Mexico.)

MANGELSDORF, PAUL C. *Corn: Its Origin, Evolution and Improvement*. Cambridge 1974. (With the following, gives Mangelsdorf's side of the controversy over the origin of corn.)

—— "The mystery of corn: new perspectives," *Proceedings of the American Philosophical Society*, 127, no. 1, 215–47. 1983.

MANZANILLA, LINDA and LEONARDO LÓPEZ LUJÁN, (eds.). *Historia Antigua de Mexico*. 3 vols. Mexico City 1994 (vol. 1) and 1995 (vols. 2–3). (Collection of synthetic articles by top Mexican archaeologists covering all aspects of Mesoamerican culture and history.)

MARCUS, JOYCE and FLANNERY, KENT, V. *Zapotec Civilization: How Urban Society Evolved in Mexico's Oaxaca Valley*. London and New York 1996. (Major synthetic work spanning all aspects of pre-Columbian Zapotec history.)

MARQUINA, IGNACIO. *Arquitectura Prehispánica*. Mexico City 1951. (In spite of its age, still useful for plans and drawings of major sites and buildings.)

—— (coordinator). *Proyecto Cholula*. Mexico City 1970. (Various reports on the Mexican investigations of the 1960's at this major site.)

MARTÍNEZ DONJUAN, GUADALUPE. "Los olmecas en el estado de Guerrero," in *Los olmecas en Mesoamérica*, ed. John E. Clark, 143–63. Mexico City 1994. (A synthesis of work at Teopantecuanitlan.)

MATOS MOCTEZUMA, EDUARDO. *The Great Temple of the Aztecs*. London and New York 1988. (Semi-popular account of the spectacular excavations at the remains of the most important structure in the Aztec empire.)

MEDELLÍN ZENIL, ALFONSO. *Cerámicas del Totonacapan*. Xalapa, Veracruz 1960. (Illustrations of Remojadas pottery and figurines, but with an outdated chronology.)

MILLER, ARTHUR G. *The Mural Painting of Teoti-huacan*. Washington 1973. (Beautifully illustrated volume on Classic Teotihuacan palace murals.)

MILLER, MARY ELLEN. *The Art of Mesoamerica from Olmec to Aztec*, 3rd edn. London and New York 2001. (A concise and well-illustrated introduction to all of Mesoamerica.)

—— and KARL TAUBE. *The Gods and Symbols of Ancient Mexico and the Maya: An Illustrated Dictionary of Mesoamerican Religion*. London and New York 1992. (Immensely useful dictionary and guide to Aztec and pre-Aztec religion and iconography.)

MILLON, RENÉ. *Urbanization at Teotihuacan, Mexico*, vol. 1, parts 1 and 2. Austin, Texas 1973. (Excellent summary of Teotihuacan culture, along with detailed maps of the entire city.)

—— "Teotihuacan: city, state, and civilization," in *Supplement to the Handbook of Middle American Indi-ans*, vol. 1: *Archaeology*, 198–243. Austin, Texas 1981. (An important updating of the earlier essay.)

NELSON, BEN A. "Chronology and stratigraphy at La Quemada, Zacatecas, Mexico," *Journal of Field Archaeology* 24, no. 1, 85–110. Boston 1997. (Syn-thesis of work on Mesoamerica's northern frontier.)

NICHOLSON, HENRY B. "Religion in Pre-Hispanic cen-tral Mexico," in *Handbook of Middle American Indians*, vol. 10, ed. Robert Wauchope, Gordon Ekholm, and Ignacio Bernal, 395–446. Austin, Texas 1971. (The essential work concerning Aztec religion.)

NIEDERBERGER BETTON, CHRISTINE. "Paléopaysages et archéologie pré-urbaine du Bassin de Mexico," 2 vols. *Collection Études Mesoaméricaines* 1–11. Mexico City 1987. (Late Archaic and Preclassic occupation in the Tlapacoya region, Valley of Mexico.)

OFFNER, JEROME. *Law and Politics in Aztec Texcoco*. Cambridge 1988. (Definitive work on the unique legal system of the Aztecs.)

ORTIZ DE MONTELLANO, BERNARD R. "Aztec cannibal-ism: an ecological necessity?" *Science* 200, 611–17. Washington 1978. (Careful refutation of the Harner thesis.)

PADDOCK, JOHN (ed.). *Ancient Oaxaca*. Stanford, Cali-fornia 1966. (Excellent background material on Zapotec and Mixtec archaeology and ethnohistory.)

PARADIS, L.-I., C. BÉLANGER, D. RABY, and B. ROSS. "Le style Mezcala découvert en contexte au Guer-rero (Mexique)," *Journal de la Société des Américanistes*, 76, 199–213. Paris 1990. (Archaeolog-ical dating of objects in the Mezcala style.)

PASZTORY, ESTHER. *Aztec Art*. New York 1983. (The most complete treatment of the subject.)

—— *Teotihuacan: An Experiment in Living*. Norman, Oklahoma 1997. (Synthesis of Teotihuacan icono-graphy and aesthetics.)

PLUNKET, PATRICIA and GABRIELA URUÑUELA. "Pre-classic household patterns preserved under volcanic ash at Tetimpa, Puebla, Mexico," *Latin American Antiquity* 9:4, 287–309. Washington 1998. (Excava-tion of a Preclassic village with preserved house groups.)

POHL, JOHN M.D. and BRUCE BYLAND. "Mixtec land-scape perception and archaeological settlement patterns," *Ancient Mesoamerica* 1, no. 1, 113–31. 1990. (Identifies a host of toponyms found in the codices.)

—— and —— *In the Realm of 8 Deer: the Archaeology of the Mixtec Codices*. Norman, Oklahoma 1994. (The most important addition to Caso's original readings.)

—— and ANGUS McBRIDE. *Aztec, Mixtec and Zapotec Armies*. London 1991. (Strikingly illustrated popu-lar work on native Mexican warfare.)

POLLARD, HELEN PERLSTEIN. "The construction of ideology in the emergence of the prehispanic Taras-can state," *Ancient Mesoamerica* 2, 167–69. 1991. (Perceptive study of the origin and nature of the Tarascan kingdom, based on the re-analysis of ethnohistoric sources.)

—— *Tariacuri's Legacy: the Pre-Hispanic Tarascan State*. Norman, Oklahoma 1993. (Synthetic study of the Tarascan kingdom.)

POPE, KEVIN O. et al. "Origin and environmental setting of ancient agriculture in the Lowlands of Meso-america," *Science* 292, 1370–73. Washington 2001. (Early maize near La Venta, Tabasco.)

PORTER, MURIEL N. *Tlatilco and the Pre-Classic Cultures of the New World*. New York 1953. (Diffusionist explanation of Tlatilco, but still the best treatment of this important Preclassic site.)

PROSKOURIAKOFF, TATIANA. "Varieties of Classic Cen-tral Veracruz Sculpture," *Carnegie Institution of Washington, Contributions to American Anthropology and History*, no. 58. Washington 1954. (Pioneering definition of the Central Veracruz style.)

Relación de Michoacan (1541). Transcription, prologue, introduction, and notes by José Tudela. Madrid 1956. (The primary ethnohistoric source on Taras-can culture.)

SAHAGÚN, FRAY BERNADINO DE. *General History of the Things of New Spain*. Translation from the Nahuatl by Arthur J.O. Anderson and Charles F. Dibble. Santa Fe 1950–69. (A massive scholarly encyclo-pedia of almost all aspects of Aztec life by its greatest student. Book 12 presents an absorbingly interesting account of the Conquest from the native point of view; Sahagún would later refute this in a pro-Spanish work.)

SANDERS, WILLIAM T., JEFFREY R. PARSONS and ROBERT S. SANTLEY. *The Basin of Mexico: Ecological Processes in the Evolution of a Civilization*. New York 1979. (Results of a massive survey of settlement pat-terns in the entire Valley of Mexico from earliest times through the Conquest.)

SANDSTROM, ALAN. *Corn is Our Blood: Culture and Ethnic Identity in a Contemporary Aztec Village*. Norman, Oklahoma 1991. (Sensitive rendering of contemporary Nahua world view.)

SÉJOURNÉ, LAURETTE. *Un Palacio de la Ciudad de los Dioses, Teotihuacan*. Mexico City 1959. (Very well-illustrated account of excavations in a luxurious palace of the Teotihuacan elite.)

SMITH, MARY ELIZABETH. *Picture Writing from South-ern Mexico: Mixtec Place Signs and Maps*. Norman, Oklahoma 1973. (Analysis of the Mixtec writing sys-tem, from a linguistic and art-historical perspective.)

SOUSTELLE, JACQUES. *The Daily Life of the Aztecs*. New York 1962. (A very readable introduction to many aspects of Aztec life and culture.)

SPORES, RONALD. *The Mixtec Kings and Their People*. Norman, Oklahoma 1967. (Good general account, written when Mixtec archaeology was still in its infancy.)

—— *The Mixtecs in Ancient and Colonial Times.* Norman, Oklahoma 1984. (An update of the preceding.)

STARK, BARBARA L. and PHILIP J. ARNOLD (eds.). *From Olmec to Aztec: Settlement Patterns in the Ancient Gulf Lowlands.* Tucson 1997. (Synthesis of data on human occupation from throughout Veracruz.)

STIRLING, MATTHEW W. "Stone monuments of southern Mexico," *Bureau of American ethnology, Bulletin* 138. Washington 1943. (Early report on Olmec and post-Olmec sculptures and sites.)

STOREY, REBECCA. *Life and Death in the Ancient City of Teotihuacan: A Modern Paleodemographic Synthesis.* Tuscaloosa, Alabama 1992. (Life and health in the Classic metropolis as seen through the bones.)

TAUBE, KARL A. "The Teotihuacan Spider Woman," *Journal of Latin American Lore* 9:2, 107–89. Los Angeles 1983. (Identification of the "Great Goddess" of the ancient city.)

—— "The iconography of mirrors at Teotihuacan," in *Art, Ideology, and the City of Teotihuacan,* ed. Janet C. Berlo, 169–204. Washington 1992. (Mirrors as military paraphernalia in early Mexico.)

—— "The Temple of Quetzalcoatl and the Cult of Sacred War," *Res* 21:53–87. Cambridge 1992. (Crucial account of Teotihuacan war iconography in the light of the spectacular dedicatory offerings.)

TOLSTOY, PAUL and LOUISE I. PARADIS. "Early and Middle Preclassic culture in the Basin of Mexico," *Science,* 167, 344–52. Washington 1970. (Should be read together with Niederberger Betton, loc. cit., for a comprehensive view of the first Preclassic cultures in the Valley of Mexico.)

TOWNSEND, RICHARD F. *Ancient West Mexico: Art and Archaeology of the Unknown Past.* London and New York 1998. (Important account of recent archaeological discoveries and revised history of the region.)

—— *The Aztecs,* revised edition. London and New York 2000. (A succinct account of Aztec history and life by a leading art historian.)

TROIKE, NANCY P. "Prehispanic pictorial communication: the codex system of the Mixtec of Oaxaca, Mexico," *Visible Language* 24, 1, 75–87. Pittsford, New York 1990.

URCID SERRANO, JAVIER. *Zapotec Hieroglyphic Writing.* Washington 2001. (Definitive summary and analysis of the Zapotec script and calendar.)

VAILLANT, GEORGE C. "Excavations at Zacatenco," *Anthropological Papers of the American Museum of Natural History,* 32, pt. 1. New York 1930.(With the following, reports pioneer excavations in Preclassic occupations of the Valley of Mexico, in the pre-radiocarbon era.)

—— "Excavations at El Arbolillo," *Anthropological Papers of the American Museum of Natural History,* 35, pt. 2, New York 1935.

VON WINNING, HASSO. *La Iconografía de Teotihuacan.* 2 vols. Mexico City 1987. (Detailed study of important symbols in use in the Classic city.)

—— and NELLY GUTIÉRREZ SOLANO. *La Iconografía de la Cerámica de Río Blanco, Veracruz.* Mexico City 1996. (In-depth study of one aspect of Classic Veracruz ceramics.)

WAUCHOPE, ROBERT (ed.). *Handbook of Middle American Indians.* Austin, Texas 1964– . (A multi-volume series covering all aspects of life in Mesoamerica.)

WEAVER, MURIEL PORTER. *The Aztecs, Maya and Their Predecessors.* 3rd edn. New York 1993. (The most extensive one-volume coverage of Mesoamerica as a whole.)

WHITECOTTON, JOSEPH W. *The Zapotecs: Princes, Priests and Peasants.* Norman, Oklahoma 1977. (History and anthropology of a major Mesoamerican people, from earliest times to the present.)

WHITTINGTON, E. MICHAEL (ed.). *The Sport of Life and Death: The Mesoamerican Ballgame.* New York and London 2001.

WILKERSON, S. JEFFREY K. *El Tajín: A Guide for Visitors.* Xalapa, Veracruz 1987. (Beautifully illustrated handbook to the ruins.)

WINFIELD CAPITAINE, FERNANDO. "La estela 1 de La Mojarra, Veracruz, Mexico," *Research Reports on Ancient Maya Writing,* 16. Washington 1988. (Reports on the discovery of Mesoamerica's longest hieroglyphic text, in the early Isthmian script.)

WOLF, ERIC (ed.). *The Valley of Mexico: Studies in Pre-Hispanic Ecology and Society.* Albuquerque 1976. (Papers presented at a School of American Research Conference; the subject matter is heavily ecological.)

ZANTWIJK, RUDOLF A. VAN. *The Aztec Arrangement.* Norman, Oklahoma 1985. (The organization of the Aztec capital city, state, and empire by a structural anthropologist and expert in Aztec ethnohistory.)

List of Illustrations

All maps and drawings are by Dr Patrick Gallagher, unless otherwise indicated.

Colour plates

I Olmec colossal head, San Lorenzo, Veracruz. Photo Colin McEwan.

II Offering No. 4 at La Venta. Photo Michael D. Coe.

III Jade celt from Tomb E at La Venta. Middle Formative period. Photo Jorge Pérez de Lara.

IV Jade female figurine from Tomb A at La Venta. Photo Jorge Pérez de Lara.

V "The Acrobat", from Burial 154 at Tlatilco. Early Formative Period. Photo Jorge Pérez de Lara.

VI Hollow clay figurine from Atlihuayan. Early Formative Period. Photo Jorge Pérez de Lara.

VII Pyramid of the Moon, Teotihuacan. Photo Antonio Attini/Archivio White Star.

VIII Stone mask with turquoise mosaic. Teotihuacan style, Early Classic; mosaic Aztec. Photo Jorge Pérez de Lara.

IX Patio of the Quetzalpapalotl Palace, Teotihuacan. Photo Michael D. Coe.

X The Great Plaza of Monte Albán. Photo Antonio Attini/Archivio White Star.

XI Effigy urn, Monte Albán. Photo Jorge Pérez de Lara.

XII Plumbate-ware jar covered with mother-of-pearl and other shell mosaic in the form of a face of a bearded man emerging from the jaws of a coyote. El Corral Temple, Tula. Photo Jorge Pérez de Lara.

XIII Detail of page 37 of the Codex Vienna. Photo Michael D. Coe.

XIV Folio 2 of the Codex Mendoza. Photo Michael D. Coe.

XV Statue of Coatlicue. Photo Jorge Pérez de Lara.

XVI Aztec shield of feathers and gold trim. Photo courtesy Museum für Völkerkunde, Vienna.

XVII Life-size ceramic figure of an Aztec Eagle Warrior from Eagle House. Photo Salvador Guilliem, courtesy of the Great Temple Project.

XVIII Chacmool, from the Temple of Tlaloc, Stage II of the Great Temple. Photo Salvador Guilliem, courtesy of the Great Temple Project.

XIX Wooden Aztec mask with turquoise mosaic and shell. © Copyright the British Museum, London.

Frontispiece: Monument 1, San Lorenzo, Veracruz. Photo courtesy Matthew W. Stirling and the National Geographic Society.

1 Map of major topographical features of Mesoamerica.

2 Central highlands of Mexico, near Puebla. Photo Michael D. Coe.

3 *Chinampas* in the vicinity of Xochimilco, Valley of Mexico. Photo Michael D. Coe.

4 Native language groups of Mexico.

5 Sites of the Early Hunters and Archaic periods.

6 Clovis point from the Weicker Ranch, Durango. Based on J.L. Lorenzo, "A fluted point from Durango, Mexico" (fig. 141).

7 Animal head carved from the sacrum of an extinct camelid. Photo courtesy Instituto Nacional de Antropología e Historia.

8 Fossil human skull from Tepexpan, Valley of Mexico. Photo courtesy Instituto Nacional de Antropología e Historia.

9 The second fossil mammoth from Santa Isabel Iztapan. Photo courtesy Instituto Nacional de Antropología e Historia.

10 Chipped stone tools found in association with mammoths at Santa Isabel Iztapan.

11 Probable community patterns, Ajuereado phase, Tehuacan Valley. From Richard S. MacNeish, *Second Annual Report of the Tehuacan Archaeological- Botanical Project.*

12 Characteristic stone tools of the Archaic in Tamaulipas.

13 Ovoid biface of obsidian and matting fragment, Tamaulipas.

14 View of the Tehuacan Valley. Photo Michael D. Coe.

15 Cob of wild maize from the Coxcatlan phase. Photo Michael D. Coe.

16 Sites of the Preclassic period.

17 Early Preclassic ceramics, Chiapa I phase. Based on K. Dixon, *Ceramics from Two Pre-Classic Periods.*

18 Sub-floor burials at Tlatilco. Photo Michael D. Coe.

19 Pottery figurines and roller stamps from Tlatilco. Compiled from M.N. Porter, *Tlatilco and the Pre-Classic Cultures of the New World.*

20 Pottery figurine of a dancer, Tlatilco. Photo courtesy American Museum of Natural History.

21 Pottery figurine of a dancer, Tlatilco. Photo courtesy American Museum of Natural History.

22 Representative pottery vessels from Tlatilco. Compiled from M.N. Porter ibid., and from R. Piña Chan, *Tlatilco.*

23 Polychrome tripod jar, Chupícuaro culture. Photo courtesy J.J. Klejman.

24 Pottery figurine of the "pretty lady" type, Chupícuaro culture. Photo courtesy Instituto Nacional de Antropología e Historia.

25 View of the circular temple platform at Cuicuilco. Photo Michael D. Coe.

26 Standing figure of stone, Mezcala style. Photo courtesy Metropolitan Museum of Art.

27 Stone model of temple, Mezcala style. Photo courtesy Metropolitan Museum of Art.

28 Pottery house group, Ixtlan del Río, Nayarit. Private collection. Photo courtesy Hasso von Winning.

29 Pottery figure of a man striking a turtle-shell, Nayarit. Photo courtesy American Museum of Natural History.

30 Seated person holding a dish, Jalisco. Photo courtesy Metropolitan Museum of Art.

31 Pottery dog wearing a mask with human face from Colima. Museo Nacional de Antropología, Mexico.

Index